Urban Economics

Urban Economics

An Introduction

Alan W. Evans

Basil Blackwell

First published 1985
Basil Blackwell Ltd
108 Cowley Road, Oxford OX4 1JF, U.K.

Basil Blackwell Inc.
432 Park Avenue South, Suite 1505,
New York, NY 10016, U.S.A.

British Library Cataloguing in Publication Data

Evans, Alan, 1938–
    Urban economics : an introduction.
    1. Urban economics
    I. Title
    330.9173'2   HT321

    ISBN 0–631–14194–4
    ISBN 0–631–14195–2   Pbk

Library of Congress Cataloging in Publication Data
Evans, Alan W.
    Urban economics.

    Bibliography: p.
    Includes index.
    1. Urban economics. I. Title.
    HT321.E93   1985   330.9173'2   84–29773
    ISBN 0–631–14194–4
    ISBN 0–631–14195–2   (pbk.)

Typeset by Photo·graphics, Honiton, Devon.
Printed in Great Britain by The Camelot Press Ltd. Southampton

To Jill

Contents

Preface

Urban economics seems sometimes to be all embracing. To judge from lecture courses and other texts it can include, at least, the economics of race, poverty, crime, pollution and the environment, and housing. Moreover, the subject can be approached in various ways from the highly mathematical and theoretical to the descriptive. So if all the topics which are sometimes regarded as part of urban economics were covered in this book it would be two or three times the length that it is. It follows also that many readers will feel that some topics have not been covered which should have been.

In order to limit the size of the book I had to follow certain principles in defining the topics I wished to cover and the way that I covered them. Since these principles were in accord with my own views of the nature of urban economics doing so did not present any great problem.

The first principle I have followed is to regard a topic as part of urban economics to the extent that discussion of it relates to location and land use in towns. For example, I have touched on aspects of housing, in chapter 2 where it relates to residential location, and in chapter 9 where it relates to the land market, but there is no chapter on housing as such because much of the discussion of the economics of housing is non-spatial and therefore, in my view, not part of urban economics. Of course in an urban society most houses are in towns but if this were the criterion urban economics really would include almost everything.

The second principle I have followed is to write the book as a coherent whole in which the parts tie together and which is meant to be read starting at the beginning and finishing at the end. Though I am aware that few students will read the book in this way, since the order followed in the book may not be the order in which topics are dealt with in a lecture course, I can still hope that any interested reader who does actually start at the beginning and read through to the end is rewarded with an overall view of the economy of cities. The attempt to present a coherent overall view does mean, however, that there is less of a tendency than in some texts to present all the available views (and all the available references) on a subject and let the readers work it out for themselves. Doubtless students who use the text will be referred to the relevant alternative views by their lecturers so that I have few qualms about this, feeling that the gain in coherence outweighs any loss of comprehensiveness.

It is customary in a preface to a book of this kind to acknowledge one's intellectual debts. I find this almost impossible to do. My views of urban economics have been shaped in discussions and conversations over many years with very many people at the University of Glasgow, the Centre for Environmental Studies, the London School of Economics, and the University of Reading, where I have worked, and at the University College London, the University of Kent at Canterbury, and the University of Melbourne, where I have been a visiting lecturer, and at conferences, both national and international. My greatest debt is, however, to my immediate colleagues at the University of Reading, Paul Cheshire, Graham Crampton, Geoff Keogh, George Norman and Mike Stabler, with whom I have discussed ideas as I was writing this book.

The debts acknowledged above are diffuse and non-specific as I have indicated. I have one specific debt to acknowledge, however, and that is to Beryl Jones who not only typed the whole manuscript with her usual accuracy and speed but also caused considerable stylistic improvements through her comments on the resultant typescript.

Needless to say, all errors and remaining infelicities of style are my responsibility.

Alan W. Evans
University of Reading
September 1984

1

Introduction

Lady Bracknell: Ignorance is like a delicate exotic fruit; touch it
and the bloom is gone.
                                The Importance of Being Earnest Act I

Urban economics is one of the most recently developed branches of
economics. Indeed it is only within the last 20 years that the term
'urban economics' has been used, and serious research in the field
began only in the late 1950s.

Why has urban economics been so late in developing? After all,
one might have thought that some understanding of the way in
which an urban economy operated would have been seen as essential
to town planners, so that urban economics would have developed
alongside town planning earlier in the century. This did not happen,
however, with the single, notable, exception of a study by R. M.
Haig in 1926 for the New York Regional Plan Association.

The major stimulus to the analytical and empirical study of the
urban economy seems to have been, not town planning, but traffic
congestion. This also is the reason why urban economics developed
initially in America. As car ownership grew it became necessary to
try to solve the problems of congestion in American towns and
cities. These problems proved relatively easy to solve where the
congestion occurred in small towns and villages along major routes
between cities; these minor settlements could be by-passed and the
existing road upgraded, or if upgrading was not enough, completely
new freeways, turnpikes, or motorways could be built. The only
recurring problem was a tendency to underestimate the amount of
additional traffic which might be generated by the existence of the
new road, so that most of the early freeways and turnpikes reached
their design capacity very quickly.

The problem of congestion proved less easy to solve where it occurred within large cities. The construction of urban freeways and even the improvement of existing roads seemed merely to generate so much new traffic that congestion remained as bad as before. Moreover, it was found that new roads and other transport improvements caused a relocation of land uses which in turn led to a realignment or reorganization of the transport movements which the new transport system had originally been designed to serve.

It therefore seemed necessary to attempt to predict the traffic movements which would occur as a result of any transport improvement in order to ensure that its design capacity was adequate. It was shown that there was a relationship between the patterns of land use and traffic flows and that the traffic generated at a site could be predicted if the nature and intensity of land use at the site were known (Mitchell and Rapkin, 1954). Large-scale statistical transport models of traffic flows in cities were developed, based on surveys, the most well known being the Chicago Area Transport Study (1959), which aimed to model, and hence to predict, traffic movements within a city given the future pattern of land use, to allocate these trips to routes and hence to enable the construction of an optimal transport network.

It was at this stage that urban economics came into existence as researchers attempted to explain, using economic analysis, the determination of patterns of location given the transport system, and so to use their analysis to predict the effects on the pattern of land use of the construction and improvement of transport routes. The two major publications virtually coincided, Wingo's (1961) *Transportation and Urban Land* and Alonso's (1964a) *Location and Land Use*, which, although published in 1964, derived most of its information from his 1960 doctoral thesis.

In the event the contribution of urban economic theory to the solution of the urban transport problem was less than the early researchers might have hoped. By the early 1970s the construction of large-scale transport models had fallen into disrepute (Lee, 1973), and growing political opposition brought to a halt the construction of new freeways in urban areas (Hall, 1980). However, by this time urban economics had progressed sufficiently to develop independently. In small part this was because the theoretical analysis of a city with all its employment at a single centre, the original model used, was mathematically tractable and allowed the application of several high-powered pieces of economic theory to its analysis, a process which attracted several economists more widely known for their contributions in other branches of economics. (On this see Richardson, 1977, *The New Urban Economics*). This 'laying on of hands' certainly made urban economics academically respectable as a branch of economics, though one may doubt whether the results derived from these exercises justified the intellectual expertise used in their solution.

More importantly, so far as the independence, development, and usefulness of urban economics was concerned, it became apparent that even if, in the end, its contribution to solving the urban transport problem was relatively small, it could make important contributions to the more traditional disciplines dealing with the study of the city – town planning and land or real estate management – and to the analysis of government policies for dealing with urban problems.

LAND-USE PLANNING

As we have already suggested, one would have thought that the relevance of an economic analysis of urban areas to town planning would have been obvious. Indeed a stimulus to the development of urban economics parallel to that given by transport problems was the commissioning by the Regional Plan Association of detailed studies of the New York region. Unlike the work of Haig which they had commissioned some 30 years earlier, these studies did not remain as isolated pieces of work. In looking at all aspects of the economy of a large city they showed the way in which urban economics could be an applied and empirical study rather than purely theoretical (see for example Vernon, 1960; Hoover and Vernon, 1959; Lichtenberg, 1960).

These studies were, however, commissioned by an independent body, not by local government, and were not necessarily used in practice by those responsible for planning in the New York Metropolitan Area. In the United Kingdom even less progress had been made in this field, despite the fact that British planners have had considerably more control over what does or does not happen in the area they plan.

The reason for this lack of interest appears to be the past antipathy of British town planners to economics and economists. British town planning grew out of a concern with the physical environment and public health. In the 1930s most town planners had originally trained as architects and engineers. If town planning is seen as civic design (for example Nash's creation of Regent's Park, Regent Street, and St. James's Park) so that the aim of planning is that the result should be aesthetically pleasing, then there is no need to concern oneself with economics, or indeed with sociology or any other social science. Nor, indeed, is there any need to concern oneself with these disciplines if the aim of, say, enforcing lower densities is the prevention of disease.

Perhaps, taking the most favourable interpretation, this is what lies behind the view expressed by Sir Patrick Abercrombie, the leading British planner at the time of the Town and Country Planning Act, 1947, that the economist is a 'muddler who will talk about the Law of Supply and Demand and the liberty of the individual' (Abercrombie, 1959, p. 27). Yes, economists (whether muddled or not) do tend to concern themselves with market forces and so with what people want or are able to do at a given cost, and, in the 1940s, this was certainly at odds with the views of the planning profession. Two quotations from a 1944 conference on the new planning illustrate the mode of thought of those more junior than Abercrombie but later perhaps involved in the implementation of the planning process of which Abercrombie was the godfather.

Discussing the question, Can we induce people to move?, the Borough Surveyor of Tottenham said: 'It seems that the most difficult hurdle to surmount will be the wishes of the people of Tottenham' (Bliss, 1945, p. 35). A contributor to the discussion at the conference took an even more totalitarian view saying: 'Planning means control – you have got to put people out, tell them where to live and if somebody wants to build a factory, you have got to tell them "nothing doing in Tottenham – you must build a factory in so and so". Russia, Germany and Italy all had planned systems' (Bliss, 1945, p. 40).

How did this view change, as change it did? Why did planners become more favourably disposed towards economics and the social sciences? Primarily, I think, because although planners could lay down the controls which prevented people from doing some things, it became obvious, first, that these controls had unforeseen effects, and secondly, that it was difficult if not impossible to make people do other things which planners wanted them to do.

One response was a demand for greater powers, powers of positive planning as well as powers of negative planning. The other response was an attempt to find why planning controls were circumvented, and to find out using economic analysis what the secondary effects of planning controls would be, since these can be as important as their primary effects. The point is this. The planner can lay down, for example, that the land round a city should be designated as a green belt and should not be developed. Now if the land remains undeveloped then, in one sense, the planner has been successful. But market forces may result in responses to his success-ful green-belt policy which he may not have wanted at all. If the town becomes prosperous and employment there continues to grow, the demand for space in the town, the supply of which is restricted by the green belt, will cause prices to rise, and some people, who are unable to find accommodation in the city, will be forced to commute across the green belt. The planner wanted neither long journeys to work nor high housing costs but got them as a consequence of achieving his original objective, a constraint on urban sprawl. Although the planner might respond by seeking powers to control more effectively the growth of employment in the city, even if he does, he is also likely to realize that all aspects of the urban economy are interrelated, indeed that the city is an economic (and social) entity and not just a physical structure to be designed.

Since the planning controls imposed after 1947 did have unfore-seen consequences because of market forces, the result was that greater attention began to be paid to the social sciences by planners; indeed town planning itself became more akin to applied social science than anything deriving from architecture or engineering. In Britain town plans themselves have changed from being mainly concerned with the physical structure described in town maps, and have become more akin to the sort of documents produced by a regional or national economic planning directorate.

The primary contribution of urban economics to town planning is, therefore, at present anyway, an understanding of the ways in which the parts of the urban economic system interact – the study of positive urban economics. A second contribution, but one which is not yet regarded as important, is an analysis of what planners ought to do – normative urban economics. There is also a third area, as yet virtually undeveloped, the analysis of what planners do and the reasons why they do what they do – the economics of town planning. Since one legacy of the 'civic design' and 'public health' origins of planning is a tendency to lay down rules as to what constitutes good planning practice the analysis of this kind of problem is important. The contribution of urban economics to town planning is discussed further in chapter 12.

LAND MANAGEMENT

One field in which the contribution of urban economics is only just beginning to be developed but where, in my view, future progress will affect both disciplines considerably in the future is land or real-estate management. In one sense there has been some economic input for many years since those studying land management have usually studied land economics, but in its earlier years land economics meant the institutional, descriptive, study of land, with little analysis and almost no theory.

The development of urban economics, and the parallel development of regional economics and of environmental economics, have radically changed the nature and subject matter of land economics, and significant changes are still to occur. This is because the interests of the real-estate developer and valuer are slightly different to those of the planner. The realtor, to use the American expression, is primarily interested in land and property values, both now and in the future: the planner is more interested in the location of activities. Of course, both location and land values are in principle determined simultaneously – the level of demand at a given location determines its value, its price determines what can afford to locate there. As we indicated earlier, in practice the primary interest of urban economics has, in the past, been in location, because of its development in relation to transport and planning problems. The determination of land and property values has been regarded as of secondary importance. But future development is more likely to be concerned with land values, or, for example, with the impact of taxes, planning controls, or financing methods on property values. The foundation of the American Real Estate and Urban Economics Association and of its associated journal in 1973 is an indication of development in this direction. The land market and the impact of taxation is discussed explicitly in chapter 8 though land values are referred to throughout the book.

GOVERNMENT POLICY

Urban economics is also making an increasing contribution to the analysis and development of government policy towards towns and regions. Regional economics developed at the same time as urban economics, but its development resulted from a different stimulus. In the post-war period of prosperity it appeared that the application of Keynesian economic policies had resulted in full employment at a national level, but some regions still suffered from high levels of unemployment. So economic analysis directed at the regional level was developed to try to solve this kind of problem. Thus, just as urban economics developed primarily out of the interest of some microeconomists in transport problems, so regional economics developed primarily out of the interest of some macroeconomists in localized unemployment problems, what we would now call 'fine tuning' the economy.

Since then regional policy, at least in Britain, has become more spatially oriented and the application of urban economic theory has become more important. So whilst the application of controls to encourage industrial firms to move to the less-prosperous regions in the 1940s and 1950s could be analysed using the tools of regional analysis, study of the application of controls on office development in the mid-1960s involved an aspect of urban economics, since administrative and professional offices tend to locate in, or in relation to, cities, rather than choosing a location within a wider region. In the mid-1970s the spatial concentration of unemployment in the inner areas of the large cities, and the apparent decline of these cities, had clearly to be interpreted using urban economic analysis, and further stimulated the development of the analysis of urban labour markets (see chapter 7). The latest initiative in urban economic policy is the creation of Enterprise Zones – smaller areas in which property development is freed from controls and taxes – and their expected effects can only be analysed using many aspects of urban economics – land markets, manufacturing and commercial location, even local government finance, since one feature of the zones is that firms pay no rates.

The main problem is that urban economics has been primarily used to analyse and criticize policies after they have been put into effect, only rarely has it been used beforehand. The question dealt with has not been, What will be the effect of this policy?, but, What were the effects of this policy and why? This lag in its application is probably an indication of its early stage of development, and so we can expect it to change in the future. In the meantime we should note that research into these policy problems has stimulated the development of the appropriate theoretical analyses, although this has probably meant that other areas which are not yet policy relevant have been neglected in consequence.

URBAN ECONOMICS IN OUTLINE

It is described above how urban economics began as the theoretical analysis of the pattern of residential location in a large city. In chapter 2 we also begin with the analysis of residential location, not only for historical reasons, but because housing actually occupies most of the developed land in any city. For this reason the overall demand for space can be treated as being mainly determined by the demand for housing space, and so it is permissible, at this introductory level anyway, to analyse the pattern of land and property values which result from the actions of households, taking the other demands for space as given.

The results of this analysis can then be used to shed light on the relative costs of different urban locations, through differences in the cost of space and the cost of labour. These costs have to be borne by the manufacturing and commerical firms which provide the jobs to which the households commute. In chapters 3 and 4 we analyse the reasons why the firms owning manufacturing plants or offices are willing to bear these costs by locating their activities in cities, particularly in or near the city centre where these costs are highest – what benefits they gain, what 'external economies' make these locations profitable.

However, all cities are not the same. The most obvious differences are in terms of size. In all national economies there exists an urban hierarchy with very few very large cities, a larger number of smaller cities, and very many small towns. The interaction between the costs and the benefits of location in cities of various sizes which we have analyzed in chapters 2, 3, and 4, allow us to examine, in chapters 5 and 6, the reasons why such an urban hierarchy exists, and to analyse its characteristics.

Chapter 7 deals with urban change. The prediction of the effects of changes in transport costs was, after all, the original stimulus to the development of urban economics. Having shown the progress that has been made in the analysis of the economic structure of cities in the earlier chapters, in chapter 7 we use this to show how improvements in transport and telecommunications cause changes to occur in the economic structure of cities, and so demonstrate, we hope, that some progress has been made in providing answers to the original problems.

However, urban change puts a strain on the operation of the urban economy, and in the succeeding four chapters we examine the economics of the urban labour market (chapter 8), the land market (chapter 9), the system of local government finance (chapter 10), and the urban transport system (chapter 11). Each of these responds to changes in the urban economy of which it is a part, and these responses may create further problems; the reader will not need to be reminded of recent controversies over inner-city unemployment, derelict land and property, local government expenditure and its control, and the subsidization of public transport.

In chapter 12 we discuss the economics of planning the urban system – the objectives of town planning, the choice of methods, and the effects of the planning controls used.

In the book we have almost exclusively discussed the economy of cities in developed Western economies. In the final chapter (chapter 13) we evaluate the relevance of our analyses to cities in the less-developed world, discussing particularly the features which distinguish these cities from those we have dealt with in the rest of the book.

One question has still to be dealt with in this introductory chapter before we can begin the analysis of the economy of cities and that is, Why do cities exist?

WHY CITIES EXIST

There is one necessary condition for some form of urban place to exist. There must be some agricultural surplus. If this condition is fulfilled then towns may exist for other reasons – economies of scale in production, the uneven distribution of resources, the needs of government.

If the population working on the land do not produce a surplus over and above what is required to maintain them at subsistence level, then there is nothing left over to support those who are not engaged in agriculture. This surplus may be extracted by force or custom to support a warrior or priest class (Mumford, 1961). But if towns exist for economic rather than military reasons the surplus must be traded by the farmers for goods or services produced in the towns. This is most likely if there are some economies of scale in production. After all, if there were not, the farmers and peasants could either eat better or use part of their time in producing manufactured goods and they could produce them as cheaply as any town worker. To some extent, of course, this is what has happened. But if a person, or group of people, in other words a firm of some kind, can produce the goods in markedly less time than the peasant or his family, then the peasant will find it worth his while to import the good from the town and trade surplus agricultural produce for it.

These economies of scale may arise within the firm. The 'internal economies' may be due to the division of labour and the resultant increase in productivity due to specialization in particular tasks. Adam Smith, the founder of modern economics, ascribed economic growth mainly to the economies gained through the division of labour, pointing out also that the division of labour is limited by the extent of the market so that 'there are some sorts of industry, even of the lower kind, which can be carried on nowhere but in a great town' (Smith, 1776, p. 15).

The economies of scale are also likely to occur within the firm because of the use of specialized machinery, machinery which is too expensive and too specialized for each peasant to purchase for himself, but which allows the firm to produce the good more quickly and more cheaply than each individual farmer when it is manufacturing a large quantity. In practice, of course, since specialized machinery usually requires skilled labour, the two kinds of internal economy may be difficult to distinguish.

The economies of scale may also arise outside the firm. The 'external economies' occur when the grouping together of firms in a particular place allows them, for example, to use common services and suppliers, to create a market, to share the cost of training labour. These external economies are a particular feature of large diversified cities, as the various firms gain advantages from their concentration together in one place.

Although economies of scale are the primary reason for the growth of cities, they may also come into existence at particular locations because of the uneven distribution of resources. Most obviously the geographical concentration of mineral resources encourages the growth of mining towns and villages, which as in the American West or in Australia may grow quickly with a boom, and, as quickly, disappear or become ghost towns when the ore is worked out. A natural harbour or a crossing point on a river may also be the reason for a settlement, as Sydney has grown up because of its fine natural harbour. But note that the settlement cannot exist solely for that reason, there must also be some reason for trade through the port or across the river; the trade must include either some part of the agricultural surplus or goods manufactured elsewhere because of economies of scale of some kind or the minerals extracted in some other part of the country. So the settlement of Sydney could grow and develop initially only with the trade of New South Wales with the rest of the world.

Another reason for the growth and existence of cities is their role as centres of government. Until recently this used to be relatively unimportant, but it became more important towards the end of the middle ages when it became possible, with more efficient tax systems, for king and court to settle down at a single place rather than travelling from place to place being supported by the host area. In more recent times it has become feasible to create administrative capitals functioning almost solely as government centres, such as Washington, Canberra or Brasilia.

In the case of most major cities the various reasons for urban location and growth tend to be naturally reinforcing. London, for example, was located at a point on the River Thames where ships trading with Europe could be brought upstream, and where it was also possible to maintain a river crossing, at first a <u>ford</u> or ferry but later a bridge. This favourable location encouraged its growth as a commercial centre trading with Europe and its growth was assisted by the eventual location of the seat of government at Westminster just upstream from the City of London. The presence of the court, and the existence of the port, encouraged the growth of trades specializing in the manufacture of imported goods, particularly luxuries for sale to the court and its ladies.

So not only was London the major trading and manufacturing centre for South-east England, it was also a major port and also the centre of government, and these three functions combined caused it to become a specialized manufacturing centre. Moreover, the concentration of commercial and trading functions eventually encouraged further commercial development, developments which also occurred in one way or another, in other world cities. For example, the banks developed out of the practice of the goldsmiths taking and storing other's gold and lending the proportion of it which they could safely assume would not be withdrawn. In London the maritime insurance market grew up as those taking on the business began meeting at Lloyd's coffee house. The stock exchange came into existence in a similar way. The size of the city as a commercial and trading centre ensured the existence of enough people interested in insurance, or in trading stocks, so that a market could come into existence trading not in goods, as markets had done previously, but in 'rights' of one kind or another.

This growth of the very large, predominantly commercial, world cities in the nineteenth and twentieth centuries was dependent on developments in other fields, initially on improvements in transport. It is not enough that the agricultural sector should be able to produce a surplus over and above subsistence level, it must also be able to trade this surplus for the goods produced in the towns and cities, and to do this it must be possible to transport goods economically. When transport was slow and expensive then only small towns could exist because agricultural produce could only be transported from the area immediately surrounding any town. When transport improvements occurred at the earliest stages of the industrial revolution – through improvements in road surfaces or the construction of canals – so they allowed the transport of the greater agricultural surplus resulting from the simultaneous agricultural revolution to more distant, expanding towns. The age of steam continued this development, as food could be imported from the most distant parts of the world and in return manufactured goods exported. Moreover, the fact that the manufactures produced in the towns could be traded nationally and internationally encouraged increased economies of scale and the specialization of towns and cities in particular kinds of manufacture – for example, the cotton towns or the steel towns – as plants became larger and labour more specialized.

The growth of the world cities such as New York, London, or Tokyo, in the late nineteenth and early twentieth centuries was dependent on another kind of transport improvement, the ability to transfer information more rapidly over long distances, initially using improved postal services and the electric telegraph, and later wireless and the telephone. By these means the office functions could be separated from the manufacturing functions of companies, and insurers, bankers and brokers of various kinds could arrange transactions which were actually completed thousands of miles away. So in London the underwriters of Lloyds could move from insuring ships docked in the Port of London to insuring ships on the other side of the world which might never sail near Europe; the brokers in the various commodity exchanges could move from trading commodities which lay nearby in the ships and stores of the port to trading rights to these commodities anywhere in the world. Over time the functions of these large cities changed from trading goods to trading rights to goods, from shifting goods to shifting paper.

Nowadays it is possible that developments in the ability to transfer, store and process information, in other words in information technology, will lead to the transfer of many office functions out of the cities and so to a reduction in the size and status of the great metropolises. We shall discuss this later in chapters 4 and 6; in this brief survey we have been concerned with the processes which have generated urban growth in the past. As technology changes in the future so cities will continue to change. The urban economist must attempt to explain and to predict the pattern of change.

FURTHER READING

Perloff (1973) discusses the development of urban economics with reference to the United States and McKean (1973) discusses critically the nature of urban economics. The development of cities from pre-history to the present day is studied in depth and at length by Mumford (1961). Urban history has itself developed rapidly as a subject at the same time as urban economics, with studies such as those by Rudé (1971) or Dyos (1961). These studies are of interest in themselves but of course the economic topics are mixed in with and almost inseparable from political, social, planning, architectural and other aspects. Keen students of the economics of urban areas cannot confine their studies only to economics, however.

2

Residential Location

Lady Bracknell: You have a town house, I hope? A girl with a
simple unspoiled nature like Gwendolen could hardly be expected to reside in the country.
The Importance of Being Earnest Act I

As we noted in the introduction, modern urban economics has
largely sprung from a theory of residential location developed in the
late 1950s. This theory has come to be called the 'trade off' theory of
residential location because it represents each household as choosing
its location by 'trading off' housing costs, which tend to fall with
distance from the city centre, against transport costs, which tend to
increase with distance from the centre. The theory's usefulness is that
it helps to explain not only the pattern of residential location, as we
show in the second section of this chapter, but also the pattern of
land values in the city, as discussed in the third section. It is because
of this that is has come to be a core theory of urban economics.
Most of the land within an urban area is used for housing, so to a
large extent variations in residential land values can be treated as
determining all land values. But since variations in the cost of space,
both within large cities and between different cities, are going to be
crucial in determining the location of other activities within and
between cities, a theory which explains what these variations are
likely to be helps to explain what the locational patterns of these
other activities are likely to be.

Before the 'trade off' theory was developed, the explanation of
residential location patterns was based on what has since become
known as the 'filter down' or 'historical' theory which we consider
first. This was based on the observation that in general the newest

housing tended to be occupied by the wealthiest households, whilst older housing 'filtered down' to poorer households: the pattern of residential location is, therefore, dependent on the historical pattern of development in the city, since it is explained in terms of the age and quality of housing.

There is no doubt that the 'trade off' theory is methodologically a better theory than the other in that it explains more, particularly the pattern of land values, but its supremacy has had the effect of emphasizing the demand side, household preferences for different locations, and playing down the importance of the supply side, the historical pattern of development. Just as both supply *and* demand are important in determining any price – in Marshall's phrase; 'We might as reasonably dispute whether it is the upper or the under blade of a pair of scissors that cuts a piece of paper' (Marshall, 1920, p. 348) – so both supply and demand must be relevant to the determination of patterns of location and will eventually be incorporated into the theory of residential location.

One way in which the past pattern of development may affect the present location of households in different income groups is discussed in the fourth section. It is shown that high-income households are more likely to occupy lower-density areas and an area is more likely to be developed at a lower density if it is controlled by a single land owner.

The density of development is one cause of residential segregation, if only of different income groups. Other factors which may cause residential segregation in terms of income, class, or race are discussed in the fifth section – environment differences, social preference, and differences in the services required – and in the final section we briefly consider yet another factor, the impact of differences in the services provided in different local government areas, a factor which is important in the United States, but which is less important in countries with a more centralized form of government, such as the United Kingdom.

THE FILTER DOWN THEORY

The earliest version of this theory was developed inductively by E. W. Burgess in the early 1920s to explain the pattern of residential location in Chicago. He observed that in general the higher the income of any household the further it lived from the centre of

Chicago; moreover, because of the rapid development of Chicago in the nineteenth century, it was also true that the newer the housing the further from the centre it was located and therefore that the highest-income households lived in the newest housing furthest from the centre and the poorest households lived in the oldest housing nearest the centre. Thus the pattern of location was explained by the 'filtering down' of housing. As the city expanded so the richest households moved on to the newest houses on the edge of the city, leaving their former housing to be occupied by slightly lower-income households – and so on until at the centre of the city the very oldest housing was vacated by the poorest households as they moved outward into very slightly newer housing and their former housing was demolished and replaced by the offices and shops of the expanding Central Business District.

The theory has been given various names. It has been described as social ecology because its concepts were based on the ecological concepts of invasion and succession. Burgess argues that the growth of the population of the city results in an expansion of its area and a consequent 'tendency for each inner zone to extend its area by the invasion of the next outer zone' (Burgess, 1925, p. 50) so that a particular site served a succession of users. To geographers it has been the 'concentric zone theory' because Burgess represented the 'ideal construction of the tendencies of any town or city to expand radially from its central business district' as consisting of a series of concentric zones.

Economists on the other hand, concentrating not on the pattern itself but on the economic forces which are supposed to cause the pattern have called it, as I have, a 'filter down' theory. Moreover, the pattern of concentric zones is, in terms of the description of the economic process, accidental, so that it need not occur even if that description were accurate. An old city which was not increasing in population might have newly built houses occupied by the wealthy anywhere in the city, the pattern of location depending solely on the pattern of housing replacement. It is for this reason that Alonso called it a 'historical theory' of residential location.

A variant of the historical theory was published by Hoyt in 1939. He argued that a high-income sector would become established in a city for topographical, sociological, or historical reasons, for example, along a lake front or along a fast transport route. This sector would migrate outwards with the growth of the city; some upper-middle-income households might occupy new houses in adjacent sectors, but otherwise 'occupants of houses in the low rent categories tend to move out in bands from the centre of the city mainly by filtering into houses left behind by the high income groups' (Hoyt, 1939, p. 120). Thus the economic processes are the same as in Burgess's theory save that, for various reasons – social, prestige, environment, etc. – high-income sectors exist in the outer parts of the city. It follows that the pattern of zones and sectors is to some extent accidental, since they would not necessarily occur in the same way in a city which was not expanding. Thus the filter down theory could be correct even if a pattern of concentric zones or of sectors did not exist. The theory is primarily a theory of housing occupancy which can also be used to explain the pattern of residential location.

It should be noted that the filter down theory, as an explanation of either housing occupation or residential location, is a positive theory rather than a normative theory. Conceptually a positive theory explains what happens and can be used to predict what will happen if circumstances change.' A normative theory shows what ought to happen, what will maximize welfare, and what the consequences for economic welfare will be of any change, either in terms of economic efficiency or in terms of the distribution of welfare.

The filter down theory describes and explains; it does not show whether the process ought to happen. Moreover, I know of no analysis of filtering in terms of welfare economics. Even if it could be accepted, intuitively, that the process of filtering down was economically efficient, it does not seem equally plausible that the process is equitable. Indeed a situation where the poorest get the worst housing and the richest get the best seems, on the face of it, inequitable.

Nevertheless, the notion that filtering down is optimal was the principle on which the American policy of urban renewal was based in the 1950s and 1960s. It was thought that the enforced demolition of the oldest, and therefore the worst, housing occupied by the poorest households and its replacement by housing for the highest-income groups (so called middle-income housing) would result in the improvement of the housing of all income groups, but particularly those at the bottom of the scale, as each group moved into newer, better-quality, housing.

In fact, of course, things did not turn out like that. The poorest households did move into the next best available housing, but, since they were unable to afford anything more than they had paid before,

the housing became more overcrowded and its condition deterio-
rated. The policy therefore appeared to have displaced, at great cost,
the worst housing conditions and the poorest households from one
part of the city to another.

The cost of the policy and recognition of its defects eventually led
to its abandonment. The British policy of clearing slums and
replacing them by new local-authority housing for the groups which
had been displaced was of course different in kind since the filtering
'chain' was broken into by the provision of new homes for the
poorest groups.

THE TRADE OFF THEORY

It is possible that the increasingly obvious inadequacies of the filter
down theory in the 1950s helped to stimulate the development of an
alternative theory, but the obvious cause, as we indicated in chapter
1, was increasing concern over traffic congestion and the transport
problems in cities, the consequent attempt to model transport flows
within cities as a function of land use, and the incentive to create a
theory which related land use to the transport system. Certainly, of
the two authors who laid the foundations of the theory, Wingo
(1961) and Alonso (1964a) and two later developers of the theory
Muth (1969) and Evans (1973a), only one, Muth, was primarily
interested in housing as such.

Whilst the filter down theory assumed that household location
depended on housing conditions, in the trade off theory it was
assumed that housing conditions in any area would depend on, or
adapt to, the kind of households which located there. Whilst the
former was, in economic terms, a supply-side theory, the latter was
clearly a demand-side theory.

The basic assumptions of the trade off theory are as follows. There
is a large city with a single central business district to which all
workers commute. It is located on a flat plain with no topographical
features. The transport system carries commuters from all the
suburbs to the centre with equal efficiency. There are no externalities
of any kind and housing can be costlessly adapted. Since everything
else has been assumed away the only factor which the household has
to consider in choosing its location is the cost of the journey to work.
However, the attempt to minimize these costs results in a high
demand for inner-city locations and this causes the cost of land and

housing to be higher in the inner city than in the suburbs. Indeed competition for sites will result in land values being highest at the centre of the city and falling at a decreasing rate as sites further and further from the centre of the city are considered. The relationship between the cost of housing and distance from the city centre will be as shown in figure 2.1a. The cost of transport to the centre will be as shown in figure 2.1b. A household in choosing its location may be thought of as considering the costs of alternative locations, both transport costs and housing costs, and choosing to locate at the cost minimizing location – shown as C in figure 2.1c. (In travelling out from the centre of the city the household bears higher transport costs but is compensated by lower housing costs – thus in choosing its location it 'trades off' transport costs against housing costs; which explains the name of the theory.)

How is the pattern of location determined? Each household has three factors to consider in choosing its location. First, the amount of space that it requires. Clearly, if it wanted a large amount of space the savings from locating further from the city centre would be great, and one would expect large households to locate furthest from the centre, as they do in the English and American suburbs. Secondly, there are the two components of transport cost, the direct cost of travel, i.e. the fare paid to the transport company or the running costs of a private vehicle, and the opportunity cost of the time spent travelling. Various empirical studies have shown that this time is valued at about 25 per cent of the traveller's hourly wage rate.

Clearly, therefore, if the household's demand for space remains constant whilst the number of journeys to work increases the household will find that it could save money by moving closer to the centre. Thus one would expect households in which a high proportion worked to be located close to the centre, whilst households in which, say, only one person worked would be located further out. This also appears to be the pattern in British and American cities.

As a household's income increases its demand for space increases, which should lead it to locate further out from the centre, and the value of travelling time increases which should lead it to locate nearer the centre. Which of these two forces dominates depends on the exact relationship between the increase in the demand for space and the increase in income, i.e. the elasticity of demand for space with respect to income. If this elasticity is generally high, certainly if it is above one, the richer households will locate on the edge of the city,

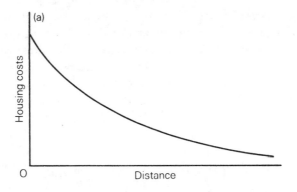

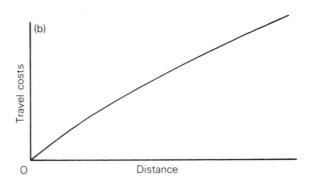

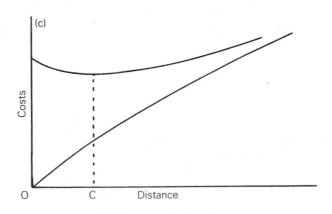

FIGURE 2.1

and the poorer at the centre. If it is generally low, certainly if it is close to zero, the richer households will locate close to the centre and the poorer at the edge. In Britain and America the average elasticity is probably just under one with the result that both patterns occur, although the dominant pattern is that of the richer households living in the outer suburbs. Unfortunately there is little information on the income elasticities in European or Latin American cities, although the theory suggests that, given the pattern of location, one would expect that income elasticities were lower than in Britain and America.

MARKET EQUILIBRIUM IN THE CITY

The importance of the trade off theory is not only that it provides a reasonably good explanation of patterns of residential location, but also that it provides the basis for an analysis of the location of other activities in the city, which the filter down theory cannot do, and for a general equilibrium analysis of the city.

The basic tool of analysis is the bid-price curve developed by Alonso (1964a). Take any household and suppose that household, with given tastes, income etc., is offered space adjacent to the city centre at a certain rent per unit of space. This is indicated in figure 2.2 by OC, where rent is measured along the vertical axis and distance from the city centre is measured along the horizontal axis. Suppose now that we choose another location within the city, more distant from the centre, and ask the household to state the price per unit of space that it would have to pay at that location, in order to be indifferent between the original location adjacent to the city centre and the location at that distance. The rent at the more distant location must be lower, given that all land is the same, there are no externalities, and all work places are at the city centre, because the cost of reaching the centre is higher. This procedure can be carried out at other locations and a schedule of prices and distances can be obtained. From these a bid-price curve can be constructed such as CC' in figure 2.2. It will be appreciated that the bid-price curve is similar in construction to an indifference curve used in the basic analysis of consumer behaviour.

Just as a complete set of indifference curves can be obtained, so a complete set of bid-price curves can be derived covering all possible combinations of prices and distances. By setting a price higher than

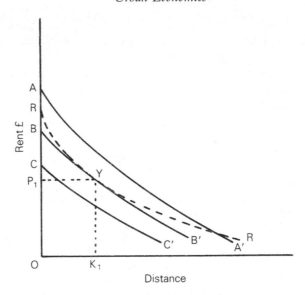

FIGURE 2.2

OC adjacent to the city centre, say OA, the household could be asked to define another bid-price curve AA'. Since at any location the household would be paying a higher rent, this curve represents a lower level of welfare. In any set of bid-price curves, the lower curve represents the higher level of welfare.

If the rent gradient is known, then the household's choice of location can be represented as saying that it attempts to find the price/distance combination which lies along the lowest attainable bid-price curve (and, therefore, represents the highest level of welfare). This equilibrium location is shown in figure 2.2 by the tangency of the bid-price curve BB' with the rent gradient RR at Y fixing the household's optimal location as at a distance OK_1 from the centre, paying a price per space unit of OP_1.

The above analysis takes the rent gradient as given. The usefulness of the bid-price curve concept is that the rent gradient can in principle be obtained from the bid-price curves, i.e. from household preferences. This can most easily be seen in the simplest case, where all the households in the city are assumed to have the same tastes, etc., and so to have identical sets of bid-price curves. Suppose that figure 2.3 shows some of this set of curves; in equilibrium the rent

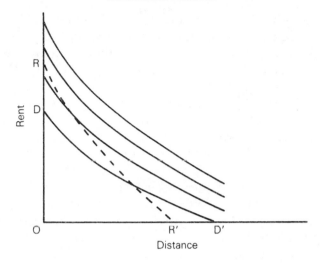

FIGURE 2.3

gradient must lie wholly along one of the set of curves, but not necessarily one of those shown. For suppose it did not but initially lay along, say, RR'. Then all households would find that their optimal location would be at R', for this would be on the lowest attainable bid-price curve. If they attempted to move towards R' this would raise prices at R' and prices elsewhere would tend to fall. The adjustment would continue until the rent gradient lay along a bid-price curve, say DD'. Which bid price would depend on the population of the city, and so on the area required to accommodate it. A rent gradient lying along DD' would, if the price of land outside the city can be ignored, ensure that an area of land of radius OD' would be developed. If the population of the city were larger, a larger area would have to be developed and the rent gradient would have to lie along a higher bid-price curve. If it were smaller it could lie along a lower bid-price curve.

Armed with this analysis we can go on to make some predictions about things other than residential location – variations in wage levels, and the factors determining the location of firms. An implication of the analysis is that, *ceteris paribus*, the population of a larger city might be expected to be worse off than the population of a smaller because their housing and/or transport costs are higher. It follows that there must be other benefits to living in a large city either in terms of the greater range of consumer services available, or in terms of higher wages. The evidence suggests the benefits to be a little of both, but certainly wages are higher in the larger city. Moreover, if the rent gradient is higher, the cost of space is higher at all distances from the centre so that the cost of space is going to be higher, for all users, at the city centre. Thus the commercial and industrial users will have to pay both higher wage rates and higher space costs in larger cities, and they must gain some advantages from their location. Similar reasoning would suggest that the space costs of commercial and industrial users will fall with distance from the city centre, as also will the cost of labour since the housing or transport costs of the employees will be less. The advantages which the firms might gain from a central city location are discussed in the following three chapters.

Finally, bid–price curves can be used to show that the rent gradient must have the shape shown in the diagrams in this chapter, i.e. rents, or house prices, will tend to fall with distances from the centre at a diminishing rate. Supposing there are two sets of households in the city, one with steeper bid–price curves than the other. The equilibrium rent gradient must lie along sections of curves in both sets. A possible solution is shown in figure 2.4 where the rent gradient lies

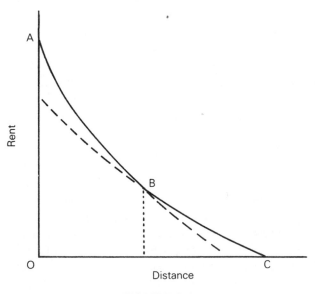

FIGURE 2.4

along one bid-price curve AB, and the other BC. The land market is in equilibrium if the households with the steepest bid-price curves can be accommodated in a circle of radius OR, and the others in a ring of width RC. Note that those with the steepest bid-price curves can always outbid the others for locations closer to the centre, whilst those with the least-steep curves can always outbid the first group for locations further from the centre. This will be generally true. Households with the steepest bid-price curves will be able to outbid others for locations closer to the city centre, and the rent gradient lying along sections of bid prices of all the households will be steepest close to the centre but diminish in slope as distance increases, as assumed in the earlier analyses.

We have shown that the trade off theory is useful not only as a theory of residential location but also as a theory explaining the general variation in property values and land values both within cities and between cities. Moreover, there is considerable evidence that land values do change in the way predicted; some of this evidence was drawn together by Clark (1966) and is shown in figure 2.5. As the graphs in the figure show, however, there are large variations in land values which are not accounted for by distance from the centre even though in most cases this factor is important. The trade off theory appears to do a reasonably good job in explaining the general pattern of location and land values in a large city, but variations in smaller towns or over sectors of large cities may be unexplained. This is not surprising: the assumptions on which the theory is based appear to be quite restrictive – a single work place at the city centre, uniform travel costs, no topographical features, costless adaptation of housing, and no externalities of any kind. Clearly variation in any one of these will affect the pattern of location. The first two of the assumptions are probably relatively unimportant, however, in that the predictions of the theory can easily be modified to take account of location patterns where there are a number of workplaces or where travel costs are not uniform in all directions (Evans, 1973a, chapters 10, 12). The other assumptions are more important, however. They may have been made initially for the same reason as the others, to simplify the mathematics, but it is considerably more likely that their relaxation will alter the predicted pattern of location. In particular the assumption that housing can be costlessly adapted assumes completely unimportant the very factor that the filter down theory assumed to be the most

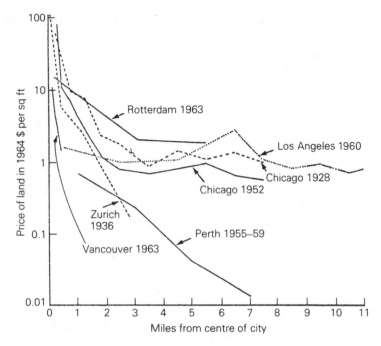

Source: Clark (1966)

FIGURE 2.5
Land values in some major cities

important. Moreover, the assumption that there are no externalities assumes away the problems of density, etc., that most concern town planners. It is these latter problems which we consider in the following sections.

One last point must be made regarding the trade off theory. In that theory the economic forces pushing the household to choose its location are differences in housing costs and differences in travel costs. If those differences are large, as they will be in a large city with a very dominant city centre, then these economic forces will be very powerful and the trade off theory will explain the general pattern of location very well. If the differences are small, as they will be in a small town, those economic forces will be weak, and other factors, such as those we shall be talking about in the next three sections, which do not vary in their importance with city size, will be relatively stronger, so that the trade off theory will explain the general pattern of location relatively badly.

RESIDENTIAL DENSITY

One way in which the trade off theory of residential location can be modified is to recognize that households are not indifferent to variations in residential density but prefer to live at lower rather than higher densities. This modification was carried out by Mirrlees (1972) and Evans (1973a, 1977). The assumption is supported, with respect to Britain and America at least, by econometric studies of house prices.

If households were indifferent to residential density then the optimal density of development of an area would be that at which the (capitalized) rent which households were willing to pay for an additional house in that neighbourhood would be just equal to the cost of building it, and this density of development would be the density at which the area would be developed by profit-maximizing builders.

This is illustrated in figure 2.6, where density is measured along the horizontal axis and costs are measured along the vertical axis. The relationship between density and the average cost per housing unit is shown by the curve OB and the marginal cost curve is the

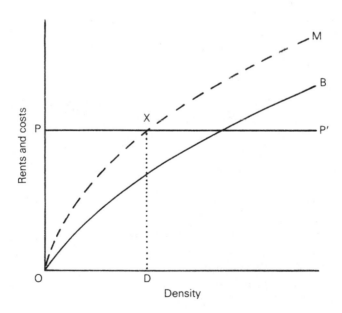

FIGURE 2.6

curve OM. If the price per housing unit at some location is indicated by OP on the vertical axis, and the price does not vary with density, then the demand curve at that location is PP'. The profit maximizing density OD is indicated by the point, X, at which price equals marginal cost.

Where rents were higher, the density of development would be higher since, as the marginal-cost curve shows, the cost of development increases as density increases. Since rents, according to the trade off theory, would tend to be higher in the inner areas of large cities, we would expect densities to be higher, a prediction from economic theory which is generally supported by the empirical evidence.

If residential density does matter to households, so that they prefer lower to higher densities, then the construction of an additional house in a neighbourhood, since it increases the density of the area, reduces the welfare of all the households in that area. If the area is being developed by a large number of builders, none of them will take this into account with the result that the density of development will be too high. Some form of government intervention may therefore be necessary, the most usual form of intervention being a zoning system or a set of controls limiting the density at which areas can be developed.

But the reduction in the welfare of the inhabitants of an area resulting from the increase in density due to the construction of an additional house in an area will be reflected in a reduction in the price per house they are willing to pay. If an area is being developed by a larger number of builders this factor can be ignored by them, since the fall in prices is almost entirely borne by the other builders. If, on the other hand, the area is being developed by a single developer he will take this into account since all the fall in prices due to the increase in density will be borne by him. He therefore has an incentive to develop the area at a lower density; indeed, he should develop it at the optimal density, the density to which the local authority should limit development anyway.

This is illustrated in figure 2.7. OB and OA indicate the average building cost per dwelling and the marginal cost, both as a function of density. The average-revenue curve for the entrepreneur developing the whole area is shown by the line RR', which slopes downwards since the higher the density of development the lower the price per unit. To maximize his profits he should take account of the fact that an

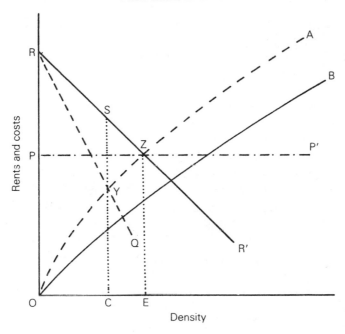

FIGURE 2.7

increase in density of one unit results in a fall in the price of all units, and this is indicated by the marginal-revenue curve RQ. The profit-maximizing density is OC, as indicated by the intersection of the marginal-revenue and marginal-cost curves at Y. This is also the welfare-maximizing density since the developer, in taking account of the fall in price, is in fact taking account of the fall in welfare of the residents as density increases. At a density OC the cost of providing an additional house, CY, is just equal to the benefits accruing to the occupier of the house (the price he pays, CS) less the reduction in everybody else's welfare from the increase in density (i.e. SY).

If development occurs piecemeal, the average-revenue curve facing the developer of each individual site is more or less horizontal, e.g. PP' in figure 2.7. This is because any increase in density on that site does not significantly affect the price he receives for housing on that site, and so each developer need not take it into account.

Long-run equilibrium will occur when this horizontal average-revenue curve passes through Z, the intersection of RR' and OA.

This fixes the density at OE. It can be seen that density is, in some sense, too high (and the price too low) since the density is fixed without taking into account the effect of increases in density on the welfare of the area's residents.

The assumption that households are not indifferent to variations in residential density appears to concern only the demand side, rather than the supply side. But what we have shown above is that differences in the ownership of land will affect the density of development, i.e. there will be an interaction between the demand and supply side. Will these differences also affect the pattern of residential location? It would appear so. It seems plausible to assume that higher-income households care more about, or, rather, are willing to pay more to achieve, a better environment than lower-income households. The latter will have little over after paying for food, clothing, shelter and other basic necessities, and therefore will be unwilling to pay a high premium for lower-density housing. Higher-income households will be more willing to pay a premium. It follows that, in the absence of any other influences, if an area is developed by a single developer he is likely to develop it, not only at a lower density, but also for a higher-income population than if the area is developed piecemeal by a large number of developers who will build at a higher density for a lower-income group. There is some evidence to support this in urban history – a study of the nineteenth-century development of the London suburb of Camberwell attributes some of the differences between development in the north (Peckham) and south (Dulwich) of the suburb to differences in the pattern of land ownership (Dyos, 1961), and a study of the history of eighteenth-century London attributes some of the differences in the development of the East and West Ends of London to the fact that in the East End land ownership was fragmented, while in the West End land was owned in large estates such as the Portman, Bedford and Grosvenor estates (Rudé, 1971). These estates are well known for their tree-lined squares, a pattern of development which would be impossible if large areas of land were not owned by a single landlord.

Thus the ownership of land in the past and the historical pattern of development is likely to affect the present pattern of location, a conclusion which helps to integrate the demand side with the supply side and takes us a step toward an integrated theory of residential location, particularly in so far as it involves the modification of the assumption that housing is costlessly adaptable to the needs of whatever group finds its optimal location there.

The discussion also takes us a little further in ascertaining the optimal pattern of location. We have shown that the optimal density can be achieved by controls or by a unified land ownership. The controls did not exist in the past, so that only those areas developed by a single developer were likely to have been developed at the optimal density, and these were also likely to have been developed for occupation by high-income households. The argument therefore provides an economic justification for something which is probably intuitively accepted anyway; namely, that housing built some time in the past for occupation by low-income households was likely to have been built at too high a density, particularly, if, as seems likely, the demand by low-income households for environmental attributes such as low density tends to increase over time as incomes rise with economic growth.

SOCIAL AGGLOMERATION

Some externalities, which are of particular relevance to the determination of residential location, but which have been very neglected in analyses of the economic theory, are those which lead people of the same type to want to live close to each other. Apart from the desire for particular kinds of local government service which we shall analyse in the next section, there are three kinds of external economy which have this effect. By analogy with the external economies which lead to industrial agglomeration, I have called these social agglomeration economies.

First, there is the tendency for people to want to have as neighbours those they would expect, with a high probability, to be friends with. The geographical evidence suggests that people's friends usually live nearby, and the evidence from social phychology tells us, if we should need telling, that people tend to make friends with those who have similar characteristics to themselves. It follows that we would expect, *ceteris paribus*, that people with high incomes would tend to try to live amongst other high-income people and people with low incomes would want to live amongst other low-income people. Further social stratification is possible, of course, particularly in large cities, where areas may be known as having a high concentration of a particular age group, or ethnic group, or educational background. (Sometimes indeed the place name may become a description of the type, e.g. 'a Hampstead intellectual' in London.)

Secondly, there are the different services which people of different kinds require and which, because there are economies of scale in their provision, can only be provided if the market is sufficiently large. These are most obvious in the case of ethnic minorities. Kosher butchers for Jews, for example, require a large enough market to make it profitable for them to exist. Therefore, if Jews congregate in one area these services will come into existence, and, *once they are in existence*, they provide a reason for Jews elsewhere to live in the area. The same forces apply, although perhaps less obviously with respect to different income groups (jewellers and furriers in very-high-income areas, pawn shops in low-income areas), different age groups (cafés, record shops and places of entertainment in areas where young people live), and even different educational backgrounds (bookshops for the intellectuals).

Thirdly, there is the desire for a favourable physical environment which is most easily and obviously achieved by the high-income groups. This may partly occur because some areas have topographical features which are environmentally desirable – high ground with splendid views, the edge of a lake or the banks of a river. High-income groups will be able to pay a higher premium for these locations than low-income households which, as we have remarked before, will conserve their scarce resources for expenditure on necessities. So areas which naturally have good physical environments will tend to become high-income neighbourhoods. But it is also likely that, quite apart from this, because high-income households live in larger houses with, probably, more private open space, and spend more on maintaining their houses and gardens than do the poor, they will themselves ensure that a high-income neighbourhood is an area with a good physical environment, for the environment of an area is mostly the sum of its parts.

The above analysis sets out the reasons why we should expect neighbourhoods of various kinds to come into existence. The analysis is in effect a positive theory; it explains why we should expect a certain pattern to occur. But it has normative implications. The usual finding in economics is that when an activity generates an external diseconomy, as we argued that an increase in residential density did, then that activity will probably be carried too far, in the absence of any intervention, and should be restricted by controls, by taxes or by other means. Conversely, when an activity generates an external economy then that activity will not be carried far enough, and it should be encouraged, by subsidies or other means so that the full benefit of the external economy can be obtained. In this case the addition of, say, an additional high-income household to a high-income neighbourhood, improves the neighbourhood for the other residents, by increasing the number of possible friends, by increasing the size of the market so that other more-specialized services can be provided more cheaply, and by improving the environment. The household will not take these benefits to other people into account in choosing its location, however, and therefore may choose to live somewhere else, if, say, the housing in the area is found to be too expensive.

The normative economic implication is, therefore, that the social segregation which occurs is too little and that segregation should be encouraged. But this runs counter to the often strongly held view that social segregation should be discouraged, and that social mix should be encouraged.

Of course the economic argument relates to the achievement of economic efficiency; the arguments for social mix are almost wholly non-economic relating to the political and sociological benefits of social mix. In a survey of the subject Wendy Sarkissian (1976) lists only one suggested reason which is at least partly economic (and is, from an economic point of view, probably incorrect).

(1) To improve the functioning of the city and the welfare of its inhabitants, (a) by ensuring the provision of leadership, (b) by promoting economic stability (of a city), and (c) by helping to maintain essential services at minimum expense through mix in housing.

It is not clear how social mix will promote stability, and it is probably not true that mix helps to maintain essential services at minimum expense. For example, if the poorest people require easy access to public telephone boxes, or a good bus service, they are more likely to get these services if they are grouped together in a single area rather than spread evenly and thinly amongst the rest of the population, when the scale economies of providing the services would be minimal.

The other reasons she cites are non-economic:

(2) To 'raise the standards of the lower classes' by nurturing a spirit of emulation.
(3) To encourage aesthetic diversity and raise aesthetic standards.
(4) To encourage cultural cross-fertilization.
(5) To increase equality of opportunity.
(6) To promote social harmony by reducing social and racial tensions.
(7) To promote social conflict in order to foster individual and social maturity.
(8) To help maintain stable residential areas.
(9) To reflect the diversity of the urbanized modern world.

Some of these conflict, of course – social mix cannot both promote social harmony and social conflict. This raises the doubts as to the extent to which they are correct, but for the present the point which must be made is that, although economic analysis suggests that social mix is not efficient, non-economic arguments are used to support it, and on these arguments economics has very little to say.

One possible economic approach might be to approve social segregation as being efficient, and to handle the undoubted equity problems through a grant and tax system operating between areas. Certainly this is the approach suggested by economists with respect to different local government areas, as we show in the next section.

LOCAL GOVERNMENT AND THE TIEBOUT HYPOTHESIS

The only explanation of social agglomeration which has been thoroughly analysed by economists derives from a hypothesis suggested by Charles Tiebout in 1956. He argued that if there were a number of local governments controlling different parts of the metropolitan area, each with the power to decide the quality of the services it provides and the level of taxes it levies, then each householder will choose to locate in the suburb which provides the tax and services package which it most prefers. The result would be, at the least, a tendency for each local-government area to be occupied by the same kind of household. The local-government areas would become socially homogeneous, but there would be considerable differences between the local-government areas.

The hypothesis has been analysed in depth and extensively tested against the empirical evidence for the United States (see, for example, Edel and Sclar, 1974). There, of course, metropolitan areas are governed by a large number of local authorities. The hypothesis is less relevant to the urban areas of European countries where, first, the number of governments is usually small and, secondly, central or metropolitan governments tend to limit the diversity they will allow. However, the theoretical analysis suggests that the provision of local services in this way is efficient, though it will probably be inequitable.

Take, for example, education. If the mechanism suggested by Tiebout is allowed to operate, the childless will tend to live in areas with low taxes and a virtually non-existent school system. Families with children will pay high taxes to live in areas which have good school systems. This is, of course, inequitable, but the alternative, if the two groups are completely mixed, is that school systems have to be provided for the whole area and this is inefficient (at the least the cost will be that children have longer journeys to school). It has been shown by McGuire (1974), however, that it is optimal to allow the Tiebout mechanism to operate so that the many areas provide different services, thus achieving maximum efficiency, and to achieve equity by a system of differential grants and taxes between areas, rather than attempting to solve the equity problem by enforced social mix.

SUMMARY

In this chapter we have reviewed the various theories of residential location. We have argued that the trade off theory is most useful in explaining the pattern of location in very large cities, where travel costs are high and travelling times may be long. In small towns the theory is not at all useful and other factors are more important – the past pattern of development and the ownership of land, environmental attributes, the social preferences of the population, local-government services. In middle-sized cities the various economic forces vie in importance.

We have also shown that the trade off theory can provide the framework for a general equilibrium analysis of the urban land market. This analysis predicts the relationships we might expect between the cost of space and wage costs on the one hand and the size of cities and location within cities on the other. These differences in costs have to be taken into account in explaining the location of manufacturing firms and offices in the next two chapters.

FURTHER READING

The modern economic theory of residential location was first presented formally by Alonso (1964a), but later discussions by Muth (1969) and Evans (1973) include much more empirical evidence. The discussion of residential density is carried further in Evans (1977), and of social agglomeration in Evans (1976). Critical views of the economic approach are presented by Bassett and Short (1980). A radical view of the theory of land rent was put forward by Harvey (1973) and a more recent analysis of land rent and housing from a Marxist viewpoint is presented by Ball et al. (1985).

3

Manufacturing in the Cities

Jack: You always want to argue about things.
Algernon: That is exactly what things were originally made for.
The Importance of Being Earnest Act I

Towns and cities, as we showed in chapter 1, may come into existence as trading centres, as administrative centres, or as manufacturing centres, and most cities will be all three at the same time. But the major growth of cities as manufacturing towns occurred in the nineteenth century, in America and Europe at least, after the early stages of the industrial revolution, when the shift from water and wind power to coal meant that factories could be concentrated and not dispersed, and also made possible an increase in the scale of manufacturing plant. This increase in scale, and the fact that the working population had, necessarily, to live within walking distance of their place of work meant that even single-plant towns could be fairly substantial if the plant were large enough, as for example in steel towns such as Middlesbrough.

Of more interest to the urban economist than the 'company town' are the towns and cities in which several firms and several industries co-exist. As we showed in the preceding chapter, concentration is not 'free'. It increases the demand for space in the city and increases its geographical area; so the larger the city the higher is likely to be the cost of space in the city and the longer is likely to be the average journey to work. The increasing concentration of population may also increase the impact of external diseconomies. Congestion and pollution, which might not be noticeable if the population were scattered in rural areas, become much less tolerable when people are concentrated in a small area.

These costs may be borne by the population, but if the market works efficiently they will be borne by the employing firms through higher wage costs. Since this concentration is avoidable, and so, therefore, are the higher costs, there must be economic reasons for the concentration of manufacturing in a single city or town, first, through the sequencing of production processes so that one firm's output is another's input with the consequent need to minimize transport costs through proximity, secondly, through the existence of agglomeration economies of some kind, and thirdly, because the firms and employees in the city constitute such a large market that it is worth supplying it through manufacturing plants located there.

INDUSTRIAL LOCATION

The basis of the theory of industrial location at the interregional or international level is due to Weber (1928), his work being later developed and modified by Isard (1956) and Moses (1958). An excellent summary and introduction to the theory of industrial location is due to Alonso (1964b). At its simplest the problem is one of choosing a location for a plant which processes material produced at a single source, when the output of the plant is sold at a single market. When the market is some distance from the source of the raw material, the best location for the plant, if transport costs are the only factors which vary with location, must be either adjacent to the source, at the market, or somewhere along the transport route between the two.

The Weberian analysis shows that in practice the minimum cost location will either be at the source or at the market. There are two reasons for this. First, unloading and loading goods is an expense which it is unprofitable to incur unnecessarily, and it may be avoided if the materials are processed at the point where they are produced or where the final product is sold. Secondly, fare or transport tariff structures tend to be non-linear so that the cost of transport tends to be lower, per mile, for long rather than for short distances. It follows that firms can minimize transport costs if goods are transferred from the source to the market in one long journey rather than two short ones.

The major exception to this rule occurs when goods have to be trans-shipped from one transport system to another, for example at a port. Since the goods have to be unloaded anyway it may be economical to process them at that point.

The basic argument can easily be understood if readers think of themselves as travelling from work to home by train and wishing to do some shopping on the way. The journey will almost certainly be less expensive and quicker if the shopping is done either near home or near work, rather than getting off the train at some intermediate point. If, however, the commuter travels by bus to the station and then takes the train, there is the third option of shopping at or near the station.

Which of the two or three possible locations is chosen for the plant will depend on the relative cost of transporting the raw materials and the processed product. If the cost of transporting the first is cheap and the second dear, the plant will be best located at the market, as for example are bakeries or breweries. If the cost of transport of the raw material is high, but that of the finished product is low, processing will take place at the source, as occurs for example with most ore refining or with fruit and vegetable canning or freezing. Location at a trans-shipment point will come about if, first, the cost of transporting the raw materials over the first stage of the journey is cheaper than the cost of transporting the product, and, secondly, the cost of transporting the product over the second stage of the journey is cheaper than the cost of transporting the materials. So manufacturing has often occurred at ports because bulky, low-value materials could be transferred relatively cheaply by sea, but would be more expensive to transport by road or rail than the less-bulky, higher-value, finished products.

Examples of manufacturing at a port are the tobacco industries of Glasgow and Bristol, and the food firms located in Liverpool. An example often cited in the geographical literature is the flour-milling industry of Buffalo on Lake Erie in upper New York State. A more modern example would be the oil refineries built on the coasts of Western Europe in the 1950s and 1960s.

The port as a trans-shipment point provides one explanation for the concentration of different manufacturing firms at a single location. Another can be seen in the way in which market-oriented firms will locate in an already large city to serve its population. A third is provided by the sequencing of production processes. Thus, if oil refining takes place near the market, then the products from refineries may be used by the petrochemicals industry and that industry's products may in turn be inputs to the chemicals or plastics industries before reaching the final consumer in finished form.

In this way a concentration or agglomeration of firms and industries may occur. The sequence may be linear, in the way that we have described above, with one firm's finished product being another's raw material, but the situation will be more complex when the inputs of one group of industries are the inputs of several others. An example of this is the engineering industry in Birmingham and the West Midlands where the manufacturers of machine tools, pressed steel, electrical equipment, and so on, supply to the car, motor cycle, cycle, and other industries.

This kind of concentration is dependent both on transport technology and economies of scale in manufacturing. In the nineteenth century goods could be shipped long distances by sea, canal, or rail but short distances only slowly by horse and cart. There was, therefore, a considerable incentive to minimize these short-distance transfers. The result was a concentration of industry in towns and cities, particularly in ports, on the sites of raw materials such as the English coal fields, or at major markets such as London. Reductions in transport costs since then, and the growth of cheaper, faster road haulage, has tended to weaken the need for proximity, and containerization has reduced the advantages of manufacturing at ports. These changes have led to the dispersal of manufacturing away from the conurbations and large cities.

Even in the nineteenth century, however, an industry might locate in a number of small industrial towns rather than in a single large city – see, for example, the Lancashire cotton towns. The costs of concentration – high land costs, high labour costs, congestion and pollution – mean that for concentration to be advantageous some additional benefits, some external economies, must usually be additionally gained from it. It is to these agglomeration economies that we turn next.

AGGLOMERATION ECONOMIES

Agglomeration economies, which describe the economies or cost reductions which are possible if a group of firms locate near to each other, were first explicitly discussed by Weber. Other researchers have given these economies other names. Lichtenberg (1960), and Vernon (1960) in studies of the manufacturing industries of New York described them as external economies and made some attempt to define them. Isard (1965) distinguished urbanization economies from localization economies, the latter referring to the economies derived by firms in a particular industry from locating near to each other, and the former referring to the economies derived by the firms in many industries from locating in the same area. Although this might be a useful theoretical distinction to make, in practice it is extremely difficult to distinguish the one from the other.

In principle, however, these economies, whatever one calls them, arise because of the existence of some kind of service or supply which is either not available elsewhere or is more expensive elsewhere. In this the term external economies is probably more meaningful than the others. The economies are scale economies which are external to firms or industries which are concentrated there. The increased demand because of the concentration together of these firms allows other firms which provide supplies or services to grow larger. In the case of a number of these firms there are economies of scale, which may be very great, so that they can provide these services or supply cheaper if they are supplying a larger concentrated market. The economies are thus external to one group of firms, those which are mainly exporting their goods and services out of the city, but are internal to others, those which are mainly selling goods and services to the first group.

The operation of the agglomeration economies, and the way in which they serve to encourage urban growth can be demonstrated using Wilbur Thompson's illustration of the growth process (Thompson, 1966, p. 13), one obviously inspired by the growth of cities in the American mid-west. Suppose a small town is already in existence serving the trading needs of the surrounding rural community. If a meat-packing plant is located in the region it may be located in this town because there is already a labour supply. If a second meat-packing plant is to be located in the region, it may also be placed in this town because some of the labour is now trained in the necessary skills and bidding some away from the existing firms may be cheaper than training them from scratch.

Now, where a single firm might have to import supplies, for example meat-cutting tools, from some distance, if there are two firms located in the town their joint demand may be large enough to make it profitable for a meat-cutting tools manufacturer to be located there. The presence of this firm, and the supply of trained labour already in existence, now constitute external economies which make the town even more attractive to any further meat-packing firms intending to locate in the general region. If there are economies of scale in the manufacture of meat-cutting tools, any further increase in demand if any new firms locate there further reduces the cost of making them and the price at which they can be sold. It is clear that the interaction between demand and the cost of production increases the attractiveness of the town to new firms as a number of firms already there increases. The only things preventing 'excessive' concentration are the increased costs of concentration already mentioned – higher land costs, higher wage rates, congestion, pollution – and, in this case, the dependence of the meat-packing firms in the city on a supply of meat which must come from the surrounding area.

In sum, the concentration of firms at a single location increases the size of the market for those other firms supplying goods and services to them. This increase in market size allows the supplying firms to take advantage of any economies of scale and hence to provide these goods and services more cheaply; the cheapness of these goods and services relative to other locations where the demand is less encourages firms which use these goods and services to locate there; and so on. If the goods and services are provided to firms in a single industry then we can describe them as localization economies, and if to firms in several industries as urbanization economies, but since such a clear distinction is rare – firms are unlikely to supply only firms in one industry – for practical purposes the division is, as we have said, of little use.

One other kind of external economy we have already mentioned in passing. It arises, when there are a number of firms employing labour with similar skills, from the existence of this pool of skilled labour which can be drawn upon by firms setting up in business or expanding, or, indeed, in filling any vacancies. Since there are likely always to be vacancies occurring, unless the firm is contracting, its labour costs are likely to be less because this pool of labour exists. Once again the skills can be peculiar to a particular industry or more general.

A third kind of external economy is similar to the above. It arises when services and suppliers exist in an area even though there may be no economies of scale, and it applies to new or expanding firms. Take the case of an urban area with a large number of firms and a large amount of space. Because of natural turnover a company wishing to set up in business is more likely to find space available here than in a smaller town. In the latter case the plant would have to be built from scratch, and the costs of starting up would be that much greater. Once again the space may be particular to an industry or it may be general. The argument is also applicable to services. If a service is available from a large number of firms the very new company is more likely to find a firm with some spare capacity so that it can obtain the service at the same price as existing firms. In a small town with fewer firms providing the service this might be more difficult.

THE INNER CITY INDUSTRIES AND THE INCUBATOR HYPOTHESIS

Manufacturing firms in certain industries seem to be more likely to be found in or near the centres of large cities than others. Lichtenberg (1960) and Vernon (1960), in the study of the New York economy, described these as external-economy industries, because they felt that their presence there, and their ability to pay the high costs of a central city location, were mainly due to the fact that they benefited from the kind of external economies outlined above. They defined these industries as, (a) women's and children's clothing and allied products, (b) fur, leather goods, toys, dolls, and jewellery, and (c) periodicals, publishing, and printing.

In quantitative importance by far the most important of these inner-city industries were women's clothing and printing. For example, of the new manufacturing plants set up in inner London between 1970 and 1978, and which were reasonably successful in that they still existed in 1978 and employed more than 20 people, 38 per cent were in the women's clothing industry and 27 per cent in the printing industry (Nicholson *et al.*, 1981). They are not only important in cities such as London or New York. Cameron (1980) found that 26 per cent of the new plants set up in Glasgow between 1958 and 1968 were in clothing and footwear, and 11 per cent in paper, printing and publishing. Looked at in another way, 83 per cent of all new printing firms, 62 per cent of all new clothing and footwear firms and 72 per cent of firms producing leather goods set up in the Glasgow area in that period were set up in the inner city. Less than half the new firms of other important industries were set up in the inner city of Glasgow.

But why should such firms find an inner-city location attractive? Vernon and Lichtenberg's explanation runs as follows. In general, demand for the products of firms in these industries is highly variable because of changes in fashion. A women's clothing firm may make 'dresses' but the characteristics of the 'dress' produced by the firm will have to be changed rapidly if fashion changes or the product fails to sell. Similarly a publisher may produce a magazine but the content of the magazine changes from week to week. The products of the clothing firm and the publisher are highly 'perishable' in that whilst they may be in demand this week they may not the next. Nobody wants to buy yesterday's news or yesterday's fashions.

The variability of the demand for the products of these firms, and the fact that the characteristics of the product may have to be changed rapidly after relatively short production runs, means, it is argued, that plants in these industries remain small since there are few economies of scale available, and that they carry low stocks or inventories either of materials, work in progress or finished products. The aim is to get the product out of the plant and on the street as quickly as possible.

The firms can service and prosper even though they are small by clustering together and obtaining, as external economies, the economies of scale which would be internal to a large firm. The services which the firms cannot supply for themselves because they are too small are supplied by others because, in total, the demand is large enough. Examples are the specialist hauliers which transport clothing from manufacturer to retailer. Specialist suppliers may even exist, such as those supplying trimmings to the 'rag trade' which can carry stocks and so allow the manufacturers, with more variable demand, to carry less. Other advantages of concentration are the availability of skilled labour and suitable factory space, and, particularly in the women's clothing industry, the fact that the buyers from the shops can more easily tour the showrooms to determine what they will buy.

This clustering together not only allows existing firms to be both small and profitable but also allows new firms to start small so that the capital which must be risked in producing an 'unstandard product' in a necessarily high-risk business can be minimized.

Clustering reduces the risks borne by firms in the industries in another way. Fashion changes and production requirements change. The manufacturer has to discover not only what is selling in the shops now but to try to discover what will sell later. There is inevitably a time lag, however short, between production and retail.

It is advisable to know what everyone else is producing, and location in the same area as the other small firms will increase this knowledge and reduce the uncertainty.

This analysis of the reasons for the location of these particular industries in the inner areas of large cities is more of a hypothesis than a complete explanation. The majority of the firms in these industries do not locate in these areas, even in the women's clothing industry. Virtually all of the production which can be standarized takes place outside the inner cities, for example the production of large quantities of dresses for multiple retailers like Marks and Spencer. The analysis explains the location of only a small part of several industries, even though these may be the important manufacturing industries in the inner areas.

Nevertheless, out of this analysis of the location of the inner-city industries evolved what has come to be called the incubator hypothesis. Lichtenberg noted that the industries which tended to locate closest to the centre of New York were those in which production in the region was dominated by small firms. And also that within other industries the smaller firms tended to be located closer to the centre of the city than the larger. Martin (1969) found this also to be true of London. On the basis of these findings the New York researchers hypothesized that the inner city might act as a kind of incubator or nursery for newly formed manufacturing firms. The entrepreneur would find it easiest to start his new small firm at a location near the centre of the city. There, floor space would be readily available for rent, employees could be hired from a pool of labour with various skills, and other firms would be able to supply goods and services so that the entrepreneur need neither stock the goods nor provide the service for himself. Just as the existence of particular external economies allowed the entrepreneurs in the fashion-oriented, inner-city industries to minimize the capital they wished, so it was argued that the existence of general urbanization economies would allow new entrepreneurs to minimize the capital they risked in their new businesses. When any firm was successful and became less risky, so it would provide services for itself, hold larger stocks, and generally have less need to rely on the external economies available in the inner area. These successful businesses would then become larger and, as they did so, migrate from the central city to the suburbs and smaller towns. The centres of the large cities would therefore act as incubators for new firms and new development in the national economy, this new development, in the version suggested by Thompson (1968), filtering down to the rest of the spatial economy.

This is an attractive hypothesis but in practice there is little evidence to support it. What there is we have already stated, namely that, on average, within any industry the smaller firms tend to locate closer to the centre than others, and that, on average, industries dominated by small firms are located nearer the centre than others. But studies of firm 'birth rates' in various American cities found little evidence that the birth rate was higher in the inner cities than elsewhere in the urban area (Struyk and James, 1975). Moreover a study of the movement of new firms in New York found few new firms migrating from the centre to the periphery (Leone and Struyk, 1976). All these studies were carried out using aggregate data and with this sort of data it is difficult to know what sort of results one would need to either confirm or refute the hypothesis, in particular, what sort of birth rate one would expect to find and how many firms one would expect to migrate.

One case where less aggregate data has been used is a study by Fagg (1980) of new firms in Leicester. He found that the new firm birth rate was higher in the inner city than in the suburbs of the conurbations, but was, however, no higher than in the old industrial villages in outer Leicester. This suggests that it is not external economies which might be causing a higher birth rate in inner Leicester, but rather the existence of cheap, second-hand premises, since these are also available in the old established industrial villages in the outer area of the conurbation.

Direct evidence as to the motives of entrepreneurs can, however, only be obtained by interview or questionnaire and this kind of study has now been carried out in a sector of inner London. Nicholson *et al.* (1981) found, in their survey, that none of the new manufacturing firms, mainly in engineering, occupied new industrial premises. On the other hand, there was no evidence at all that the firms took advantage of any other external economies which were supposedly available in the inner city – suppliers of goods and services were mostly decided on the basis of contacts made prior to the firm's foundation, and there was no predisposition to use firms located nearby in the inner city.

However, if these firms do not locate in the inner city for the reasons specified in the incubator hypothesis, why do they locate there? After all, as we stressed at the beginning of this chapter, there are costs involved in such a location, and these must be compensated by some other benefit. The study by Nicholson *et al.* (1981) suggested, on the basis of interviews with the founders of the firms, that in general they located in the inner city because they found there a market for their products. For example a large number of new engineering firms were providing services or supplies to the printing industry of inner London. Many others were supplying the construction industry of the city. The interviews revealed that this market orientation might actually exist even where it was not obvious. For example one firm manufactured specialist pipework which was installed in chemical plants all over the country; however, the firms to which the pipework was sold had their head offices in London so that the discussions involved in selling the pipework actually took place there.

This research suggests that the incubator hypothesis can be rejected. The external economies of the inner city are a minor factor in inducing new firms to locate there. They are more likely to locate in the inner city because that is where they find the market for their products. But these findings also suggest that the analysis of the location of the inner city industries should be reconsidered, for this interpretation is also applicable to these industries. The analysis earlier in this section stressed the way in which these firms needed to respond quickly to changing demands. But an implication of this is that the demand comes from the city centre or the inner city, not from elsewhere in the city or the national economy. Printing firms are located close to the commercial centre because that is their market, and because speed in the production of a printed document is often essential, particularly those being printed for firms in the financial market. This is certainly true of printing. It would also seem likely to be true of the clothing industry. It seems reasonable to assume that the small fashion-oriented clothing firms located in the inner cities are mainly selling to the fashionable shops and boutiques of the city centre. So these manufacturing firms are located in the inner city mainly because their market is there. In turn, of course, the boutiques can respond to fashion more quickly because these small firms are located nearby and can change their production quickly. The firms in this sector of the industry therefore necessarily remain small and flexible. And the result is a pattern of production which relies on the external economies available because there are a large number of small firms in the same area, the pattern of production and the external economies being those described at the beginning of this section.

The point that is being made is that the external economies exist because the firms are there, and to a large extent they are peculiar to those firms not general to any firm in the inner city. The manufacturing firms which locate in the inner city are therefore there because of the market it provides. If there are enough of them in a particular industry external economies may be generated which increase the attraction of the location. But the external economies are particular to the industry and not general, and are not a function of city size or the size of the industry.

SUMMARY

In this chapter we have shown why manufacturing firms should choose to locate in larger towns and cities, despite the higher costs of such locations. The principles of industrial location set out by Weber suggest three reasons; first, the output of some firms is the input of others and these firms may locate close to each other to reduce transport costs; secondly, some places, particularly ports, may be trans-shipment points and goods and materials unloaded there may be processed before being sent on; thirdly, large towns and cities are in themselves markets which attract plants making products for sale to these markets.

The concentration of manufacturing plants together in one place may itself generate agglomeration economies of one kind or another, as the size of the market allows for economies of scale in the provision of services, supplies and factors of production. These agglomeration economies themselves encourage other firms to locate in the same area in order to benefit from these economies.

Firms in certain industries, particularly women's clothing and printing, have often been found to be concentrated in the inner areas of large conurbations, and the considerable external economies due to this concentration are obtained by these firms. But these firms appear to locate where they do because they market their products in the central city. The external economies they generate do not seem to encourage new small firms in other industries to locate in the same area as the incubator hypothesis suggests.

But the core of almost every large city is not a manufacturing centre but an office centre. Manufacturing is usually located in the adjacent inner areas. The reasons for this central location for offices are discussed in the next chapter.

FURTHER READING

The theory of industrial location was initially developed by Weber (1928) and modified by Isard (1956) and Moses (1958). An excellent introduction is given by Alonso (1964b). Empirical evidence on patterns of location is given more copiously by Hoover (1948) and Smith (1981). The study of industrial location within cities was stimulated by the New York Metropolitan Region Study. Hoover and Vernon (1959) and Lichtenberg (1960) are still of interest. Recent studies of the location and movement of industry in British cities are given in several papers in Evans and Eversley (1980). Of these Massey and Meegan stress the effect of industrial organization, a topic which is emphasised in contributions to Hamilton (1974). Intra-urban industrial location was recently and comprehensively surveyed by Scott (1982). The incubator hypothesis is discussed and, in the end rejected, by Nicholson et al. (1981).

4

Offices and Office Location

Algernon: If it was my business, I wouldn't talk about it. It is very
vulgar to talk about one's business. Only people like stock-
brokers do that.

The Importance of Being Earnest Act II

Until the nineteenth century towns and cities were primarily trading
centres. After the industrial revolution the larger towns and cities
came to be manufacturing centres; now in the twentieth century the
major urban centres are centres of administration. Note how recent
this development is. Certainly there has always been some central
government administration in the capital city but until the nineteenth
century even this was small. The possibility of any administrative
activity being physically separated from the activity being administered was limited by the impossibility of communicating the
decisions made. Only the development of efficient systems of
transferring information – a rapid postal system, and, later, systems of
telecommunications – allowed the growth of office centres.

But, as we have remarked in earlier chapters, the concentration in
close physical proximity of large numbers of firms raises the costs of
a location there to those firms. The cost of floor space is certainly
higher, the cost of labour is likely to be higher and there are increased
external diseconomies such as pollution and congestion. If firms are
prepared to bear the cost involved in locating in the city centre they
must gain some benefits from this location, probably in the form of
urbanization, agglomeration or external economies, and it is those
economies which we shall mainly be examining in this chapter.

Offices are not one single kind, however. There are basically three
groups of offices, first, those involved in the insurance, banking and

finance industry, secondly, the administrative offices of firms primarily engaged in manufacturing, retailing, transport and so on, and thirdly, the offices of those firms providing business services to other offices – accountants, lawyers, advertising agencies, marketing consultants, etc. We shall discuss the first group, the financial complex, in the first section of this chapter, and administrative offices in the second section. The location of the firms providing business services are primarily determined by their need for proximity to the other groups so we shall not discuss them separately.

The characteristics of the office industry should be noted. Offices are at an intermediate stage of production – they do not deal with the final consumers of products, neither are they directly engaged in production. This does not mean that office activities are unproductive though they are viewed as such in some Marxist literature; for example, Baran and Sweezy (1966) regard them as part of the surplus extracted by 'monopoly capital' from the product of labour.

One reason for a somewhat negative view of office activities is that offices deal with intangibles. They do not actually handle goods but they deal in the rights to goods. If not that, then they may simply be collecting, processing and transferring that almost unquantifiable thing, information. If they are doing neither of these things they will be providing services; and these services are of a particular kind since they are often devoted to minimizing risk – insurance in case the unexpected happens, auditing to ensure that there is no error or fraud, legal advice to ensure the firm falls into no legal pitfalls.

In the third section of this chapter we shall discuss the nature and characteristics of the information dealt with in offices and in the final section we shall consider the way in which developments in information technology will affect office location.

INSURANCE, BANKING AND FINANCE

It appears to be universally true that the insurance, banking, and finance industries are concentrated in the largest city in any country. They are not necessarily located in the capital city, and the capital city is not necessarily the largest city. There are numerous examples of capital cities which are the centres of government but which are not major financial centres – Washington, Canberra, Berne, Ottawa, and so on. This suggests that the concentration of employment in the financial sector in a particular area – for example Wall Street or the

City of London – and the attraction of this area to head offices and business services is the major factor determining the growth and size of the largest city in an economy. Thus in central London, according to the 1971 Census, over a quarter of a million people were employed in insurance, banking, and finance, more than a fifth of the total employed in the conurbation centre. It would almost be true to say that this quarter of a million on its own would make the conurbation centre of London larger than any other in the United Kingdom.

In most cases the growth of the financial complex at a particular site seems to have been almost accidental, and based on the original development of a city as a major port for the import and export of goods. The initial development was promoted as various services came into existence to facilitate trade. Banks became proficient in handling the finance of foreign trade, arrangements came to be made for the insurance of ships and their cargoes, commodity traders dealt in goods which had been landed, and shipping brokers handled the allocation of shipping contracts.

This development, once under way, gave the major port an advantage over others which it was difficult to match. The insurers, bankers, and brokers acquired an expertise and achieved such a size and prestige that when it eventually became possible, because of progress in posts and telecommunications, they could finance and service trade elsewhere in the national economy or in the rest of the world.

Moreover, they could remain at the same location even when the reasons for their location there originally became irrelevant. The City of London grew up as a centre financing trade through the Pool of London, the stretch of the Thames adjacent to the City downstream from London Bridge. Growth in the size of ships has caused the port facilities to move steadily downstream so that now few goods pass through docks within Greater London let alone inner London. But this does not matter. The commodity brokers – for example – now handle the rights to goods, not the goods themselves, and the goods to which the rights are traded may be thousands of miles away. The growth in telecommunications has allowed both the centralization of dealing and the decentralization of goods handling.

A similar kind of story can be told with respect to New York City. Although not initially dominant, Philadelphia was the new nation's capital between 1790 and 1800, New York's harbour ensured that it grew rapidly as a port, so that from 1800 to 1830, . . . New York's proportion of the nation's foreign trade rose from 9 per cent to 37 per cent. Growth fed on growth [so that] long before the Civil War . . . activities which had sprung from the Port were already beginning to develop an independent reason for existence . . . New York took the lead in marine insurance . . . but later on the companies which had grown on marine business came to thrive on domestic property risks. Similarly the Region's lead in banking could be traced partly to the importance of foreign commerce as a generator of bank business. (Vernon, 1960, chapter 2)

The tendency for a location to become fixed for the financial firms, and for it to remain despite other locational changes indicates that the firms find a substantial financial advantage in locating close to each other in a single centre. This financial advantage must be due to the external economies or agglomeration economies available at the city centre, and these we will find are similar to those found by firms in manufacturing industries from locating close to each other. First, clustering together is a method of reducing uncertainty. The firm which is located close to its rivals can be sure of obtaining information as quickly as they do. If it were elsewhere, it might not come into possession of information as rapidly as the others, and, lacking this information might sustain substantial losses. Of course the existence of advanced systems of telecommunication reduces the risks involved in a physical separation, but one thing that must be remembered in considering information transfer is that the quality of the information varies with the method of transmission. At the bottom end of the scale is the printed word. The telephone, higher up the scale, allows the hearer to gain increased knowledge from tones of voice, hesitations, corrections, and so on; television additionally gives information on facial expression, whilst at the top of the scale is the face-to-face meeting. In dealings involving large sums of money it is scarcely surprising that the personal meeting should be the preferred means of communication, though where speed is essential the telephone has an advantage.

So the foreign exchange dealers, who operate in a world-wide international market, but have to act very quickly to take advantage of small fluctuations in exchange rates, tend to be located in the financial centre but to deal largely by telephone. Stock brokers operate not only by telephone but also through a trading floor where dealers meet. The offices of brokers have to be within a short walk of the floor, but the transfer of information is in two directions. The brokers in the office communicate by telephone with their clients and with their representatives on the floor of the exchange. The presence of the dealers on the floor ensures that all the firms have the same information, none is at a disadvantage, and that this information can be transferred back to their offices and hence to their clients.

Physical concentration and personal contact ensures the rapid transfer of information. In particular physical contact through the trading floor of the stock exchange or any other exchange ensures that the number of meetings and so the number of possible transfers of information is maximized. The trouble with a letter, or even a telephone call, is that the writer or caller has usually to have a specific question to ask. In many circumstances what information is required, what question is asked, is not known. By maximizing the possibility of random information transfer the risk of not having this information, whatever it is, is minimized. It is because of this that trading floors, whether the stock exchange, commodity exchanges, Lloyds, or any other, have continued to exist despite efficient postal services, the telegraph, the telephone, television, or information technology.

A second kind of external economy occurs as the concentration of firms in one place increases the size of the market and so allows services to be provided at a lower cost because of economies of scale. Indeed sometimes the services would not be provided at all were the market smaller. One of these 'services' we have just mentioned. The existence of a large number of dealers in a single place allows for joint facilities, the use of which can be shared by all, such as the trading floors of the exchanges.

The growth of the market allows specialists to exist within the industry. Stock jobbers or brokers who specialize in dealing in the shares of a group of companies and who are therefore more expert than they otherwise would be: a financial market such as Wall Street or the City of London attracts branches of foreign banks who then are able to provide an expertise in the finances and financial systems of their own country which a domestic bank could not provide.

Market concentration also allows specialist services to come into existence outside the industry. For example accountants with specialized knowledge of some aspect of the tax system, or lawyers with expertise in advising on or interpreting the law in some other country. Note that uncertainty is a factor here too. No firm knows at the beginning of a period all of the services which it will require. It knows only that as conditions change and new information is acquired some of these specialists will have to be consulted. The specialists themselves do not know who their future clients will be, only that in the nature of things they will be consulted by enough firms to make the provision of the service profitable.

These services and information transfers require personal contact between executives and professionals, but the number of executives actually involved in such transfers is relatively small, certainly only a small proportion of the total number in the offices of the firms in the insurance, banking, and finance industry. The other employees – secretaries, accountants, clerks, typists, and so on – support in one way or another, the activities of the executives. Information is stored, processed, and transmitted to the executives by the supporting personnel, and the executives use it in their transactions outside the firm, in turn relaying their decisions back to the supporting personnel to be put into effect.

This 'dual role of the elite', as it was called by Robbins and Terleckyj (1960), is what makes a central city location expensive. Space has to be provided at prime rents and labour employed at premium wage rates in order to carry out these routine functions which in practice have little need for direct contact with the rest of the central city. There is, therefore, considerable economic pressure on firms to decentralize routine functions, and this can be done if there is little need for contact with the executives or if the necessary information can be transmitted by low-grade slow methods. For example the major British clearing banks often act as registrars for public companies, recording share transfers, keeping the share register and handling dividend payments. This function has little connection with other banking functions and has generally been decentralized – Lloyds Bank registrar's department is in Worthing, 70 miles south of London, the National Westminster Bank's department is in Bristol, 100 miles west of London. At each of these locations space and clerical labour are cheaper than they would be in the capital city. Even if the administrative function is more central to the activities of the financial institution it may still be decentralized if this is possible. So Lloyds of London maintain the administrative offices handling the accounts of its 'names', the members of the underwriting syndicates, at Chatham some 30 or 40 miles to the east of the insurance exchange.

Even within the financial complex itself some institutions appear to have a greater need of, and are therefore willing to pay more for, centrality than others. The study by Robbins and Terleckyj (1960) of the New York financial markets, working on the basis of an analysis of the apparent flows of information between institutions, identified a financial 'core', trading in securities, loans and so on through the money market, an 'inside ring' of bank-loan and investing departments, and insurance-investing departments, and an 'outside ring' of bank and insurance offices, brokers and dealers which dealt with the paper work and other lending, selling and servicing financial activities. Goddard (1968), using statistical methods to identify groups of activities within the City of London which located in close proximity to each other, similarly picked out a 'financial core' comprising the British clearing banks and insurance companies and a 'financial ring' comprising foreign banks, investment trusts, and some other financial firms. Thus even within the square mile of the City of London the different locational requirements of the different activities resulted in noticeable differences in location patterns.

ADMINISTRATIVE OFFICES

The head offices and regional offices of manufacturing and commercial firms gain the same advantages from a central city location as the offices in the financial sector. There is the same need to reduce uncertainty by maximizing personal contact, for executives to be in touch with those in other firms and in the financial sector in order not to be put at a disadvantage. The desire to reduce uncertainty is probably less important to this group than to financial firms; more important are the services which are available in larger cities, not only the accountants, lawyers, and so on which are important to the finance industry but also, for this group, the banks, insurance companies, and other financial institutions which now provide services to these firms. Again, it cannot be predicted which services will be required. The head office, even the regional office, deals with the problems which cannot be dealt with at a local or plant level and these problems are unstandardized, necessarily so. What is certain is that some of the services will be required.

Once again the same factor expands the cost of a central city location as it does for the financial institutions. Although relatively few executives may be involved in consultations and personal meetings with those in other central-city firms, the administrative office of the company will also include a number of routine functions supporting the decision-makers. Moreover, in the case of the administrative offices the ratio of routine to non-routine functions is likely to be higher than for a financial firm, and it may be more difficult to split off and decentralize separate routine functions. The head-office functions move as a unit, and therefore must usually be centralized or decentralized *en bloc.*

Analysis of the pattern of location of the head offices of the largest British industrial companies, as listed in *The Times* 1000, shows that the larger the company the more likely it is that its head office will be in the largest city (see figure 4.1). The largest ten industrial companies all have their headquarters in central London, 88 per cent of the largest 25 do so, 70 per cent of the largest 100, and the proportion declines until, of those ranked between 801 and 1000 in order of size, only just over one-fifth have their head offices in central London. Since the population of the London metropolitan area is slightly less than one-fifth of the total population, it is clear that the head offices of the smaller companies are distributed roughly in proportion to the population. They are still most likely to be located in the major city

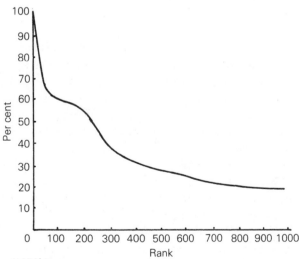

Source: Evans (1973b)

FIGURE 4.1
Percentage of companies having their head office in London, ranked by turnover 1971.

TABLE 4.1
Location of the headquarters of the 500 largest United States industrial corporations, 1975

Metropolitan area	Number of corporation head offices	Companies %	Assets %
New York	136	27.2	36.7
Chicago	47	9.4	7.2
Los Angeles	23	4.6	4.8
Cleveland	20	4.0	3.8
Philadelphia	18	3.6	3.0
Pittsburgh	15	3.0	6.0
Detroit	14	2.8	7.5
San Francisco	13	2.6	3.4
Minneapolis–St. Paul	13	2.6	1.7
Boston	12	2.4	1.0
Houston	11	2.2	2.8
St. Louis	11	2.2	1.9
Dallas	6	1.2	0.8
Tulsa	4	0.8	1.5
Cincinnati	4	0.8	1.0
Total	347	69.4	83.1

Source: Stephens and Holly (1981)

in their region. Table 4.1 shows that 401 of the 500 largest American industrial corporations had their headquarters in just 15 metropolitan areas. Moreover comparison of the column showing the percentage of companies in each area with the column showing the percentage of assets controlled by those companies clearly shows the way in which the larger corporations are concentrated in a relatively few regional metropolises.

Why should these patterns occur? Why should larger corporations locate their head offices in larger cities, and why should they disproportionately locate them in the largest city? There are a number of reasons, all of which are interrelated.

First, the head office of a company deals, as we have already stressed, with unstandardized, non-routine, problems. In a small company the executives are more likely to be dealing both with the routine problems of production and with these non-routine problems. The larger the company becomes the more probable it is that the functions are split so that some executives are dealing with

routine problems and some with the non-routine problems. Therefore, the larger a company is the easier it is to split the decision-
making functions between sites with routine production decisions
being made at plant level and non-routine, unstandardized problems
being dealt with at the head office.

Secondly, the larger company is more likely to be a multi-plant
operation. In a single-plant company the activities of the head office
and the plant are closely interrelated, but where there are a large
number of plants the attachment of the head office to the activities
and location of any one plant is likely to be weak, because a high
proportion of head-office activity relates to other plants. So it is
easier to separate the head office from the plant and locate it in a
major city.

Thirdly, this city may be a regional or national metropolis, but the
larger the company the more likely it is that it sells to a national or
international market, and that its production is also not concentrated
in a particular region but is on a national or international scale. So a
company operating on this scale is likely to locate its head office in
the major city.

Fourthly, a company of substantial size operating at a national or
international level is likely, at some level, to be politically important,
and, therefore, to be engaged in discussions, of whatever kind, with
central government and this is a reason for locating its head office in
the major city if this is also the capital.

Finally, if the above factors still do not take the headquarters of the
large company to the major city, the prestige factor may just tip the
balance – the notion that location in a major city rather than a small
town is, in some sense, more prestigious.

Clearly, as we noted earlier, these factors are all interrelated. The
larger the company the more likely it is that it has a large number of
plants, is operating on a national and international scale, and that it is
conscious of its size and prestige and political importance.

That size alone is not the crucial factor can be seen in the context of
an exception to the rule that large companies locate their headquarters in the largest city. Before the renationalization of the steel
industry in the 1960s major British steel companies did not have their
head offices in London, despite the fact that most other companies of
their size did. The reasons for their different behaviour lie in the fact
that, despite being large, they did not have similar characteristics to
the other large companies. They produced a single product, steel,

which was relatively standardized, so there were relatively few problems which a separate head office might deal with. They produced this product at a single plant, or else in a few plants concentrated in particular regions, so there was little reason to move the office away from the plant or out of the region. After renationalization, of course, the nationalized industry, British Steel, located its headquarters in central London, for it was now a large multiplant company with a geographically scattered production system.

INFORMATION

Despite the fact that information is an invisible commodity, and, one would have thought, difficult to measure, a considerable amount of knowledge has been acquired about the characteristics of the information flows within the central cities, and the reasons why offices are located where they are. In Britain this came largely from research sponsored by the former Location of Offices Bureau between 1963 and 1980. Early results came from surveys of firms asking them either why they chose to decentralize or why they chose not to. These surveys showed that the most important factors leading to the choice of a central location were access to or contacts with services and customers, whilst reductions in rents, property taxes and wage costs were the factors which made firms move (Wabe, 1966; Alexander, 1979). With respect to firms decentralizing from central London it was found that small firms were willing to move as a unit within the Greater London area whilst larger firms were willing to split the head office functions, the 'elite' remaining in central London at a slimmed-down head office, and the routine decentralizing up to 100 miles from London (Wabe, 1966). It was also found that firms were unwilling to shift even routine functions further than this because of the difficulty of maintaining ease of communication between the functions (Rhodes and Kan, 1971).

Later research has tended to be aimed at an analysis of contacts between firms, for example by asking executives to maintain contact diaries in one form or another. To some extent these have confirmed the previous findings as to the pattern of contacts between sectors, with the banking and finance and legal sectors being highly interlinked with each other and with the other office groups.

The more interesting finding regarding the transfer of information concerns the classification of types of contact. It is suggested

that these fall into three groups, orientation, planning and programming (Wärneryd, 1968; Thorngren, 1970; Goddard, 1973). The
findings from a diary study of executives of central London firms are
shown in Table 4.2. It has been suggested that orientation processes
are characteristic of head offices in the national metropolis, planning
processes of group head offices at a regional centre, and programming processes of manufacturing plants at local centres (Thorngren,
1970; Stephens and Holly, 1981), but it would be stretching the
evidence to say that this thesis has been demonstrated by it.

TABLE 4.2

Characteristics of a sample of business contacts in central London

Type		Per cent	Length	Purpose	Frequency	Medium
			Modal characteristics			
I	Orientation	14.5	1–2 h	Exchange information	Occasional	Face-to-face
II	Program-ming	81.2	2–10 min	Receive information	Occasional	Telephone
III	Planning	4.2	2–10 min	Bargaining	Daily	Telephone

Source: Goddard (1973) Table 31

So the London study shows that even there the vast majority of all
contacts are of a 'programming' kind. Most of these contacts are
with other firms within the central area, although the majority take
place by telephone. Clearly the information conveyed does not have
to be of a high grade, though one may surmise that the telephone
communications will have been preceded by face-to-face contacts.

The fewest kinds of contact are 'planning processes'. They are
infrequent and involve few participants; they may often be carried on
by telephone and are usually directly related to buying and selling.

The most important type of meeting, and the type which draws
firms to the central area is the 'orientation' meeting. It is arranged
well beforehand, involves a large number of people, and is intended
to cover a wide range of material on which long-term action can be

based. Examples are the board meeting, or other kinds of committee meeting, or a meeting between executives of the firm and, say, legal or accounting advisors.

Does this research have any implications for the analysis of the decentralization of firms? The relative infrequency of contacts requiring face-to-face contact, of orientation processes in other words, has been used to suggest that many firms have, in practice, relatively little need of a central city location (see Goddard, 1973). However, against this it should be noted that the use of meeting frequency as a guide tends to understate the importance of orienta-tion meetings. If the executive makes nine telephone calls when he deals with his post in the morning and then is tied up in a meeting all day, then only 10 per cent of his contacts may be 'orientation', and 90 per cent may be 'programming'; but 90 per cent of *time* will have been spent in 'orientation'. Moreover, the importance of these orientation meetings suggests that, even though they are less frequent than programming or planning contacts, such face-to-face meetings are difficult to replace.

It has been fancifully suggested in popular discussion that the development of the electronic office will mean that the central-city office will cease to exist. Even that offices as such will cease to exist in their present form since each employee will be able as easily to sit in his/her own home in front of a computer terminal. Admittedly the most recent research on the impact of information technology on the office-property market suggests that any development in this direc-tion will be slow, if only because of the difficulty of adapting property (CALUS, 1983), but there are other reasons both economic and social.

First, and not unimportantly, people go to work for social reasons as well as to earn money. Sitting in one's home in front of a computer terminal all day is not likely to be popular, so that firms are unlikely to save on wages.

Secondly, the space for the terminal has to be found, and employers will have to compensate employees for, in effect, provid-ing their own office space. For example, in the town of Reading, one firm has assisted programmers to work at home by paying part of the mortgage cost since the home is larger than it otherwise would be. So firms are unlikely to make substantial savings on the cost of space.

But the main reasons why developments in information technology are unlikely to lead to the disappearance of the central-city office have to do with differences in the quality of information. Electronic office equipment provides for improved methods of storing, processing, retrieving and transferring relatively low-grade information. But the information which is dealt with in the face-to-face orientation meeting is of a very high grade, and this is unaffected by developments in information technology. So the economic reasons for a central-city office location remain unchanged.

It is indeed possible that these developments will increase the attractions of a central city location to firms. Improvements in telecommunications work two ways. They can assist executives in their contracts with other firms, or they can assist the transfer of information between the routine and non-routine functions. It appears much more likely the latter will be much more important simply because it deals in low-grade rather than high-grade information. Moreover developments in information technology reduce the cost of storing and processing this information. Fewer staff are required, and less space is required to house them, and to house their computing facilities. So these developments either reduce the cost of maintaining the routine functions at the central city location, or they make it less costly to decentralize them. In either case the number of staff employed at a central-city office is reduced, and the space it needs to occupy is made smaller. So the growth of the electronic office is likely to reduce the cost of maintaining a relatively small 'elite' head office in the central city. Whilst the number of people employed in the central city will continue to decline, the central cities of the major metropolises will otherwise increase in importance, as it becomes possible for firms which would formerly have located elsewhere to move their offices to a central city location.

SUMMARY

The continued decline of manufacturing industry in the major cities has meant that the largest cities today are primarily administrative centres. Management rather than production is the primary reason for their size if not their existence.

In this chapter we have explored the various factors, particularly the external economies, which allow the office industry to bear the high costs of a central city location in one of the conurbations. These economies have mainly been discussed in relation to the insurance, banking, and finance industry, and the administrative offices of manufacturing and commercial corporations. We also considered the characteristics of information and information transfer, since information is the commodity with which offices deal, and also analysed the probable impact of developments in information technology on office location.

In the next chapter we go on to consider the reasons for the existence of an urban hierarchy.

FURTHER READING

The literature on the subject is well surveyed by Alexander (1979). Goddard (1973) on linkages and location is worth reading as is the later paper by Stephens and Holly (1981) on the location of corporate headquarters. The impact of information technology on offices is discussed in CALUS (1983).

5

The Urban Hierarchy

Cecily: Oh, flowers are as common here, Miss Fairfax, as people
are in London.
Gwendolen: Personally I cannot understand how anybody man-
ages to exist in the country, if anybody who is anybody does.
The Importance of Being Earnest Act II

Perhaps the most glaringly obvious empirical fact in the whole of
urban economics is that some cities are larger than others – that in
any economy there is an urban hierarchy with few large cities, more
medium-sized cities, and larger numbers of smaller cities and towns.
An explanation of why such a hierarchy should exist is less obvious,
however, and there is still none which is generally accepted. But then
there is probably no single cause, a number of factors operate to
determine the nature of the urban system.

Acceptable explanations, however, must, at least in part, take
account of the various facts and relationships which we have outlined
in earlier chapters. The factors determining the pattern of residential
location will differ in importance between large cities and small cities
– the cost of space and the cost of travel will be important in large
cities but of minor importance in towns. More importantly, from
the point of view of a theory of city size, the industrial and
commercial structure of larger cities will differ from those of smaller
towns because costs and benefits differ. The high land and labour
costs of a location in the inner part of a large city ensure that only
those firms locate there which gain from the external economies or
other benefits of that location.

In this chapter we shall develop these hints of the basis of a theory
to provide an explanation of the urban hierarchy in an industrial

economy, and also look at other possible explanations for its existence.

CENTRAL PLACE AND OTHER THEORIES

Central place theory, as originally developed by Christaller (1933) and Lösch (1945), was, and is, an attempt to explain the locational pattern of market and manufacturing centres selling goods to the local populations within given market areas; but there is also, implicit in the theory, an explanation of the existence of an urban hierarchy. As the name central place theory implies it is based on the idea of the urban area as a trading centre or central place – a market town in other words. The smallest urban places – hamlets or villages – sell commonplace goods, food, for example, to the population of the rural areas, and there are a very large number of these small villages each selling to the population of its own small market area. In the context of pure central place theory these market areas, and the market areas of all urban places, should be hexagonal since any area can be divided up into regular hexagons with no gaps or overlaps, and, of the three regular shapes of which this can be said (the other two being the square and the equilateral triangle), the hexagon is the one which is nearest to a circle.

Above the villages in the urban hierarchy there are a smaller number of larger urban places – small towns – which sell less-commonly purchased goods, say clothing, to the populations of larger market areas. These larger areas will include some hamlets and their associated rural market areas. In turn there are still larger urban places – large towns – selling even less frequently purchased goods – furniture for example – to still larger market areas. The whole land area is thought of as being, at least conceptually, divided up into a series of nested sets of hexagonal market areas, as shown in figure 5.1. The central place system in southern Germany, the area which Christaller studied is shown in figure 5.2.

Central place theory provides an explanation for two urban phenomena, first it explains the existence of an urban hierarchy and secondly it explains the spatial structure of the urban system – the spatial relationship between cities of different sizes. A considerable amount of work has gone into exploring the mathematics of this kind of urban hierarchy (e.g. Beckmann, 1958; Beckmann and McPherson, 1970) and in non-industrial areas the predictions of the

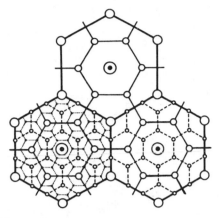

Source: Davies (1976)

FIGURE 5.1
The arrangement of centres and trade areas according to Christaller's
classical (marketing) model

theory about the spatial system are in agreement with the empirical
evidence, particularly on the plains and prairies of North America. A
good introduction to this work, and to central place theory itself has
been published by Berry (1967).

But even though central place theory has been found to give a
good explanation of the nature of the urban system in these
predominantly agricultural areas, it provides no real explanation for
the existence of an urban hierarchy in industrialized economies,
where production in towns and cities is usually not for distribution
to surrounding market areas but may be for sale throughout the
nation or for export across the world.

Because of this, various attempts have been made to construct
theories which would explain the urban system in an industrial
economy. The closest of these to pure central place theory is the
hierarchy model of the size distribution of manufacturing centres
suggested by Tinbergen (1968). In his model the smallest centres
manufacture some goods, type 1, for consumption by their own
population, all other goods being imported from outside. The next
largest towns manufacture goods of type 1 and type 2, and satisfy the
demands of their own population for these goods, as well as
exporting type 2 goods to the smaller urban places. Larger towns
manufacture three kinds of goods, types 1, 2 and 3, for their own

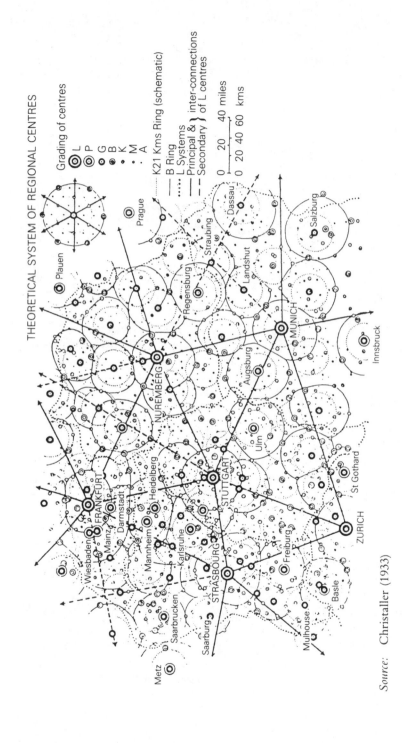

THEORETICAL SYSTEM OF REGIONAL CENTRES

Grading of centres

◎ L
◎ P
◉ G
○ B
○ K
· M
· A

········ K21 Kms Ring (schematic)
———— B Ring
········ L Systems
———— Principal & } inter-connections
– – – Secondary } of L centres

0   20   40 miles
0 20 40 60 kms

Plauen

Prague

Dassau

Straubing

Regensburg

Landshut

Salzburg

MUNICH

NUREMBERG

Augsburg

Innsbruck

Ulm

St Gothard

FRANKFURT

Wiesbaden

Mainz

Darmstadt

Heidelberg

Mannheim

Karlsruhe

STUTTGART

Freiburg

ZURICH

STRASBOURG

Basle

Mulhouse

Saarbrucken

Saarburg

Metz

FIGURE 5.2

Source: Christaller (1933)

The hierarchy of central places in Southern Germany (c. 1930). The English equivalents are: L, Regional capital; P, Provincial head city; G, Small state capital; B, District city; K, County seat; A, Township centre; M, Market hamlet population and export goods of type 3, and so on. Since the export markets of the towns are not defined spatially, indeed it is assumed that all of the exporting firms compete with each other over the whole market, there are no market areas and the model defines no spatial structure. However, although the model explains the existence of an urban hierarchy, its assumptions, namely that manufacturing firms in larger cities only export to smaller urban places, and that the smaller places never export to the larger, are at variance with reality.

Another type of theory, to some extent developed from the mathematical analysis of central place theory, is one based on statistical theory, for example the entropy maximization model suggested by Berry (1964) or Curry (1964). Taking this approach all cities are viewed as randomly subject to various forces, some leading to growth, others to decline, so that the city size distribution is, therefore, the result of these forces, working randomly. It can be shown that defining an hierarchy which obeys the rank–size rule as one in which the second ranking city is half the size of the largest, the third ranking one a third the size of the largest, and so on, the nth ranking being one nth the size of the largest, then a city–size distribution which obeys the rank–size rule is the most probable distribution of a given population in a given number of cities. Since city–size distributions frequently do obey the rank–size rule, as first shown by Zipf (1941), the theory appears to be confirmed. Which is all very well, but once again the theory, or model, like the Tinbergen model, explains the existence of an urban hierarchy but explains nothing else. The explanation assumes that there are no systematic forces operating to increase or decrease the growth of cities in that there are no forces which are correlated either positively or negatively with city size, and this assumption is clearly incorrect. At the present time, for example, the very largest cities and the smallest urban areas appear to be declining relative to smaller cities and medium-sized towns.

AGGLOMERATION DISECONOMIES AND URBAN SIZE

An economic approach to a theory of the urban hierarchy should take account of the various costs and benefits which vary with city size. In this section we shall examine the costs and in the next the benefits.

First, and most importantly, we should expect the cost of land and floor space to be higher in larger cities. We showed in chapter 2, in the discussion of residential location, that we should expect the value of land to be highest at the centre of a city and to fall, at a decreasing rate, with distance from the centre, and that there is substantial evidence that this is generally true. Put in another way, this means that if we start at the edge of the city with marginal land at agricultural value, then, in the absence of any supply constraints, its price will increase continuously as one travels towards the centre. Clearly the larger the city, the longer the distance over which this increase takes place and the larger the difference between the price of agricultural land and the price of land at the city centre.

Another way of looking at the relationship is this – the value gradient exists, so far as households are concerned, because the cost of travel is high at the edge of the city but low at the centre. Households are, therefore, willing to pay more for housing nearer the centre so that they do not have to bear higher commuting costs, both in terms of time spent travelling and the direct, financial cost of travel. Since the distance which might have to be travelled is higher in larger cities, we should expect land values to be bid higher in the centres of these cities. In one of the few instances in the whole of economics of this kind of evidence, visible confirmation of the fact that land costs are higher, as predicted, is provided by the higher buildings and higher densities constructed in the centres of these larger cities by developers seeking to maximize their profits by economizing on their use of expensive land.

A second kind of cost which may vary with city size is the cost of labour. We should expect wages to be higher in larger cities. Those living in these cities must either pay higher housing costs, if they live near the centre, or higher commuting costs, if they live near the edge, or a combination of the two if they live in the inner suburbs. Higher land costs may also result in some goods and services being more expensive in larger cities. Therefore, *ceteris paribus*, we should expect there to be pressure exerted, either through the labour market or through collective bargaining, for higher wages to be paid in large cities. There is considerable evidence that this is so. A thorough study of United States data was carried out by Goldfarb and Yezer (1976). They concluded that differences between the wage levels in different-sized cities did not appear to be explained by other factors but were solely a function of city size. There is also some evidence that wages increase with city size in British cities (Evans, 1973a). Goldfarb and Yezer (1976) also found that, in general, wages rose with city size at a decreasing rate – indeed 'by far the largest rises and fastest rates of increase take place over the range 0–100 000 inhabitants' (p. 360). Theoretical analysis suggests that this should be so. Commuting costs increase with the distance travelled and this distance will be a function of the radius of the city. On the other hand, the size of the city, measured in terms of population, will be a function of its area. Since, as a matter of elementary geometry, the radius of a circle is a linear function of the square root of the area, this distance, the radius, will increase at a decreasing rate as area increases. So, in principle we should expect commuting costs, and hence wages, to increase at a diminishing rate as city size increases. It may be noted that the same argument is applicable to land costs; the cost of floor space would be expected to increase at a decreasing rate as city-size increases, though there is little empirical data which could be used as evidence relating either to the increase or the rate of increase.

American evidence on wage levels is, however, complemented by evidence on the relationship between the average cost of living and city size. The evidence is clear that the cost of living increases with city size. Hoch (1977) found that, on average, the cost of living rose by 5 per cent as the population rose tenfold – i.e. it rose by 5 per cent as city size went from 10 000 to 100 000, from 100 000 to 1 million and from 1 million to 10 million. On the other hand, Hoch found that, on average, wage levels rose by 9 per cent as population increased tenfold. It follows, therefore, that either the population of the larger cities is better off in real terms than the population of smaller towns, which is unlikely, or, more probably, that there are other costs of living in larger cities which are not measured by changes in indices. These may be 'money costs not picked up in the conventional cost of living index', or non-market or unpriced costs such as 'time costs of the journey to work, air pollution and noise, and the psychic costs of crime not covered by insurance premiums' (Hoch, 1977, p. 53), and lack of access to the countryside. On the other hand, some at least of the residents of large cities may be compensated by the availability of consumer goods and services which the size of the market makes it economic to provide – theatre, for example, concert halls, professional football or cricket are more likely to be available in a larger city and their quality is likely to be better, the larger the city. Indeed Cropper (1981) suggests that these consumption externalities outweigh unpriced consumption diseconomies such as pollution, noise, or congestion. These external diseconomies still exist, however, and to the extent that they are borne by firms direct and not by the residents, constitute a third group of costs which we would expect to increase with city size. To the extent that they are borne by the residents we would expect them to be reflected in higher wages as the evidence shows they are in the United States, and so to be borne by the firms indirectly. The cost of the external diseconomies which the firms bear directly are more difficult to estimate – possibly the most important is congestion – but they probably increase with city size as wage levels do, and the differences in costs caused by these external diseconomies are probably of the same order of magnitude as the differences in wage levels.

AGGLOMERATION ECONOMIES AND URBAN SIZE

Since the cost of space increases with city size, and since the cost of labour also increases with city size, so compensating employees for the higher costs of living and working in larger cities, it follows that firms locating in these cities must pay more for land and labour (and bear greater external diseconomies) than if they located in smaller towns. It follows that for an urban hierarchy to continue to exist in stable long-run equilibrium, the firms in these larger cities must gain benefits from their location which compensate them for these higher costs. As we have shown in chapters 3 and 4, these benefits are represented mainly by the agglomeration economies (or external, localization or urbanization economies) available in a large city, and partly by the size of the market which encourages some firms to locate there to serve it. The size of the market is indeed all important since it not only attracts firms but also increases the 'economies' available. Its size allows new firms to come into existence and new services to be provided because the demand is great enough in the large city to support them, i.e. to allow them to take advantage of possible economies of scale. Moreover, the larger the market, the larger is the labour force and the wider its range of skills, and also the wider the range of available floorspace and of the services and supplies which are readily available. All these factors tend to reduce the costs of firms located there since they are likely to be able to find the goods and services they want more easily and at a more reasonable price than in the smaller towns.

The advantages of location in the large city will vary from firm to firm, however. Some firms or activities mainly require cheap labour and cheap floor space and have little need for specialized business services. An example is the textile industry which since its beginnings as an industry has tended to locate in small towns gaining whatever localization economies are possible from a loose regional grouping rather than concentrating together in a single large city. At the other extreme are the head offices of firms and the various firms providing specialist financial services. They use space intensively and may require access to a wide but essentially unforeseeable range of services. Therefore they are likely to wish to locate in the centre of a large city.

These agglomeration economies, their nature and existence, have been discussed at length in the two preceding chapters; it is apparent from that analysis and from casual empiricism that they exist. Proof of their existence by statistical means would seem to be difficult, but in fact, in the last decade or so, a number of increasingly sophisticated attempts have been made to measure the impact of city size on productivity with respect to US cities. These attempts have been hampered by the absence of data relating to the stock of capital, but can and do use measures of output, labour inputs, and wage rates. In general the results show an increase in productivity with city size, but at a diminishing rate. For example, Sveikauskas (1975) found that a doubling of the urban population appeared to be associated with a 6 per cent increase in labour productivity. More recently Carlino (1979, 1982) has attempted to distinguish between the influence of urbanization economies, localization economies and internal economies of scale. He found the latter to be relatively unimportant so that 'one must look to external economies to explain economies of scale for establishments which are located in metropolitan places' (Carlino, 1979, p. 371). Of the two kinds of external economies he finds localization economies to be less important than urbanization economies as factors leading to urban concentration. Or to be exact, his regression results showed the localization economies variable to be positive and significant for 5 of the 19 industries studied, and the urbanization economies variable to be positive for all industries and significant for 12 of the 19. Moreover, urbanization diseconomies were found to exist for all the industries, with the variable being significant for 10 of the 19.

The empirical evidence thus confirms the existence of agglomeration economies which increase the productivity of firms in larger cities. Moreover, these economies, as we would expect, vary in importance for different kinds of industries. On average, however, Carlino (1982, p. 105) found that agglomeration economies outweighed diseconomies for populations less than 3.3 million, and diseconomies outweighed economies for urban populations greater than that. This gives some measure of the importance of agglomeration economies, but it should be noted that the various studies have concentrated on manufacturing industry, and the average of those. Clearly some industries will find their optimal city size to be larger than this and others to be smaller. Moreover, it is apparent that the largest cities tend to be dominated by industries providing services rather than manufacturing, so that the agglomeration economies for services would possibly indicate a larger 'optimal' city. The difficulty of measuring output for service industries suggests that it will be some time before any satisfactory analysis of their agglomeration economies is undertaken.

THE ECONOMICS OF THE URBAN HIERARCHY

We now have the following assumptions, based on deductions, and confirmed where possible by the empirical evidence. First, land and labour costs increase with city size but at a diminishing rate. Secondly, productivity also increases as city size increases because of agglomeration economies, also at a diminishing rate. Thirdly, firms and industries have different preferences as regards their preferred size of city. On these assumptions we can now develop an explanation of the existence of the urban hierarchy in an industrial economy (Evans, 1972). This explanation is based on the idea that firms which find themselves in the 'wrong'-sized city will either have to move or go out of existence. Firms which are in cities which are too large will be undercut by their competitors who will face lower bills for wage and floor space. Firms which are in cities which are too small will be undercut by firms in larger cities who, despite bearing higher costs for labour or floor space, benefit from the external economies of city size. This will result in a hierarchy of the kind we observe basically because it takes a large number of firms to form a large city but very few, possibly only one, to employ all the labour force in a small town. The result, if the number of firms preferring to locate in a small town is the same as the number wishing to locate in a large city, is a number of small towns but very few large cities.

The way in which the city formation process can operate can be illustrated as follows. Suppose we start off with a number of firms which require cheap labour and land and have no need for and would gain no advantage from the external economies – business services, specialized labour, etc. – of a larger grouping. In the absence of any other systematic forces the initial location of the firms would be a random scatter of small, single-firm, towns. But other economic forces do operate and so some locations may be more favourable than others – river crossings and natural harbours, for example. Some firms will locate at these advantageous locations and so larger towns will be formed. They would be formed even in the absence of agglomeration economies because the advantages of the sites would outweigh the possible increases in costs – diseconomies – caused by the growth of the city. These towns, however, because they are in existence and because of the size of the market, will now begin to generate external economies, so they will become favoured locations for firms which can benefit from these external economies and will grow in size because of this. This increase in size will displace some firms who would find a better location in a smaller city. They will have to move or else the rise in the cost of labour and space will increase their costs making them uncompetitive and putting them out of business, their customers being served by firms in other, smaller, towns. In this way a hierarchy will come into existence.

But why should this hierarchy be one of the kind we observe in practice, one in which there are more smaller towns that there are larger towns, and where this appears to be true for any pair of size classes?

It was originally suggested (Zipf, 1941) that the size distribution generally corresponds to a rank-size distribution – the city which is ranked nth in order of size has a population one nth of that of the largest city (e.g. the fourth ranking city will have a population one-quarter that of the largest). Later researchers have shown that the rank-size rule does not generally hold even though it may often be a good approximation. A great deal of attention has been paid to what is called the primate distribution where one or two large cities dominate, and it has been suggested that this is a characteristic distribution in developing economies, but there are a number of counter examples to this. In an exhaustive study Sheppard (1982) concludes that the rank-size distribution 'has patently failed as an empirical norm . . . There does not seem to be any justification for the rank size rule on theoretical grounds ... There is also little evidence to suggest that other city size distributions can be better identified with a unique set of social processes' (p. 148). Nevertheless all city-size distributions which have been discussed and observed accord with the stylized description above – there are fewer larger towns than smaller towns.

But in fact there are only two other possible city-size distributions. The first would be that all cities are equal in size. But this does not exist anywhere, and the analysis above shows why it will not exist so long as some activities obtain greater benefit from the external economies of larger cities than others.

The second possibility would be that the number of cities in any size class did not decrease as average city size increased; but either remained the same or increased, so that there would be the same number or more large cities as small cities, e.g. there would be at least as many cities in the range 1 million to 2 million population as there were large towns in the range 500 000 to 1 million population, and at least as many of these as there were small towns and villages in the range up to 500 000 population. Again this kind of distribution does not exist in practice, but the analysis does not prove that it could not. It is, however, inherently improbable. For such a hierarchy to be formed by the process described earlier then if there were a given number of firms locating in cities of a given size, there would have to be more than double that number of firms wishing to locate in cities of double that size ... and a hundred times as many wishing to locate in cities of a hundred times the size. Whilst this is possible over some part of the city-size range, it is not likely at the top of the range. Unless there is an infinite population there has to be a maximum city size. And it seems improbable to say the least, that at this maximum size, with at least as many cities of this size as any other, and with more firms wanting to locate in this city size than in any other, that there should be no larger cities and no firms would want to locate in larger cities.

In the absence of any information as to the city sizes which are preferred then it seems most plausible to assume that the probability distribution of city-size preferences is a normal distribution so that the number of firms wishing to locate in cities of different sizes increases up to some city size but then diminishes. If this were so then, although the number of cities of new size class might increase as average city size increased, after some point the number of firms per size class would tend to diminish in the way that is observed in practice. A proof that if the formation of groups by firms or households with like preferences is a model of city formation, then the most probable distribution is one of the kind we observe is given by Beguin (1982).

SUMMARY

In this chapter we have examined the various theories of the urban hierarchy, looking first at central place theory, and statistical theories, and then going on to examine the economic forces which would tend to affect city size, and the way in which these forces will cause an urban hierarchy to come into existence. The relevant economic factors, the costs and the benefits of city size and their implications, are discussed again in the following chapter where we consider the concept of the optimal city size and other facets of the problem of size.

FURTHER READING

Berry (1967) provides a good introduction to central place theory. Various aspects of the economics of urban size are discussed in the collection of papers edited by Cameron and Wingo (1973), and theory and evidence are surveyed by Richardson (1973b). Hoch (1977) attempts to measure various goods and bads associated with city size.

6

City Size, Structure, and Growth

Jack: When one is in town one amuses oneself. When one is in the
country one amuses other people.
The Importance of Being Earnest Act I

In the previous chapter we analysed the economic factors determining the structure of the urban hierarchy; there we were considering the whole set of cities in the economy. In this chapter we will still be concerned with city size but considering, now, each city on its own, and considering the economic factors which determine its growth and size. This chapter appears more policy oriented than chapter 5, but that is because governments tend to be more overtly concerned with the problems of individual cities than with the more abstract concept of the urban hierarchy.

In the first section we discuss the concept of the optimal city size. It will be apparent from the preceding chapter that there is no such thing. Nevertheless, the idea that there is an optimal city size has influenced the planning of many new towns and cities, and although there is not some definite optimal city size, it is also clear that there must be some optimal planned size for a given new town intended to fulfil certain functions at a given location. In that context the discussion of the optimal city size is not unreasonable.

The second aspect of city size we discuss is the degree of industrial diversification. To some extent industrial diversification is related to city size. In the preceding chapter we discussed agglomeration economies as though they were a simple function of city size. However, in truth they are related not only to size, but also to the degree of diversification and to the average size of plants in the city. This complicated relationship suggests also that these factors will affect the pattern of urban growth and we discuss this in the next chapter.

Just as there is no single theory of the urban hierarchy there is also, I suspect, no single theory to explain differences in urban growth rates. Cities perform various functions within the national economy, selling their goods and services to markets which may be local, regional, or national. Their growth will depend on growth in these markets and on their ability to compete in them, and several factors have to be considered.

One factor which may cause growth or improve a city's chances of growth is innovation, whether in new products or new firms. Moreover, the amount of innovation has also been thought to be affected by a city's size and by its industrial structure, and we discuss the possible interrelationships.

We end the chapter with some comment on a topic to which little systematic attention has been paid in urban economics – the spatial relationships between cities of different size and their pattern of growth. Central place theory is the only theory of the urban hierarchy which explains both the size distribution *and* the spatial distribution of cities. Most economic analyses, as in the preceding chapter, have sought to explain only the size distribution and have done so in a non-spatial context; but spatial relationships are also important.

OPTIMAL CITY SIZE

The analysis of the economics of the urban hierarchy in the previous chapter suggests that there is no such thing as an optimal city size even though there might possibly be an optimal city-size distribution. It is probable, however, that for any particular city within the urban hierarchy there is an optimal size. Certainly this is an idea which is not merely of theoretical interest, as is shown by the attempts of post-war British governments to control the growth of large cities by green belts and other planning instruments, to create new towns, and to expand existing towns. All these interventions indicate that a view has existed as to the optimal size for the various towns involved, although the drift upwards in the larger populations of the British New Towns from 40 000 for the first to be planned to 250 000 for the last, indicates that this view may have changed over time.

A possible economic approach to the theory of city size was suggested by Alonso (1971), one analogous to the theory of the firm. In figure 6.1 costs and benefits are measured along the vertical axis and the total population of the city along the horizontal axis. Clearly some heroic assumptions are being made in order to be able to represent the economic factors in this way. In particular it is assumed that costs and benefits vary only with city size and not with, at the least, urban form and density, and that these costs and benefits, whether internal or external, can be measured.

Thus, the average cost curve AC is supposed to take into account all costs of whatever kind, whether private costs, public costs or social costs – the cost of land and labour which we have already mentioned, the cost of local-government services, and the cost of congestion, pollution, and crime. The assumption has often been that average cost per capita falls over some range as population size increases but then begins to rise. In some discussions this minimum cost point, population P_n in figure 6.1, has been regarded as in some

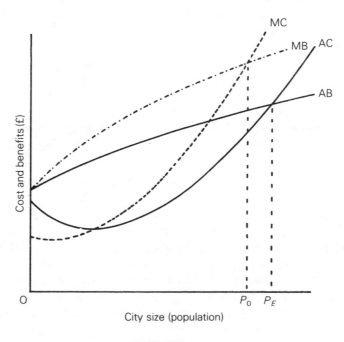

FIGURE 6.1

sense the optimum, for example in discussions of the optimal size of a local government area. Empirical studies have generated a wide range of possible minima, however. Gupta and Hutton (1968) found the population served which resulted in the lowest average long-run cost for various government services ranged from 50 000 for ambulance services to 1.4 million for administrative costs, though in most of their studies there was no clear minimum. The Royal Commission on Local Government (1969) argued that a population of at least 250 000 was necessary to attain the economies of scale possible in management and administration. The costs of local-government services are discussed further in chapter 10, but here we should note that the optimal size of a local-government area is not the same as the optimal size of a city. Several towns can lie, and often do, within the same local-government area, and a large city can be split amongst several. The population which results in the minimum cost of services is useful to know, therefore, but does not indicate the optimal population of a city. For this it is necessary to know the benefits.

In theory we can draw the curves marked AB and MB in figure 6.1, showing respectively the average benefit and marginal benefit. These benefit curves should take into account the preferences of householders and the social and private benefits of agglomeration, the wider range of consumer services available in larger cities and the agglomeration economies available to manufacturing and commerce. As we indicated in the preceding chapter, however, the economic benefits of agglomeration vary from firm to firm and from household to household. Although it is possible that the average cost and marginal cost curves (AC and MC in the figure) will not vary from city to city, being dependent solely on the variation in costs with city size, the average benefit and marginal benefit curves which can be drawn are those for one set of firms or households for which benefits happen to vary identically with city size.

Elementary economic theory would suggest that the optimal size of city would be at a population P_o where the marginal cost of an extra person in the city is just equal to the marginal benefit; at any greater population the additional cost would be greater than the additional benefit. Basic welfare economic analysis would also suggest that the population would grow beyond this if entry is unregulated. Since the average benefit per head is higher than the average cost per head, in-migrants would apparently gain a net benefit up to the point at which average benefit equalled average cost as indicated by the intersection of the curves AC and AB giving a population P_E. This line of argument appears to lie behind the various attempts to control the size of large cities, namely that there is market failure, and although individual in-migrants receive a net gain from moving to the city their net gain is outweighed by the loss imposed on the existing residents. The average size of any city is, therefore, greater than the optimum.

This argument suffers, however, from the fact that it treats each city as existing in some sort of isolated state in which people can choose to migrate to the city and although the economic impact of their in-migration is considered, the impact of their emigration from other towns and cities is ignored. But, as we argued earlier, there is no single optimal city size, though there might be an optimal city-size distribution, primarily because the benefits resulting from increases in size vary from household to household and from firm to firm. As a result, as Price (1978) argues, the urban hierarchy is unlikely to deviate much from the optimum. Suppose a middle-sized city expands through in-migration as suggested above. Then if in fact there is no demand for that sized city in the economy then either some of the households who would prefer to live in a small city will move out to a smaller city or the firms which would find their optimal location in a smaller city will either move or go out of business as they become unprofitable relative to firms in smaller cities. Thus, unless there is a permanent shift in demand the system will return towards the optimum. Moreover, Price argues that provided the preferences of firms and households are such that they are fairly indifferent to a wide range of city sizes 'a freely migrating population will adjust to produce a system of city sizes not far short of optimal . . . [although] no implication should be read that those externalities which can be varied in a city of a *given* size [e.g. pollution] are in an optimal state' (Price, 1978, p. 80).

He qualifies this conclusion further by pointing out that some households may be unwilling or unable to move, particularly the elderly, and, therefore, may suffer as the town they live in expands or contracts through the movement of the more mobile. With regard to firms the adjustment costs may be the insolvency and failure of firms which do not move and the frictional unemployment which results from firms going out of existence in one location but employing the more mobile in another. All this, however, is fairly theoretical since change in urban size is usually slow. The general principle would appear to be that a stable urban hierarchy does not generate large social costs through cities becoming too large (or too small).

INDUSTRIAL STRUCTURE

In the discussions of agglomeration economies and of the city size distribution we have implied that agglomeration economies are a linear function of city size; indeed this is an explicit assumption in the discussion of optimal city size above, most obviously in figure 6.1. But the industrial structure of a town is important as well as its size in determining its characteristics, its costs and its benefits. In a sense this is recognized in everyday discussion – cities are known not only by their size but also by what is the dominant industry – a steel town, a textile town, etc.

This mode of speech is most likely to be a true characterization, and is most likely to be used, when the town is small and dominated by one or two large plants. For as we showed in chapter 3 large plants which have no need of the external economies of the large city are most likely to be located in smaller towns. It is less likely to be a true representation of a large city, and so is less likely to be used, for the growth of the city is likely to have resulted in a more diversified employment structure.

A view of the relation between the degree of industrial diversification and city size was suggested by Thompson (1965) when he set out the stylized picture of the growth of a city to which we have already referred in chapter 3. The meat-packing firms which were the first firms in the town were joined later by tool manufacturers and shoe firms, local business services and local consumer services as the city increased in size.

> Our hypothetical urban area is now moving up in rank in the hierarchy of cities. As it becomes first a provincial and then a regional capital, its rising status is explicitly recognised by an industrial structure which changes to reflect its new role. The first step, usually, is to export a growing range of services to nearby cities of the next smaller size. With growth, however, the metropolis may extend its reach to embrace the whole nation or a very large portion of it for a much narrower group of services.
>
> Even local manufacturing tends to become more diversified and self sufficient, as the growing local market attracts the branch plants of outside firms. (Thompson, 1965, pp. 12–15, edited)

This schema is clearly modelled on the growth of the mid-western towns where growth through these stages took place in less than 100 years. The implication of this schema is that larger cities will have a more diversified structure than smaller towns. But is this true? Clemente and Sturgis (1971) and Crowley (1973) tested the hypothesis and found that the degree of diversification did indeed increase with city size. But size did not explain all the variation in the level of diversification; indeed in their study of Canadian cities, Clemente and Sturgis found that it explained, at best, less than 50 per cent in 1951, and less than 36 per cent in 1961. But if size explains such a small proportion of the degree of diversification then it follows that cities of the same size might have widely differing industrial structures, from which it follows that the external economies would also be different.

The significance of differences in industrial structure was first pointed out by Chinitz (1961), in an article contrasting the economies of New York and Pittsburgh. He argued that Pittsburgh, the less diversified city, its economy dominated by a few large steel companies, would have a lower level of agglomeration economies than would a city with a more diversified industrial structure such as New York, even after allowing for differences in size. He gives several reasons why this should be so.

First, large firms are able to provide services internally, and are less likely to buy them in from outside. Their size allows them to provide in themselves a market large enough for the service to attain the available economies of scale. So in a city dominated by large plants which can internalize services fewer services are likely to be provided externally. Thus there are fewer services available for use by smaller firms.

Secondly, in a city dominated by large companies, decisions regarding their financial needs and requirements are likely to be dealt with by the banks and other financial institutions at head-office level. The branch will have less experience in financing smaller firms, and so is less likely to be willing to provide finance. Moreover, small entrepreneurs who have cash available for investment are likely to invest in neighbouring firms. Large companies are more likely to invest elsewhere. So in a city dominated by small firms finance will be more readily available for other small firms than in a city dominated by large firms.

Thirdly, entrepreneurship is scarcer in a city with a large-plant economy. As Chinitz (1961) puts it 'the son of a salaried executive is less likely to be sensitive to opportunities wholly unrelated to his father's field than the son of an independent entrepreneur' (p. 284). Being an entrepreneur where many are seems less difficult and less risky than where few are.

Fourthly, Chinitz points out with respect to Pittsburgh that the employment structure of the steel industry, particularly shift work, resulted in fewer women being employed. In my view, there is a more general argument relating to the labour force. Where there are a few plants in a single industry the workforce is likely to be relatively immobile and to lack a diversity of skills, since each plant will tend to employ a large number of people all using the same skills. The narrow range of skills in the labour force makes it more difficult and expensive for new small firms to obtain a labour force.

In his original article Chinitz expresses some doubt as to the feasibility of testing his hypothesis, but Carlino (1980) has attempted to do just that. Using several measures of urban scale he attempts to discover the extent to which they are correlated with output in various cities in various industries. These variables include a measure of industrial diversification, the population of the cities, and the total number of firms in a city. He finds that 'the external economies of scale are an important force in an understanding of agglomeration economies for manufacturing establishments . . . [but] the empirical analysis does not generally suggest that these forces of scale are either influenced or offset by urban industrial specialisation' (Carlino, 1980, p. 348). On the other hand, the 'findings reveal the importance of external economies of agglomeration – especially urbanisation economies [measured by the number of firms in the city] – as a contributor to total economies of scale in metropolitan manufacturing' (Carlino, 1980, p. 349). In other words, Chinitz's hypothesis is confirmed if he is interpreted as saying that a large number of small firms increases the economies of agglomeration, but not if he is interpreted as saying that it is industrial diversification that increases the economies of agglomeration. Carlino interprets the hypothesis as referring solely to the degree of industrial diversification, and on that basis it is 'largely unsupported by the empirical analysis' (Carlino, 1980, p. 349). My own interpretation of Chinitz's hypothesis is that the number of firms is more significant than the degree of diversification. It is not industrial structure in terms of the range of industries which is important but industrial structure in terms of the average size of plant. On this interpretation, I believe Carlino's work to confirm the hypothesis.

URBAN GROWTH

Industrial diversification, city size and agglomeration economies are also relevant to the discussion of urban growth, as we shall show later. Indeed Chinitz's original discussion is related to the question as to the extent to which the generation of new firms in a city with a high level of agglomeration economies would cause growth or at the least prevent its decline.

But what do we mean by urban growth? In most discussions, whether academic or not, urban growth means population growth. But when we talk about growth in terms of a national economy we usually mean growth of national income or income per capita. There is a significant difference in emphasis and it is worth noting the reason. It is implicitly assumed that any rise in income per capita in a town, because of an increased demand for labour there, would be swiftly damped by in-migration, just as any fall in demand will be reflected in unemployment and out-migration. In other words, urban economic growth is likely to be observable in terms of population growth, even if some residual differences in income and wage levels remain (although urban decline may more obviously be seen in unemployment).

What are the causes of urban growth? There is in fact no single theory which can explain the growth of particular cities. Any city must fit into the urban hierarchy. Unless the whole hierarchy is growing, as, for example, it may in the early stages of industrialization as the rural population migrates to the towns, then the reason or reasons for a change in the relative position in the urban system of a particular town will lie outside that system. There are, therefore, a number of possible explanations for the growth of a particular city.

THEORIES OF URBAN GROWTH

The first and most obvious possibility is that the causes of growth have to do with the location of markets or, more probably, resources. The growth and prosperity of Aberdeen in the 1970s was primarily due to the discovery and exploitation of oil in the North

Sea. An earlier example is the growth of Melbourne and San Francisco in the nineteenth century following the discovery of gold in Australia and California. The exhaustion of the gold fields meant that both these cities declined in importance relative to their rivals, Sydney and Los Angeles. The rise of the west-coast British ports of Bristol, Liverpool and Glasgow was stimulated by the growth of trade with the Americas, Asia, and Australia. The recent growth of British trade with Europe has caused them to decline in importance relative to the east-coast ports. This is a 'school geography' approach to the analysis of urban growth, but that does not mean that these geographical factors are unimportant; the opposite is true, these factors are the most important determinants of urban growth which is why they are mentioned in the school books but for all that they are often neglected by economists interested in more 'economic' factors.

A second possible cause of urban growth is growth in the population that the city or cities serve. To the extent that cities act as central places, then any increase in the population in their market areas, or hinterlands, means that it becomes economic for new services to be provided in existing cities. As population density increases the area which needs to be served to achieve the necessary economies of scale falls, and the existing cities, or some of them, move up the urban hierarchy whilst new low-level centres may come into existence. Higgs (1969) found this to have happened in the American mid-west in the late nineteenth century; the most important determinant of the growth of any city was the rate of growth of the population in its hinterland. In a more industrialized area, however, it is doubtful whether such an explanation would be applicable.

A third possibility is that the growth of cities is due to urban agglomeration economies. Whilst the two other explanations depend on Weberian industrial location theory, and on central place theory, so it is inevitable that agglomeration economies, at the core of urban economics, should be used to explain urban economic growth, and attempts have been made to build agglomeration economies into a theory of urban, or rather, regional growth (Richardson, 1973a; von Böventer, 1975) or alternatively to explain differences in the growth rates of cities by differences in agglomeration economies (Williamson and Swanson, 1966; Stanback and Knight, 1970). Of course agglomeration economies have something to do with the size of cities; we have, after all, argued that they are the primary factor causing large cities to exist. It follows that they must have had something to do with the growth of these large cities to their present size. Scenarios can show the way they would operate – once a city grows to a certain size it becomes economic for certain services to be provided; these may be new services or they may replace imported services; the existence of these services attracts manufacturing and commercial firms and plants which 'export' outside the city.

But this process of growth is not self-sustaining because growth causes diseconomies. In von Böventer's words

> (i) If a centre grows larger and larger absolutely, additional immigrants have to overcome greater and greater distances if the same rate of growth of the labour force is to be maintained;
> (ii) intra-metropolitan distances grow with the expansion of the city, and commuting distances also rise on the average – furthermore, people have to spend more and more time travelling if they want to spend weekends in the country; and
> (iii) with rising incomes and rising population numbers, wages and land values assume values which make large centres less attractive for many firms and even employees though they may become more attractive than ever before for certain other lines of business (those that push the former ones out) and also certain other households; and the fact that there is also
> (iv) in many parts of the centre, sites may not be available any more in the desired quantities. (von Böventer, 1975, p. 14)

The result is of course that the attractions of this large city are reduced and firms and households move to other towns and cities which are nearer to their optimum size. As a result there is a process of regional dispersion. Thus this approach is less a theory or urban growth than of regional growth, since it implies the growth of the whole urban system.

The approach can be used, however, to analyse the growth of single cities, or a single-city size, over a short period of time, such as a decade or so. For example Stanback and Knight (1970) found middle-sized cities to be growing faster than smaller or larger cities in America in the decade 1950–60. Differences in growth rates of this kind are less likely to be due to the absolute level of agglomeration economies in those cities than to temporary disequilibrium differences between the benefits derivable from the agglomeration economies and the costs of locating there because of the diseconomies. In the 1950s, for example the growth of private-car transport and the construction of urban freeways was unlikely to improve the transport systems of very large cities with efficient public-transport systems, congested roads, and where high land values restricted freeway construction, but would have its greatest impact in medium-sized cities. So the reduction in the costs of location in these cities would encourage firms and households to migrate there so pushing up the costs, in the way von Böventer points out, and damping down the growth process.

THE PROCESS OF GROWTH

Whatever the cause of growth, the process of growth can be analysed in economic terms. Growth in one sector of the urban economy has multiplier effects on the rest. The growth of employment in the docks, say, or in a factory, causes people to migrate to the town and generate further employment as the in-migrants spend their income in the town, and rent or buy housing there. Moreover, if the goods they purchase are manufactured in the town this in turn generates further multiplier effects.

It was on the basis of this relationship that distinctions began to be made by American planners, even in the inter-war years, between basic and non-basic industries, or export and service industries, see Pfouts (1960). It was felt that some industries, typically manufacturing, produced goods which were exported outside the city and so generated income for the city. These were the basic or export industries. Other industries provided services and sold goods to the population of the city and to other firms there; these were the service or so-called non-basic industries. 'So-called' because many felt that these industries could not truly be regarded as 'non-basic', a somewhat emotive adjective, since they were the industries which were likely to remain in the town as the basic industries changed, with, for example, ship-building declining but being replaced by light engineering. The use of the export/service terminology avoids this semantic argument and draws attention to the fundamental argument, namely that if the export (basic) industries expand this will in turn cause an expansion of the service (non-basic) industries.

There are, nevertheless, several problems with the use of the concept of the economic base in practice. First, as one might expect, the proportion employed in export industries tends to decrease as city size increases. In other words, cities become more self-sufficient as they increase in size as trade takes place internally rather than externally. Services which are either not available or have to be obtained from elsewhere in a small town are readily available in a larger one. Figure 6.2 shows a representative employment ratio in retailing for some United States cities; the way this ratio increases as city size increases is readily seen. However, this introduces a second problem. Presumably one reason for the increase in the ratio is that some goods – furniture or jewellery, for example – are only widely available in large cities so that residents of small towns travel to these larger cities to buy them. Thus even with such an obvious service industry as retailing some of the sales may actually be 'for export'. This same problem is likely to be even more true for other industries.

Because of these problems, extensively reviewed in a volume edited by Pfouts (1960), emphasis began to be switched in the 1960s towards the use of the multiplier, a concept derived from Keynesian economic analysis, and towards input–output analysis. Instead of trying to analyse changes in terms of employment in different kinds of industries the multiplier relies on the use of financial data, arguing that an increase in incomes in an area will result in greater expendi-

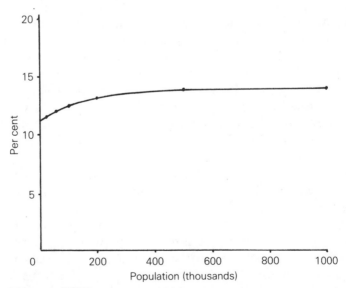

Source: Momsett (1958)

FIGURE 6.2
Percentage of all employed persons in retailing as a function of city size.
Cities in the south and west of the United States 1950

ture in an area and hence a further increase in income, and so on. Empirical analysis tended to show that the multipliers, for smaller towns at any rate, were rather low. Tiebout (1960) found the multiplier to be only 1.04 in an early study of Winnetka, a small town outside Chicago (see also Troy, 1965; Friedly, 1965), and their results led to a loss of interest in the topic, for urban economic analysis at least.

Input–output analysis has been used (see e.g. Isard and Langford, 1971) to measure the impact on an area of growth caused, e.g. by the location of a new steel plant. The interrelationship of all industries was recognized, in that each industry's inputs were the output of others, so that with an accurate input–output matrix the precise impact of any change could be measured. The extensive data requirements of this technique have slowed its development though work continues; but a discussion of this technique takes us somewhat outside the consideration of urban growth since, as we have indicated, its main use has been either in the study of short term, but large, changes in small areas, or in the analysis of regions, where the input–output coefficients are more likely to remain stable over time.

SIZE AND GROWTH

The relationship between size and the rate of growth is not simple. Figures 6.3 and 6.4, derived from Robson (1973), show the relationship between urban size and the rate of growth for British cities in the last decade of the nineteenth century. The scatter of points in figure 6.3 shows the very great variation in the growth rates of the smaller places and the rather smaller variation in the growth rates of the larger cities. The middle line in figure 6.4 connects together the mean points for each of eight size groups, and the upper and lower lines show the mean ±1 SD. These lines confirm and reinforce the impression given by the scatter of points that the variation in growth rates is much greater for small towns than larger cities. And also indicate that the variation in growth rates of all cities is so great that city-size differences can explain very little of this variation. Robson carried out similar investigations for each intercensal period between 1801 and 1911 and although throughout the nineteenth century the mean growth rate was positively related to city size the wide variations in the growth rates meant that the relationship was not statistically significant.

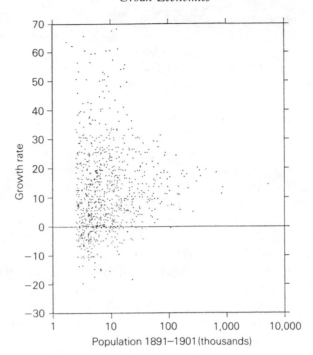

Source: Robson (1977)

FIGURE 6.3
Urban growth of cities in England and Wales, 1891–1901

Thompson (1965) in the first published text book on urban economics hypothesized that this would be the pattern – a wide variation in the growth rates of small towns and a smaller variation in the growth rates of large cities with these large cities having average or above average growth rates. The most important reason for this is that the industrial mix in a large city is likely to be close (or closer) to the average for the nation as a whole. 'With growth and size comes industrial diversification, and even a random blending of young, mature and decadent industries tends to produce local growth rates which deviate only slightly from the national average rate, or the rate applicable to the surrounding region' (Thompson, 1965, p. 22). The smaller the town the more likely it is that employment is dominated by a single firm or industry, so that the growth of the town is dominated by the growth of that firm or

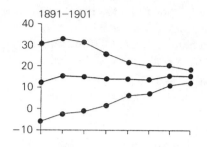

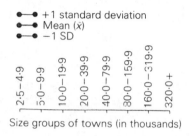

Source: Robson (1977)

FIGURE 6.4

Mean and dispersion of growth rates of cities in England and Wales, 1891–1901

industry. The result can be seen in figure 6.3. Some small towns grew very rapidly whilst others grew slowly and even declined.

Thompson suggested two other reasons, both political in nature, which would make the growth of large cities irreversible. First, 'with a larger population comes greater electoral strength' (Thompson, 1965, p. 22) which makes these cities difficult to ignore and means that signs of urban decline are more likely to lead to intervention by higher levels of government. Secondly, 'tremendous amounts of fixed capital have been sunk in social and private overheads in the very large urban area – streets, sewers, schools, water mains, electric power lines, stores and housing – so that (it would be) uneconomic to abandon so much immobile capital' (p. 22).

Since the mid-sixties when Thompson wrote this, after a period when big cities have in fact declined, experience suggests that these two arguments suffer from defects. First, although big cities have a lot of votes, the other side of the coin is that doing anything for them is very expensive. There is a strong temptation for governments to appear to respond but in actuality to do very little. The policies of successive British governments towards the inner areas of the major conurbations since the late sixties are an illustration of this. These cities could not be ignored, but the responses have been a series of small-scale experiments, initiatives, or research which cost little but gave the impression that someting was being done. For example, as an experiment, Enterprise Zones provided various incentives for firms to redevelop and invest in small parts of several inner areas. The experiment is to be monitored and evaluated but it lasts for 10 years so that large-scale expenditure is put off to the future. The cheapest initiative of all is research, such as the Inner Area Studies of the mid-seventies, into the nature of the problem. Nothing can then be done until this research is completed (when economic conditions, the problem, or the government will have changed).

With respect to Thompson's other argument, although it is true that the investment in social infrastructure is too great to be abandoned, still complete abandonment is never a possibility, only a reduction in the population of the city. Since much of this infrastructure is likely to be old and in need of replacement, or to be heavily congested, the counter-argument is that a reduction in population may not be uneconomic if it means that some things do not need to be replaced, and new investments are not made unnecessarily. A slow rate of decline means merely that investment to replace or renovate existing infrastructure, which would have had to take place in the large city if the population stayed, now takes place in the areas to which the population has moved.

Thompson puts forward two further arguments in support of the view that large cities are less likely to decline. First, 'a large local economy becomes almost self-justifying as a rich product market. New industries . . . are likely establish branch plants in this large local market, sustaining local growth' (Thompson, 1965, p. 23), or slowing the rate of decline. Secondly, 'a large urban area is more likely to give birth to new industries at critical points in its life cycle than is a small urban area' (p. 23). This view may simply be based on the law of large numbers.

> To illustrate, suppose that an entrepreneurial genius occurs only once in every 10 000 births, then a 50 000-population urban area,

with say, 1000 births per year will produce this key person only once every ten years, on the average. This area may not have a new industrial savior ready at the time of critical need, whereas the 500 000-population urban area, spawning a genius a year, almost certainly will. (Thompson, 1965, pp. 23–4)

This argument is not that helpful to the large cities, however, since the 'entrepreneurial genius', recognizing a declining city when he sees one, may choose to exercise his talent more profitably elsewhere. But it has also been argued that large cities encourage and stimulate innovation and it is this argument that we consider in the next section.

CITY SIZE AND INNOVATION

The view that large cities provide a favourable environment for new firms and industries – that they are 'more than proportionately places of creative entrepreneurship' (Thompson, 1968, p. 55) – is another version of the incubator hypothesis that we discussed in chapter 3. The external economies of the large metropolitan area, it is argued, make it a favourable location for an entrepreneur to start a new firm – the services and suppliers which are already there, the skilled labour which is already trained, the factory space to rent – all mean that the capital risked in a new enterprise can be minimized. Innovation – new firms and new industries – is therefore more likely in a large city than a small town. As the industry matures, however, 'the production process becomes rationalised and often routine', and the high labour costs of the large city 'become excessive when the skill requirements decline and the industry, or parts of it, "filters down" to the smaller less industrially sophisticated areas where the cheaper labour is now up to the lesser occupational demands' (p. 56).

In this version of the incubator hypothesis the incubator is not the inner city but the whole large city, and maturing firms do not decentralize to the suburbs but move out down the urban hierarchy. We found in our discussion of the first version of the hypothesis that there was little evidence to support it – new firms appeared to locate in the inner city because of the market potential of the location. With this second version there is once again no direct evidence to support the hypothesis, plausible though it may sound. What evidence there is suggests, once again, that it is the size of the market that is important.

In the geographical literature there is some evidence regarding the diffusion of certain kinds of innovation down the urban hierarchy. The argument, in this literature, is that information about the innovation is likely to be available first in the largest city and that this information will then be diffused down through the urban system.

All of the evidence of this kind of innovation diffusion, or filtering down to use the terminology in the economic literature, relates to 'a specific kind of innovation, a new service provided to customers resident within a limited distance of its location, for example, fire brigades, Rotary Clubs and hospitals, television stations, building societies, telephone exchanges and gas works' (Nicholson *et al.*, 1981, p. 59, references omitted). These services would seem to have been established first of all in large cities because this maximizes the size of the initial market and so minimizes the risk of failure. This interpretation fits in with the results of research into the adoption of technical innovations, where it was found that the innovations tended to be developed for and first adopted in areas where the market was largest.

The conclusion must be that although the evidence supports the hypothesis that new *consumer services* serving a local market will be first adopted in larger cities, and this view is supported by economic analysis of the process of adoption of innovations, there is no evidence that new *manufacturing* firms selling to a national or international market will locate first in the larger cities and then filter down the urban hierarchy. As we found in the earlier discussion of the incubator hypothesis, it is the size of the market which is important in determining the location of firms in the large cities, not the available external economies.

THE SPATIAL DISTRIBUTION OF CITIES

The spatial distribution of cities of different sizes is one area of research which has been largely ignored in urban economics. As we indicated in the previous chapter, central place theory provides an explanation of both the size distribution of cities and their spatial distribution in a rural area. But the economic theory of city size set out there explains only the size distribution in an industrialized region not the spatial distribution. But, even in an industrial economy in which central place theory is largely inapplicable, there must still be economic relationships between cities which influence the pattern of urban settlement, even if that pattern of settlement is not fully determined by those relationships. The physical locations of most industrial cities are determined by geography and geology – river crossings, harbours, iron and coal deposits, and so on – but the spatial relationships between them and with market centres in the rural areas must explain, at least in part, why some become large and some remain small. These relationships remain somewhat obscure, however.

The one field of inquiry in which spatial relationships between areas have been considered is in discussion of the role of the growth centre as an instrument both of regional policy and of development policy (Richardson, 1981). The concept of the growth centre derives from that of the growth pole in economic development. The growth pole is an industry or group of industries which is developed intensively in an economy in the expectation that its development will stimulate the growth of others, those which supply it for instance, and so generate growth. The growth centre is a town or group of towns in which new investment in industry and infrastructure is concentrated in the expectation that its development will stimulate growth in the surrounding region.

The theoretical discussion of this concept suggests that in practice the development of the growth centre will have both positive and negative effects on the economy of its hinterland. The negative effects, called 'backwash' or 'polarization', occur when the centre's development reduces growth in the hinterland as industries prefer a location in the rapidly developing centre to location in the more backward hinterland. The positive effects – 'spread', 'dispersion' or 'trickle-down' – occur with the diffusion of innovations, investment and different attitudes to growth through the hinerland. Unfortunately the negative effects appear likely to be evident earlier than the positive effects, and a net positive effect may only be visible after many years, possibly decades (Richardson, 1976). This considerably reduces the attraction of growth-centre policies. First, from an economic point of view, the long delay before any benefits are perceived may make the rate of return from investment in growth-centre policies too low compared with other alternatives. Secondly, from a political point of view if the benefits are only perceived after 10 or 20 years this is well beyond the time horizon of most politicians, and so growth centres may be abandoned when the negative effects are felt and before positive effects are perceived.

A further problem with the application of growth-centre policies in practice is that growth-centre policies call for the concentration of investment in a few cities, whilst political expediency suggests that each region should have its share of available investment. The result may be, and often has been, the naming of a large number of places as growth centres with too little investment being put into any of them to make the policy effective.

Despite an extensive conceptual discussion of how a growth-centre policy might work, there has been little empirical investigation of the spatial relationships between cities. One of the very few studies of this kind was carried out by von Böventer (1969), studying migration into West German cities in the period 1956 to 1966. He argued that smaller cities would gain some advantage from proximity to a big city because the agglomeration economies of the large city would be available, albeit in attenuated form, to firms and households in the smaller town. These advantages would decline with distance. On the other hand, proximity to the large city would mean that firms and households might prefer to locate in the larger city because it provided more locational advantages. A greater distance from the larger city would give the smaller a greater hinterland of its own, and so increasing distance from the large city would make it attractive as a location. von Böventer found some support for his view in the period 1956 to 1961: immigration to smaller cities decreased with increasing distance from a larger city up to a certain distance as access to agglomeration economies decreased, after this 'pessimum' distance in-migration increased as hinterland effects dominated.

Little further work along these lines has been done but the approach indicates the factors which should be taken into account in analysing the spatial relationships between cities. The findings are particular to the time and place however, since as we have indicated earlier the measurement of growth in a town is not in fact a measure of the available agglomeration economies but of the extent to which the value of those economies exceed the costs of the location. Over time these relationships will change.

In earlier years one would have expected hinterland effects to have dominated as the growth of the larger cities during the industrial revolution occurred at the expense of the smaller towns. In effect the large city cast its 'shadow' over the surrounding area depriving the smaller towns of growth as a larger tree prevents the growth of others by depriving them of light. But the extent of the 'shadow' and its effect will change as technical, social and economic factors change.

An empirical example of this shadow is given by analysis some years ago of the usage of United States airports by Taaffe (1956). He showed that if one calculated and mapped the number of passenger movements per thousand resident population for each city then, in 1950, smaller cities within 150 miles of larger cities had a lower figure than one would expect. This 'traffic shadow' occurred because people from the smaller cities would travel overland to use the larger cities' airports because of the greater number of destinations flown to and the more frequent service. But the extent of this traffic shadow would depend on demand and on aircraft technology. If demand increased then the extent of the traffic shadow might diminish as more frequent services to middle-sized cities in the outer part of the traffic shadow became viable. On the other hand, if the economic aircraft size became larger then one would expect the traffic shadow to become larger as services became concentrated at the larger airports. One would expect that over the 30 or more years since Taaffe's research, the demand factor would have been dominant during the first 15 or 20 years, but that the advent of the wide bodied jets would have caused the traffic shadow to become greater since about 1970.

SUMMARY

In this chapter we have looked at various aspects of the urban economy connected with the interrelationships of city size, industrial structure and growth. We first considered the factors which would determine the optimal size of a city, one of which was the degree to which agglomeration economies varied with city size. Then we showed these economies will vary not only with size but also with the industrial structure of the city both in terms of industrial mix and average plant size.

Agglomeration economies also figured in the discussion of urban growth since urban economists have argued that they may be a major determinant of growth. Other factors are, however, at least as important, particularly the size of the resources and markets which the city's industries trade in. The relationship of city size to growth was also discussed because urban size, and also industrial structure will affect a city's chances of secure growth. Innovation was also considered to be a factor which might be affected by urban size.

We ended this chapter with a brief discussion of the spatial relationships between cities, since the size and growth of cities are affected by their proximity to others both larger and smaller.

In the next chapter we switch from discussing growth, presumed to be in the longer run, to change, the short-run adjustment of the urban economy to changes in the technical and economic factors which have previously determined its structure and size.

FURTHER READING

The paper by Chinitz (1961) is well worth reading. As stated at the end of the previous chapter, the literature on the economics of urban size was surveyed by Richardson (1973b). On urban growth and agglomeration economics see Richardson (1973a), and von Böventer (1975). Richardson (1976, 1981) has also surveyed the role of the growth centre in regional development.

7

Urban Change

Lady Bracknell: What number in Belgrave Square?
Jack: 149.
Lady Bracknell [*shaking her head*]:   The unfashionable side. I thought there was something. However, that could easily be altered.
Jack: Do you mean the fashion, or the side?
Lady Bracknell [*sternly*]:   Both, if necessary, I presume.

The Importance of Being Earnest Act I

In the preceding chapters we have aimed to explain the economic structure of cities. The analyses have been essentially static rather than dynamic although we have commented from time to time on ways in which cities have changed and are changing. In this chapter we shall try to bring together and expand the various points which have been made in order to comment explicitly on the changing urban economy.

One of the most important causes of change in terms of its impact on urban location patterns is a change in the intra-urban transport system, whether in terms of new routes, changing speeds or changing costs. For a century and a half the cost of urban transport has fallen and transport speeds have risen. The long-term trend has been interrupted occasionally, for example by the oil-price increases of the seventies, but generally these changes have been the most important affecting the urban economy in the long run.

Other factors causing changes in urban structure in the long run have been increases in incomes and demographic changes and also changes in production technology and improvements in the speed of transferring information.

The objective in this chapter, as we have said, is to explain the process of change in the urban economy and the way in which other events will cause change. To predict those events would of course be more useful, but whilst we can predict the effects of events, it is not within the economist's ability to predict the events themselves, from developments in information technology to oil-price embargoes, which will cause the changes to take place.

In the first section of this chapter we begin by analysing the effect of reductions in transport costs on the pattern of residential location in a large monocentric city. We then go on to discuss the impact of technical change on the location of employment, whether manufacturing or services, and then to analyse the process of gentrification and its cause.

TRANSPORT IMPROVEMENTS AND RESIDENTIAL LOCATION

As we indicated in chapter 2, the trade-off theory of residential location was developed in response to the problems caused by increasing traffic congestion in cities primarily to explain or predict the effects of large-scale urban road construction. We shall show that the theory predicts the short-run effects, but that these short-run changes are modified in the longer run by changes in employment location in response to the short-run changes.

It will be remembered that the basic assumptions of the theory are that the city is large and monocentric, located on a flat plain with no topographical features. All radial transport routes are equally efficient; there are no externalities and housing can be costlessly adapted. By elimination of other factors these assumptions mean that the only factors left to be considered by the household in choosing its location are the cost of the journey to work and the cost of housing. The former increases with distance, and so the attempt to minimize travel costs by the households, given that all work is at the city centre, results in the cost of housing and land being highest near the centre of the city and falling at a decreasing rate as distance from the centre increases.

Suppose that, before any transport improvement, the equilibrium relationship between the cost of housing and distance is as shown by the line RS in figure 7.1(a) and the initial relationship between transport costs and distance is as shown by the solid line OA in figure 7.1(b). The household's choice of location is then shown in

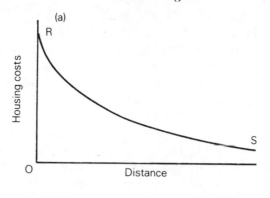

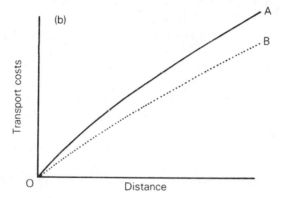

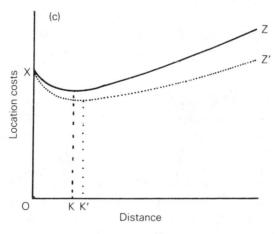

FIGURE 7.1

figure 7.1(c). The solid line XZ shows the way in which the sum of housing costs and transport costs vary with distance from the city centre. The household's optimal location is at the distance from the centre at which its total location costs – housing plus travel – are minimized, and this is represented in figure 7.1 (c) by the distance OK.

The result of any improvement in transport speed and/or reduction in transport cost is to reduce the cost of travelling a given distance. An improvement in travel speed has this effect because part of the cost of commuting is the opportunity cost of travel time, which appears to be about a quarter or a third of the wage rate. If further can be travelled in a given time the cost of travelling per mile is reduced. The effect is similar to a reduction in the direct cost of travel and is represented in figure 7.1(b) by the dotted line OB.

The change therefore alters total location costs, and this change is indicated in figure 7.1(c) by the dotted line XZ'. With no initial change in housing costs there is no change in total location costs at the centre of the city, but they fall by larger and larger amounts as distance from the centre increases. Therefore, the optimal location of all households changes. The new optimal location for the household whose costs are represented in figure 7.1(c) is shown as being at OK' miles from the centre. Each household has an incentive to move outward, for in the short run the housing cost curve stays the same, so that the savings from travelling any distance remain the same but the costs of travelling any given distance are reduced. The lower cost of travel makes it worth while travelling further to obtain greater savings in housing costs.

This is true only in the very short run, however. The attempt by households to move further out leads to a fall in the demand for housing in the inner areas of the city and an increase in the demand in the outer areas. As a result house prices and land values fall in the inner areas and rise in the outer areas so that the housing cost gradient will become less steep. The incentive to move outward is then largely eliminated although in the longer run redevelopment in the inner areas and new construction in the outer areas will lead to a gradual decentralization of the population. This decentralization is illustrated in figure 7.2 which shows the changes in population density in London between 1801 and 1941.

Other changes will also occur in the longer run, however. The reduction in the cost of transport and consequential fall in housing costs means that employers do not now have to pay so high a wage

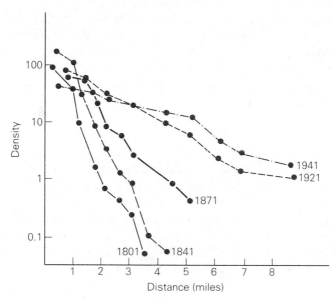

Source: Clark (1951)

FIGURE 7.2
Density gradients – London 1801–1941

premium to employ labour at the centre of this large city. Nor is the cost of space so great. The external economies of a location there remain the same, however, since they are related to the size of the city and its industrial structure. Since these economies remain the same but the costs have fallen, the centre of the city becomes a more favourable location and new firms and industries may now grow up there rather than in some smaller town. This growth in employment will lead to the migration of people from the smaller towns to the larger city, all this of course assuming the absence of any government intervention to prevent it, as would have been true in Britain until 30 or 40 years ago. This in-migration will lead to an increased demand for space in all parts of the city so that, in the longer run, housing costs will not fall as far as one might assume from the short-run analysis. The city becomes larger both in population and in area. The wage premium is therefore also greater. The firms at the centre lose some of their advantages as the cost of space and of labour is greater, but gain because of the greater urbanization economies of the larger city.

This analysis explains the growth of the larger cities over the last century and a half relative to the smaller towns as being a consequence of long-term reductions in the real cost of transport and increases in transport speeds. A general increase in the comfort of travel would have also had an effect, since it increases people's willingness to travel further (i.e. reduces the opportunity cost of time spent travelling). So, at least until recently, transport improvements have dominated technical changes on the production side, such as the telephone, which might have led to decentralization to small towns.

The development of private-car transport as a major commuting mode, primarily since the 1950s, has had a slightly different effect to other transport improvements. Because of high land values and the density of existing development it has been too costly to provide an exclusive urban motorway system in the very large cities, and congestion has prevented many from commuting by car to the centres of the very large cities. As a result this most recent development in transport technology has affected the largest cities most of all as they have declined relative to the middle-sized cities and smaller towns.

Changes in transport costs may affect the pattern of location of households relative to each other as well as their location relative to the centre. The higher the income level the higher is the value of travel time. So an increase in the speed of travel, which reduces journey times, cuts the cost of travel to higher income groups by a larger amount, both absolutely and proportionately, than it cuts the cost of travel to lower-income groups. This means, following through the argument set out above, that an increase in the speed of travel provides a greater incentive for high-income groups to move outwards and so is likely to lead to a decentralization of high-income households relative to low-income households. On the other hand, a reduction in the cost of transport will have the opposite effect. It reduces the cost of travel for lower-income groups by a greater proportionate amount than it reduces the cost of travel for high-income groups. For the latter, travel time accounts for a greater proportion of the cost; therefore a reduction in the direct financial cost of travel is relatively of less importance. So a reduction in the cost of travel is likely to lead to an outward movement of low-income households relative to high-income households. A third possible change, an increase in the comfort of travel would have the same effect as an increase in the speed of travel since the economic effect is to reduce the opportunity cost of travel time. In sum a fast, expensive, comfortable, commuter system would lead to higher-income commuters living on the edges of a dispersed city. A slow, cheap, uncomfortable transit system would tend to have the opposite effect, resulting in more compact cities with higher-income groups living much nearer the city centre. The general pattern of change over the years would seem to indicate that increases in the speed and comfort of travel have tended to outweigh reductions in travel costs with respect to the relative location of different income groups, for the suburbanization of the higher income groups has, at least until recently, been a dominant feature of large cities.

RETAILERS AND WHOLESALERS

The decentralization of the residential population away from the centres of cities because of transport improvements encourages the decentralization of the retail trade and consumer services, since these are likely to be purchased at or near the residence rather than at or near the place of work. The decentralization of retail trade was slowed down or delayed so long as transport improvements were largely confined to the radial routes, in particular to the development and improvement of railway systems, since this encouraged travel into the centre of the city to purchase clothing, furniture, and most other things apart from food. The development of the large central city department stores, such as Whiteleys, Harrods, or Selfridges, during the late nineteenth centry and early twentieth century can be attributed to this. Moreover, the existence of efficient radial transport systems and the lack of efficient non-radial transport discouraged the growth of major suburban centres since their market area was limited by the difficulty of getting to them other than along radial routes.

The development of motor transport and the spread of car ownership in the middle of the twentieth century changed this situation. Whilst hastening the decentralization of the population it also allowed the existing suburban populations readier access to suburban shopping centres. This weakened the economic position of the central city stores, and, where planners permitted it, as they generally did not in Britain, led to the development of car-oriented suburban shopping centres built on green-field sites.

The use of motor transport, which allows circumferential travel with the same ease as radial travel, hastened the decentralization of wholesalers as well as retailers although for slightly different reasons. So long as transport is less expensive along radial routes the cheapest place to distribute to the whole city is the centre – despite having to pay more for space there – because the cost of travel increases linearly with distance from the centre (as shown by CA in figure 7.3). Moreover, setting up two or three distribution points in suburban locations is unlikely to be profitable. Even if each distributes to a sector of a city few of their customers will be on the same radial route as a distribution point and so most will have to be served at greater cost by transport along slower circumferential routes or by transport into the centre and out again.

When transport throughout the city becomes uniformly cheap and fast, however, the centre still remains the location at which transport costs are minimized for a single wholesaler distributing to the whole city but these costs only increase by small amounts if the wholesaler relocates outside the centre, as shown in figure 7.3 by the line CB (Evans, 1975). Since the cost of space declines rapidly with distance from the centre even if at a diminishing rate, it is clear that the wholesaler can reduce his space costs considerably by decentralizing

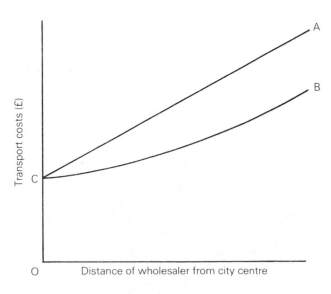

FIGURE 7.3

but will increase his transport costs only by very little. The advantages of decentralization are increased if economies of scale can still be obtained with two or three distribution centres rather than one. These can then be located well outside the centre on cheap land with little or no increase in transport costs. As a result the rate of decentralization of wholesaling with the growth of motor transport has been rapid, sometimes very rapid indeed. Between 1961 and 1966, for example, the centre of the London conurbation lost 22 per cent of its employment in wholesaling (26 000 jobs) whilst central Manchester lost 39 per cent of its wholesaling employment (10 600 jobs) (Cameron and Evans, 1973). Starting from a situation where wholesaling was much more centralized than other forms of employment its distribution is now much closer to the norm.

MANUFACTURING

Just as retailing and wholesaling have decentralized over time so has manufacturing. As Warnes (1980) has shown the process has been going on at least since the nineteenth century, although it may certainly have accelerated in the last 30 years or so. The reasons for manufacturing decentralization appear to be more varied than is true for the decentralization of residences, wholesaling or retailing. Certainly reductions in transport costs have reduced the disadvantage of being less centrally located, but other factors have been equally important. In earlier years the rapid physical growth and expansion of the city was the major factor. Former suburban locations became part of the inner city, and manufacturing firms moved out to escape the congestion and rising cost of space. For example, the Whitefriars Glass Co. which was originally located at Whitefriars in the City of London moved out to a green-field site at Harrow 15 miles to the north-west between the wars and went out of business some 50 years later as industry decentralized further afield.

This example also illustrates the two ways in which manufacturing can decentralize. A firm may actually move from one plant to another, or a firm in an inner area may decline or go out of business, while firms grow or are founded in outer areas. The evidence indicates that, in practice, in recent years at least, decentralization is not generally caused by the movement of their activities by firms, but occurs less directly, through differences between the birth rates and death rates of firms and differences between the growth rates of firms in different locations. Between 1966 and 1974, for example, less than one-third of the decline in industrial employment in inner London was due to the movement of firms, the rest was primarily due to the difference between openings and complete closures (Dennis, 1980).

In recent years there seem to have been two major factors causing the decentralization of manufacturing. First, of course, there have been transport improvements such as the spread of motor transport. This has meant that firms do not need to locate near to their suppliers or to business services or even to their labour supply and they have been able to locate in the suburbs or in small towns outside major urban areas. A second cause of industrial decentralization has been a trend towards bigger plants – large one-storey factories using mass production methods. These plants require large areas of land which are either not available or would be very costly in the inner city. So in order to find such sites at reasonable cost firms must develop sites on the periphery of the city or elsewhere.

Transport improvements and developments in production technology have probably been the most important causes of industrial decentralization, but, in Britain at least, it has also been alleged that the planning policies of local authorities have caused a decline in manufacturing in the inner areas of the conurbations. It is argued that they have been more concerned with providing housing than ensuring employment, so that the demolition and clearance of sub-standard housing and the construction of large housing estates has eliminated many small manufacturing firms as 'non-conforming uses'. Whilst this certainly happened, industrial decentralization has been as fast in countries such as the United States or Australia, with less stringent planning controls and weaker, less active, local authorities, which suggests British local governments have probably not been that important as a cause of decentralization.

Another factor which may have assisted the process of decentralization, whilst not being a cause of it, is a rising level of expectation with respect to the environment. If people like living in smaller towns in more rural environments, as survey evidence indicates that they do (see, for example, Gould and White, 1968), then if firms have less reason to locate in large cities, they are likely to be able to choose locations in the small towns preferred by their labour force or their managers. The movement of American manufacturing to 'the sun belt' (the south and south-west) from 'the snow belt' (the north-east) can be partially attributed to this as can the location of the 'hi tech' firms in southern England west of London.

Two studies suggest that the process of industrial decentralization has not been completely random, however. The external economies and the markets generated by the large cities are still attractive even though the attraction is weaker than it was. Cameron (1973) analysed the intra-urban location of new plants in the Glasgow area between 1958 and 1968 and concluded that although the new plants located further from the centre than the existing plants, 'for any given industry, there was a strong likelihood that the new plants would replicate the pattern of their parent industries with regard to access to the centre' (p. 143). New plants in industries which were relatively centralized were also centralized relative to new plants in other industries even though they located further out than existing plants in the same industry.

Similarly Keeble (1968) analysed the pattern of location of firms decentralizing from London, and found that the distance moved was correlated with size. The larger plants were moved much further from London than the smaller, which is what one might expect if the external economies of the large city are more useful and necessary to small plants rather than large.

OFFICES

Office employment is the one employment sector whose decentralization is not encouraged by reductions in transport costs or increases in transport speeds. Instead these changes allow an increase in the size of the larger cities so that a larger labour force can travel to the centre and encourages the further development of office functions at the centre where the external economies are greatest. This process, as we noted in chapter 4, has been permitted by innovations in telecommunications which have allowed these functions to be separated from the manufacturing and services being administered.

Until recently, therefore, the pattern was for office functions to be concentrated in the largest cities, but recent developments have allowed office functions to be separated from each other so that firms have been able to decentralize routine functions, leaving the elite functions more firmly in the city centre. Some large head offices have decentralized completely, however, trading off the loss of access to the external economies of the major city against the gains from lower wage costs and the lower cost of space. In Britain, planning controls have tended to keep these decentralized offices located within existing town centres, but in the United States some have located away from urban centres in rural or semi-rural environments relying on telecommunications and universal car ownership for interchanges with the rest of the world (see Armstrong, 1972).

Future developments in information technology are unlikely to significantly change present trends, as we argued in chapter 4 (see CALUS, 1983). Routine functions will be more easily carried out with fewer staff occupying less space and the data may more easily be communicated to the 'elite' staff over long distances. Since information exchange at the executive or 'elite' level is largely through personal contact it is much more difficult to decentralize elite functions than routine functions. Paradoxically, moreover, as more of the routine functions are decentralized by more firms, the fall in the demand for office space in the central city reduces rents, and possible wage costs, and thus increases the incentive to locate elite functions there. The costs are lower but the external economies, in terms of accessibility to services and contacts, are the same. If some firms respond by recentralizing their elite functions, these external economies may even be increased. Thus the wilder visions of the impact of information technology are unlikely to be fulfilled – the dissolution of the large city as an office centre as office workers sit at home by their computer terminals. More likely is the continuation of a trend which is already observable – total office employment at the centres of the large cities may fall, but the number of professionals and administrators increases, any decline being in the number of clerical workers.

GENTRIFICATION

As well as the changes in office employment outlined above – an increase in the number of professionals, executives and administrators working in the city centre and a decline in routine clerical employment – we showed earlier that the decline in manufacturing employment is expected to continue. These changes in the structure of employment in the city centre and the inner areas have caused, and will continue to cause, a change in the social and residential structure of the inner city – the 'gentrification' of inner suburbs. The older, less-well-paid, jobs in manufacturing industry and routine clerical office jobs are disappearing. To the extent that they are being replaced it is by higher-paid executive employment.

The results of these changes are a reduction in the area of the commuting field of the large urban area as its total employment declines, so that small towns at the outer edges of this commuting field become more self-contained as they cease to be mainly dormitory suburbs for the large city. The demand for working-class housing in the inner areas declines as jobs disappear. The demand for more high-income housing might be met in the outer parts of the urban area were it not for two contemporaneous social changes – an increase in the number of wives going out to work and an increase in the number of childless couples. The latter change means that these households have a lower demand for space and the former that they have a greater incentive to reduce travel costs. The result of these social and economic changes is an increase in the demand for housing in the inner city by higher-income households resulting in the displacement of lower-income households – in a word, in 'gentrification'.

In the United Kingdom other factors have been mentioned as encouraging the process – in particular home-improvement grants and the operation of planning controls but although they may have assisted the process it is very unlikely that they were the prime cause. It has occurred in cities in other countries, particularly the United States and Australia, where planning and administrative frameworks are very different. For example, Table 7.1 shows the change in the social characteristics of residents of the inner Melbourne local authorities between 1976 and 1981. The most drastic change is shown to have occurred in the suburb of Collingwood just to the north-east of the centre where the proportion in white-collar jobs has increased from 27 per cent to 40 per cent in the 5-year period.

What may hinder the process is the fact that, as we noted in chapter 2, households generally prefer to locate in the same area as others in the same income group, so that the economic forces leading to a change in the character of an area must be great enough to encourage some middle-class households to overcome this initial 'barrier'.

The process of gentrification is assisted and hastened, however, when some wealthier households have different preferences for neighbours, environment, or services – as a generalization are more 'left-wing' in outlook – and hence are willing to be the first to locate

TABLE 7.1

Changes in the proportion of white-collar workers resident in inner Melbourne
1976–1981

	Proportion of white-collar workers		
Local-government area	*Percentage of working population*		*Change in percentage points*
	1976	*1981*	*1976–81*
Collingwood	27.4	40.2	+12.8
Fitzroy	37.8	49.2	+11.4
Melbourne	49.2	54.6	+5.4
Port Melbourne	25.3	27.8	+2.5
Prahran	58.0	63.1	+5.1
Richmond	27.5	36.4	+8.9
St Kilda	46.9	49.0	+2.1
South Melbourne	41.5	52.5	+11.0
Total Inner Area	44.9	51.3	+6.4
Total Urban Area	46.6	48.4	+1.8

Source: Newman *et al.* (1984)

in a lower-income area. This 'deviant' group of middle-class households – planners, university lecturers, television people, architects, etc. – may locate there initially almost because the area is working-class but in so doing raise the status of the area as it becomes 'trendy' so that other middle-class households will follow.

SUMMARY AND CONCLUSIONS

In this chapter we have showed the way in which cities change in response to other changes in the economy. We have concentrated on changes resulting from improvements in transport, in part because the analysis of such changes was the initial impetus for the development of urban economics, in part because transport improvements appear to have been the primary cause of long-run changes in the structure of cities.

The main changes have been a decentralization of the population followed by a decentralization of employment, whether in retail or wholesale trade, in manufacturing or offices, although technical changes in production processes and in the transmission of information have assisted the latter movements. (That jobs have followed people rather than people following jobs, as is often alleged, is confirmed by Steinnes, 1982.) We have argued that this is now resulting in a major change in the spatial and economic structure of major cities. The outflow of manufacturing and wholesaling jobs from the inner city, and clerical and retailing employment from the city centre has tended to weaken the economy of the inner city. The growth of professional and administrative employment in city-centre offices provides only partial compensation as it encourages the gentrification of some inner suburbs. This weakening of the economy has been alleged to be responsible for higher inner-city unemployment, derelict and vacant land in the inner city, and financial crises in local government. To judge whether or not these allegations are true requires an understanding of the urban labour market, the land market, the local government finance, and these we consider in the next three chapters.

FURTHER READING

The determinants of changes in urban density gradients were studied using econometric methods by Muth (1969) and Mills (1970). The decentralization of industry is discussed in contributions to the volume edited by Evans and Eversley (1980). The evidence is surveyed by Scott (1982). The question as to whether the people follow the jobs or vice versa is answered by Foster and Richardson (1973), and, using more sophisticated econometric methods, by Steinnes (1982). The decentralization of warehousing is discussed by Evans (1975), and the movement of offices by Armstrong (1972) and Alexander (1979). CALUS (1983) attempts to predict the impact of developments in information technology. The economics of gentrification is analysed by Evans (1973a, 1976).

8

Urban Labour Markets

Lady Bracknell: Do you smoke?
Jack: Well, yes, I must admit I smoke.
Lady Bracknell: I am glad to hear it. A man should always have an
  occupation of some kind. There are far too many idle men in
  London as it is.

The Importance of Being Earnest Act I

It is only recently that researchers and policy-makers have shown interest in the functioning of the urban labour market. In one way this is odd, since the methods used to define urban areas for statistical purposes have often been based on the view that an urban area operates as a single labour market with people travelling between homes in one part and jobs in another. This view is evident in the definitions of metropolitan areas discussed in the first part of this chapter.

In the 1970s concern over the high rates of unemployment in the inner areas of British cities led to an opposing view being expressed – namely that the urban area was a set of separate, although interconnected labour markets – because these high rates of unemployment persisted whilst unemployment was low in the outer city. Research into the causes of high unemployment in the inner city, discussed in the second part of this chapter, tended to confirm the original view that the urban areas could be thought of as single labour markets, but in so doing shed light on the operation of urban labour markets.

Discussion of the spatial incidence of unemployment in cities in the second section of the chapter leads us into a discussion of the distribution of incomes in cities in the third section. The determinants of the level of incomes in cities and the relationship between the distribution of incomes in a city and its characteristics has been explored in several American studies. The spatial distribution of incomes and in particular the local incidence of poverty began also to be explored in some British studies in the 1970s.

British and American research has tended to follow different paths, however. One reason for this is race. Those located in the inner areas of United States cities, although just as likely to be poor and/or unemployed as their British equivalents, tend also to be mainly black or Hispanic. In consequence the inner-city problem in America has been seen as primarily a racial problem and has been investigated in those terms, as we show in the fourth section of the chapter.

DEFINING URBAN AREAS

How should the boundaries of an urban area be defined, if it must be, as far as possible, a single economic unit? One could, of course, define the area in administrative terms, by using the legal boundaries of the local government area. But these boundaries are to a large extent arbitrary and determined by past history and politics. Whilst the inhabitants of a local authority area might be roughly aware of its boundaries, and have some degree of civic pride, the dispassionate observer travelling from there to an adjacent area would often perceive them both as being part of a single functional urban area.

The significance of history and politics in defining urban boundaries can be seen in the administrative history of London. The original City of London was defined by its defensive boundaries – the Thames to the south and a wall on the remaining three sides – so that until the sixteenth century the wall and the river determined both the administrative boundary and the built-up area. There was increasing pressure to build beyond the wall, however, and from the seventeenth century onward London expanded to encompass Westminster and many formerly independent villages which eventually became part of 'London'. Despite this physical expansion the City of London's boundaries remained more or less what they always had been, and the newer suburbs continued to be governed as separate places. In 1888, however, the London County Council was set up to govern, together with a lower tier of municipal boroughs, the then built-up area of London. Thus the boundary of the local government area was for a brief period once again the same as the boundary of the built-up urban area although, anomalously, the City remained as a separate local government governing the original area of the historic walled city.

Further urban expansion meant that the County of London came only to include the inner areas of London. At the time of the 1951 Census when the statisticians set out to define a Greater London Conurbation the area they defined, which covered the whole contiguous built-up area, was some three times the size of the County of London.

Up to 1951 the urban area as an economic entity rather than as an administrative unit could be defined in terms of the contiguous built-up area. People might live in one district and travel to jobs in another, but the desire to minimize the cost of travel meant that residential suburbs and industrial areas formed one developed area. From this time on the situation became more complicated, however; after the Second World War the further contiguous expansion of London has been prevented by the creation of a green belt within the area of which further development has been effectively stopped. This limitation of contiguous development meant that the working population could no longer be accommodated within the existng built-up area when the working population of London expanded further in the 1950s. The demand for property within the built-up area caused property prices to rise until it became worthwhile for people to commute across the green belt from homes in towns and villages on the other side of it. This process was hastened by the falling real cost of transport, as car ownership became cheaper, roads were improved, motorways constructed, and railways electrified.

How then should we now define the London area? When London's government was again reorganized in 1965 the new County of Greater London covered an area slightly smaller than the contiguous built-up area. Clearly, however, London as an economic entity is considerably larger. In earlier days new commuters would have lived in new housing estates tacked on to the edge of the existing built-up area, so that the urban area could be easily defined. Nowadays commuter flows take place between urban places separated by green fields and the definition of a boundary of a functional urban area is no longer so easy.

This problem was first faced by the United States Bureau of the Census. Although there were no green belts around American cities, widespread car ownership and the construction of limited-access highways had a similar effect in encouraging discontinuous development. Their solution to the problem was the Standard Metropolitan Area used in the 1950 Census, and the Standard Metropolitan Statistical Area (SMSA) used in the 1960 and later censuses. SMSAs are formed by adding together counties (townships in New England), the American county being usually considerably smaller than its English equivalent. The central city (or adjoining cities) had to have a population of at least 50 000, and counties, to be included in an SMSA, had to fulfil two conditions. First, they had to be metropolitan in character, i.e. in general more than 75 per cent of the labour force had to be in non-agricultural employment and the population density had to be greater than 150 per mile. Secondly, such counties had to be integrated with the central city and the main criterion for deciding on the degree of integration was clearly based on a view that an urban area must be a single labour market – either at least 15 per cent of the workers *living* in such a county work in the county (or counties) containing the central city (or cities), or at least 25 per cent of those *working* in such a county live in the county or counties containing the central city (or cities). If data on commuting were not conclusive other kinds of information could be used to check on the degree of economic integration, but the main criterion clearly implies that a functional urban area constitutes a single labour market with large commuting flows between different parts of the conurbation.

A similar method of defining urban areas has been developed by British researchers for use with British data (Hall, 1971). Hall and his co-workers defined Standard Metropolitan Labour Areas (SMLAs) as consisting of a SMLA core – a set of administrative areas with a density of at least 12.5 workers per hectare, or a single administrative area with 20 000 or more workers – and a SMLA ring – administrative areas in which at least 15 per cent of the workers living there worked in the core, and which were contiguous with other areas in the core and ring, the whole group of areas having a population of at least 70 000. For a similar attempt to construct SMSA equivalent for European cities see Hall and Hay (1980).

But why should researchers and census bureaux attempt to define functional urban areas in this way? Even if one agrees with the methodology why attempt the task? One reason for doing so is to attempt to keep track of the changing nature of the urban area. For example, suppose the data for one administrative area reveal a decline in jobs or population but adjacent administrative areas are shown to grow. Is this decentralization within a single urban area or is it the decline of one city and the growth of others? The decline of an urban area may require positive policy responses to prevent high unemployment. The situation if what is observed is decentralization within a single urban area is one of the things we discuss in the next section.

INNER CITY UNEMPLOYMENT

As we have shown above, the statistical definitions of urban areas as economic entities have usually been based on the idea of the city being, in some sense, a single labour market. But what would it mean if the city were one labour market rather than several? To what extent is it true to say that it is, even when substantial commuting occurs between districts? These questions have become important in recent years in Britain as concern has increased over inner-city problems, particularly unemployment.

Suppose that there is a high level of unemployment in a particular part of the urban area. What can be done about it? It would be possible to treat this district as a kind of region. When regions of Britain have had high levels of unemployment, then, since the 1940s, the agreed regional policies have been to provide incentives or enforce controls to encourage firms to move to these regions, to build factories there and employ labour there. Several researchers have evaluated these policies and have shown that they seem to have been reasonably effective in achieving their primary goal of increasing the number of jobs in these regions, at least during the years when regional disparities were widest, in the late 1960s and early 1970s (see Armstrong and Taylor, 1978, chapter 10).

Therefore one response to high levels of inner-city unemployment would be to create incentives and controls similar to the instruments of regional policy to steer firms into the inner city. But a feature of regions is that they are separate labour market areas, even if only through sheer physical size. If unemployment is high in one region then people living in that region would find it very costly either to travel to jobs outside that region on a daily or even weekly basis, or to move house and migrate to some other region in search of employment. These costs may include the actual physical cost of movement, or the disruption of social contacts, or the loss of a local-authority house, or be caused by the fact that other members of the family are in work and, therefore, would have to find other jobs if they moved. Of course some commuting will occur across the borders, but generally these costs will discourage migration and we can treat regions as separate labour market areas.

But what of areas of high unemployment within a city? The residents of these areas who are unemployed do not face the same barriers to movement. Commuting to other parts of the city is not that expensive. Even migration – moving house – need not be that costly since social contacts can be maintained, movement may be within the same administrative area so that tenants of local authority housing may merely exchange, and other members of the family do not need to give up their jobs if they also move.

Therefore, if a factory closed down somewhere in a city it would initially throw many people who live in the surrounding area out of work, since people tend to live close to their place of employment (or choose employment close to home). At first unemployment in that area would be higher than in other parts of the city but those without jobs would seek them in other parts of the city, initially near to home but later further away. Thus vacancies in other areas would be competed for by residents of those areas and by those coming from further away. The result would be that, over time, most of those who were made unemployed by the factory closure would find jobs, the speed at which they found them depending on the general level of unemployment and vacancies. The competition for jobs in other parts of the city by those laid off by the factory closure would, however, tend to raise the unemployment rate elsewhere in the city. Thus we would expect that after a relatively short period, say a year or two, the probability of being unemployed in different parts of the city would tend to be similar, although higher than before the closure.

But how can this theory be reconciled with the fact that parts of the inner areas of the major British conurbations have high unemployment rates and that these high rates have persisted for some time? To reconcile the two we have to recognize that the average unemployment rate for an area is just that, an average. The average rate of unemployment for a city is the weighted average of the unemployment rates in different parts of the city. Similarly the average unemployment rate in a part of the city is the weighted average of the unemployment rates of the different groups of people

living in that area. At the limit of course, with a fine enough disaggregation, the position is reached where some people are 100 per
cent unemployed and the rest have unemployment rates of zero.
That level of disaggregation is too fine of course, and is uninterest-
ing, but it is well known that some groups of people have a higher
probability of being unemployed than others – those nearing retire-
ment age, for example, because if they leave a job they find it
difficult to get another; the young, because they tend to move from
job to job and to have short but relatively frequent spells of
unemployment in between. More importantly the less skilled have
higher unemployment rates than the more skilled. In 1971 the
average unemployment rate of unskilled manual workers in England
and Wales was over 9 per cent compared with rates of just over 4 per
cent for skilled and semi-skilled manual workers and under 2 per cent
for managers and professionals.

Several explanations have been put forward for the association of
higher unemployment rates with lower skill levels (see, for example,
Corkindale, 1980, p. 184), but the most important reason is probably
that employers, faced with a choice between someone who is more
skilled and someone who is less skilled when filling a vacancy would
tend to prefer the more skilled. But because of this correlation
between personal characteristics and the probability of being unemployed, it follows that areas in which the unskilled, the young, and
the elderly are disproportionately represented will have higher
unemployment rates than other areas.

But as we showed in chapter 3, the several factors which determine where people choose to live within a city will ensure that these
groups tend to live in inner city areas whilst middle-income families
with children will live in the suburbs and outer areas. So, as several
studies have shown, although the average rate of unemployment of
the resident population varies between different parts of the same
conurbation, this variation can largely be explained by differences in
the characteristics of the resident population. The unskilled labourer
will have the same (high) probability of being unemployed in
whatever part of the city he or she lives, even though the average for
the whole population will vary. (See Metcalf and Richardson, 1980;
Corkindale, 1980, but note the possibility, observed in Australian
cities, that during periods of high unemployment people living in the
outer suburbs, rather than the inner city, may suffer higher unemployment because of lack of access to jobs. See Evans, 1984.)

Of course, although economic reasoning can be used to explain the high levels of unemployment in inner areas, and to show that in terms of the probability of being unemployed people living in an inner area may be no worse off than those living in a suburb, still, from a political and social point of view, the existence of these high concentrations of unemployment may present considerable problems because of the alienation of the population. Obvious illustrations of this were the riots which occurred in London, Liverpool and elsewhere in the early 1980s. Moreover, when the general level of unemployment rises as it did at that time, then, although the proportionate increases may be the same in the inner city as in the outer suburbs, the absolute increase in unemployment will be much higher in the inner area. A general doubling of the unemployment rate may only increase the average from 3 per cent to 6 per cent in the suburbs but from 6 per cent to 12 per cent in the inner city. The social and political problems are clearly greater in the latter case.

It has been suggested by Metcalf (1975) that differences between the average unemployment rates in different cities can also be explained by differences between the characteristics of the population but this seems unlikely. We argued above that migration and job mobility within large urban areas would ensure that the probability of being unemployed was the same for any group with given characteristics wherever they were located within the urban area. The evidence tends to confirm that this is so. On the other hand, we also argued that migration between urban areas was more costly and, therefore, less likely to ensure equality in the incidence of unemployment. The evidence confirms this view – the unemployment rates of people with the same skills differ between urban areas.

These differences are, however, systematic. Migration between cities is less costly, relative to the gains from movement, for younger, more-skilled workers than for others. Moreover, the labour market for these groups tends to be national rather than local, witness the job advertisements in the 'quality' national newspapers. These factors help to ensure that the unemployment rates for the skilled, middle-income households tend to be similar in different areas. On the other hand, the unemployment rates of the less-skilled, low-income households are highest in areas of high unemployment and lowest in the most prosperous areas. Their labour markets are local – jobs are advertised in the local press or notified to the local job centre. They find migration difficult and costly relative to the difference between the wage which could be obtained and the level of unemployment benefit. In the United Kingdom subsidized local-authority housing with security of tenure increases the reluctance of such households to move long distances (Hughes and McCormick, 1981). So urban areas in which unemployment starts to rise are likely to lose their middle-income population as they migrate to jobs elsewhere, and to become increasingly working class in character (Evans and Richardson, 1981).

THE INCOME DISTRIBUTION AND POVERTY

What factors will affect the level of incomes and the income distribution within cities? One was mentioned at the end of the preceding section when we argued that areas of high unemployment will tend to become increasingly working class as the more skilled and non-manual workers move to areas where jobs are available. Another was discussed in chapter 6 when we showed that incomes will be positively correlated with city size. Various costs increase with city size, notably the cost of housing and the journey to work. Because of this the cost of living increases with city size. Households could be compensated for these higher costs by the greater range of goods and services which are available in the larger cities; the evidence is, however, that though they may be compensated to some extent in this way, wages and salaries are also higher, either through the operation of market forces or because the differences are institutionalized (as for example in the case of the various London Living Allowances).

As incomes increase with city size, so it has been documented that income inequality, measured by the Gini coefficient, also increases with city size (Farbman, 1975; Haworth *et al.*, 1978). Mathur (1970) used a different index which measured occupational mix more directly but arrived at the same conclusion. The same measure of agreement does not exist with respect to the explanation for this increase in inequality with city size.

Haworth *et al.*, (1978) interpret their findings in terms of what they call a 'monopoly' hypothesis. They argue that 'increases in size and growth raise the monopoly rents earned by those who are insulated from competition'. These include land owners since 'the price of land will rise as a city grows. Population growth will cause earnings from these assets to rise, thus contributing to greater income inequality as such wealth is unevenly distributed'. They also argue that

> a second group that is expected to benefit disproportionately from increasing city size and urban growth are certain 'monopolists' who are not likely to suffer from increased competition in either business or employment. A relatively unambiguous example of this monopoly effect in business is the newspaper industry. Due to entry barriers ... new population is not likely to entice the publication of another newspaper ... Thus, increases in size and growth are likely to raise profits in businesses that are not readily duplicated. (Haworth *et al.*, 1978, p. 3)

Their arguments have been contested (Walker, 1979, 1981). Widespread home ownership means that it is not clear that increases in the value of land with increasing city size increase inequality much. Moreover, the ownership of much urban land by companies and institutions, and so by their shareholders, and the fact that neither landowners nor shareholders need live in the cities where they own land means that even though increasing land rents through increasing city size might increase inequality in general it need not mean that inequality *within* cities is an increasing function of city size. Finally, monopoly enterprises such as Haworth *et al.*, (1978) describe are difficult to identify; even in the case of their example of newspapers, Walker (1979) observes that 'casual observation for the UK suggests that the larger the city the greater the number of newspapers produced and distributed there' (p. 341).

In my own view the perceived increase in income inequality with city size is the result of firms responding to the differing cost structures in cities of different sizes although the cost of labour increases slightly as city size increases, the cost of space increases substantially, particularly at the centre where most employment is, and where the advantages of the urban location are greatest. The result is that firms have an incentive to substitute the cheaper factors of production – labour and capital – for space. Moreover, since the absolute increase in pay with city size tends to be the same for all workers, whatever their rates of pay (*vide* the various London Living Allowances which tend to be equal absolute amounts), the proportionate increase in labour costs is greater for lower-paid workers. There is, therefore, a greater disincentive to employ lower-paid workers than higher-paid workers in the large city. The effect on employment was discussed with respect to office employment in chapter 4. The more routine functions employing large numbers of clerks are decentralized, and those which remain employ relatively skilled workers. The same is likely to be true of the manufacturing plants locating near the city centre.

Thus although it is certainly true that income inequality, as measured by the Gini coefficient, increases with city size, I would argue that it increases because a higher proportion of the population are higher paid. An area in which virtually all the population is low paid is, after all, more equal than one in which a proportion are higher paid. The measured increase in inequality may, therefore, occur but it would not seem to indicate any major social or political problem.

An alternative way of looking at the relationship between the income distribution and city size is to inquire into the proportion of the population which is, in some sense, poor. Does this proportion increase with city size? The analysis above would suggest that as the proportion of the population with high incomes should increase with city size so the proportion with low incomes should decline. Firm evidence on this is hard to obtain but Van Slooten and Coverdale (1977) found that in Great Britain in 1975 the least-urbanized region, East Anglia, had the highest proportion of households in poverty (25 per cent), whilst in Greater London there were only 15 per cent, a proportion bettered among the regions only by the rest of the south-east.

In part these figures may be misleading. The authors used an objective measure of poverty which does not take into account differences in price levels between areas. So higher incomes in Greater London may be outweighed by even higher living costs. However, the majority of those in poverty at that time were retired people living on pensions or single-parent families, rather than those who might be poor because of low wages or unemployment and their incomes tend to be mainly determined by national levels of welfare benefit. The figures are, therefore, indicative of the true state of affairs rather than strictly accurate; but given the nature of the problem accuracy is not to be expected anyway.

That poverty is high in an apparently prosperous semi-rural area and low in a great city is at odds with most preconceptions of the distribution of poverty, but this is probably because one's preconceptions are determined by what is obvious and poverty is most obvious where large numbers of the poor live in the same place, not where they are scattered evenly throughout an area. If we look around the country for areas in which the population is homogeneously poor, these areas tend to be in the inner cities of the large conurbations. So if we take the smallest area for which information is published from the United Kingdom Census, the Enumeration District (ED), inner London and the inner areas of the other conurbations have far more than their proportionate share of EDs in which a large part of the population is poor (Holtermann, 1975; Evans, 1980). There are two reasons for this. In the first place, even if the population were randomly distributed within any urban area, then since EDs are fairly uniform in size, an ED which just coincided with the area of a very small town would contain its proper proportion of the poor. In larger cities, however, purely through the operation of random distributions some EDs would be likely to occur in which a relatively high proportion would be poor (just as there would be others in which a high proportion would be rich). But, secondly, the population is not randomly distributed. As we showed in chapter 2, households in lower-income groups are likely to live in similar locations in the city, and to live near each other. In a large city the number of poor is large even when the proportion is small, so that there will always be areas in which the population is predominantly poor. But this does not make poverty an urban phenomenon. As we showed above, the proportion which is poor is 60 per cent greater in the most rural region of England than in the largest city.

The concentration of poverty in particular areas of large cities may create political and social problems, however, just as the existence of areas of high unemployment does, even though poverty, from a strictly economic point of view may be greater elsewhere. One reason for this we have already mentioned. Poverty in cities, because it is spatially concentrated, is more obvious than if the poor are scattered among the general population. This spatial concentration has another consequence. In countries with 'first past the post' electoral systems like Britain and America, political representatives are elected to represent specific areas and so in a large city some are elected to represent the areas of poverty. In a rural area where the poor are a minority they are unrepresented. Proportional representation of course operates differently.

The concentration of the poor in distinct areas may also create social problems if there are, in the jargon of economics, some externalities of poverty. Analysis suggests four possible kinds of externality, some of which might ameliorate the problem of poverty, some of which might make it worse.

First, if a large number are poor in an area then mutual understanding of the problems of others may be more likely to ensure systems of mutual support. Similarly shopkeepers may be more understanding about selling goods on credit. On the other hand, the concentration may make things worse as each household's problems make them less able to assist others, and shopkeepers become less willing to give credit when most ask for it than when few do. Moreover, charitable assistance is more able to be given when the possible recipients are few but the possible donors many.

Secondly, if the majority of the population in an area are poor, less skilled and ill educated, it may be less likely that natural leaders will emerge there, but more likely, of course, that those leaders will truly represent the poor.

Thirdly, the deliberate grouping together of the poor and those with social problems such as occurs when some local authorities locate their problem families in so-called 'sink estates' so fulfilling their statutory responsibilities at the expense of the families, will exacerbate those problems. After all, social-problem families, almost by definition, affect their neighbours for the worse.

Fourthly, the grouping together of the poor is likely to increase their alienation from society, causing class identification and unrest about their situation in society. Riots, whether minor or major, are more likely to start in the poorest quarters of the cities, witness the Toxteth, Liverpool, and Brixton, London, riots in 1981. Whilst from a far-left-wing viewpoint concentration could be seen as advantageous in providing the social conditions necessary to inflame social unrest and so spark the necessary revolution, still until this revolution comes the dispassionate observer must note that most such riots cause damage only in the poorer areas in which they occur and so, in the short run at least, worsen the living conditions of the inhabitants.

RACE, INCOMES AND LOCATION

In the United States the study of urban labour markets, and also of the spatial distribution of income in cities, has become entangled with the study of racial discrimination and segregation. The reasons for this are clear. The most obviously poor areas in the American inner cities are inhabited by blacks, and these are also the areas with the highest level of unemployment, so that it seems *a priori* obvious that the people in these areas are poor and/or unemployed because they are black.

The social or economic mechanisms which ensure this association are not completely obvious, however. Is it due to labour market discrimination, housing segregation, or is the association accidental? In the British case, where the proportion of the population which is coloured is very considerably smaller, the higher levels of unemployment in the inner cities which became evident in the mid-seventies could not be wholly attributed to any racial problems. As we have shown the initial view was that this was a problem of the inner city *per se*; people who lived in the inner city were more likely to be unemployed primarily because of the decentralization of employment. However, the economic analysis of the operation of urban labour markets suggested, as we showed earlier, that this was incorrect. The reason for the high level of inner-city unemployment was, put crudely, that those with a high probability of being unemployed, given their characteristics, tended to be concentrated in the inner city.

With respect to the problems of the black ghettoes of the cities of the United States, therefore, three possible explanations are on offer. First, and analogously with the United Kingdom case, blacks are more likely to live in the inner areas because, for historical reasons, they tend to be less skilled, and are, therefore, both poorer and more likely to be unemployed than the white population. Their location is, therefore, not due to race but to lack of skills. Secondly, the blacks' location in the inner city is due to housing-market discrimination which has resulted in the creation of the black ghettos. As manufacturing jobs have decentralized from the inner city the inhabitants of the ghettos have been unable to follow because of the discrimination in the housing market. The British in the equivalent position would be the inhabitants of inner-area, local-authority housing estates who, it is argued, may be similarly, though more benignly, trapped in the inner area by their inability to obtain equivalent (low cost) accommodation in outer areas nearer the jobs. Thirdly, labour-market discrimination may confine blacks to lower-paid jobs or prevent them getting jobs at all. Their location may be due to lack of income or skills, but this in turn is due to race.

The evidence lends some support to all three of these hypotheses.

Blacks have tended to have less training and education than whites and therefore we would expect them to be employed in less-skilled, lower-paid, jobs. Of those entering the labour market in 1930, blacks had 5.9 years of schooling and whites had 9.6 years. For 1970 the relevant figures were 11.4 years and 12.6 years. The difference had narrowed considerably but had not yet vanished altogether (Smith and Welch, 1979, p. 44). Thus, lower skill levels can explain some but not all the problems of blacks in the labour market. However, blacks are relatively more centralized than one would expect, given other characteristics. Kain and Quigley (1975) found that in the 11 largest SMSAs 53 per cent of low-income whites (incomes under $3000 p.a.) lived in the suburban rings, whilst only 26 per cent of high-income blacks (incomes over $10 000) lived in these outer areas. They found that, after taking into account other household characteristics, the location of black households tended to be closer to the centre than might otherwise be expected.

That this pattern of location results in longer journeys to work is exemplified by a study of the journey to work of employees of the Argonne factory located on the western edge of the Chicago SMSA. It was found that the journeys to work of black employees tended to be significantly longer than the journeys of white employees. Figure 8.1 clearly shows with respect to workers at the factory the longer journeys of the black workers relative to the white. Moreover, survey findings confirm that this journey pattern is not desired by blacks and therefore results from discrimination rather than choice (see Yinger, 1979).

SUMMARY

At the conclusion of the previous chapter we noted that the decentralization of manufacturing and wholesaling has tended to weaken the economy of the inner city, and has been alleged to be responsible for high inner-city unemployment. But if this were so the inner city would have to be a separate labour market from the rest of the city, indeed each part of the city would constitute a separate labour market. In this chapter we have shown that the evidence does not confirm this, rather differences between the characteristics of the resident populations in different areas seem to be the most important cause of differences in unemployment rates. Moreover the fact that urban areas function as single labour markets is assumed in the various attempts to define functional (rather than

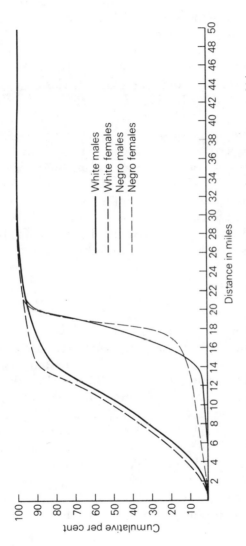

Source: Berry, B. J. L. and Horton, F. E. (1970) *Geographic Perspectives on Urban Systems* (Englewood Cliffs, New Jersey: Prentice Hall) fig. 11.4, p. 410)

FIGURE 8.1

Distance of residences from job by race and sex; employees of the Argonne National Laboratories in Chicago administrative) urban areas using commuting flows as a determinant of linkage between areas.

The high level of unemployment in the inner cities is, therefore, due both to the high level of unemployment in the country as a whole and to the fact that the people living in the inner areas are likely to have a high probability of being unemployed. In a large city the concentration of people with the characteristics associated with high-unemployment rates such as low skill levels, is more visible because of the size of the city and, therefore, because of the large number who are unemployed, even when the average rate of unemployment in the city as a whole is low. The size of the city and the concentration in one place of those who are poor tends, in the same way, to make poverty more visible in big cities, even though the evidence is that average incomes increase with city size. In the United States, discussion of poverty and of unemployment in the cities has become entangled with discussion of race, but our analysis of the evidence supports the view that poverty and unemployment in the American inner cities can only partially be explained by race, partially by the factors which have been found important in British cities.

FURTHER READING

The problems of defining urban areas and the development of the concept of the Standard Metropolitan Statistical Area are dealt with in many urban geography texts, but a good discussion is given in Chapter 8 of Berry and Horton (1970). The mainly British analysis of the economics of inner city unemployment begins with the paper by Metcalf and Richardson (1980), was furthered by Metcalf (1975) and Evans and Richardson (1981) and still continues. The classic American paper on race, housing and job discrimination is by Kain (1975) but the papers by Smith and Welch (1979) and Yinger (1979) are more recent. The reason why income inequality increases with city size is argued by Haworth *et al.*, (1978) and Walker (1979, 1980); Evans (1980) surveys the problem of poverty in the conurbations.

9

The Land Market

Lady Bracknell: What between the duties expected of one during
    one's life time and the duties exacted from one after one's death,
    land has ceased to be either a profit or a pleasure. It gives one
    position and prevents one from keeping it up. That is all that can
    be said about land.
                    The Importance of Being Earnest Act I

As urban economics has developed over the last 20 years or so the
assumption has almost invariably been made that the land market
works smoothly and efficiently to ensure that each parcel of land is
used by the activity which can pay the highest rent. Any possible
departures from this norm have usually been ignored in theoretical
analysis, though most analysts would allow that in practice speculation will cause some sites to be held off the market in anticipation of a
later, higher price.

In this chapter we look at the ways in which urban change will
affect land use, and show that although in general land may safely be
assumed to be used by the highest possible bidder, there are many
reasons why this may not be true in particular cases. The most
obvious, and the most important of these, occurs because governments intervene through planning controls to determine land use
independently of the market. Secondly, the expectations of land
owners as to what might be an acceptable price for this land may lead
them to refuse to accept a price lower than they expect to get either
now or in the future. This is called 'speculation' if the price is rising
and might be called 'inertia' if it is falling. Thirdly, the assumption
that land is always used by the activity willing to pay the highest
current rent ignores the fact that changes in land use depend upon
changes in the use of buildings and often in the buildings themselves.

The cost of redevelopment ensures that land use will change only when it is economical to replace the existing buildings. Moreover, it is possible that land may be left vacant and buildings derelict if the cost of redevelopment is higher than the possible value of any new development. This apparently odd situation has become more relevant as decentralization of industry from the centre has resulted both in vacant derelict property and a reduced demand for the sites. Fourthly, the occupiers of land may be unwilling to displace themselves, or to be displaced, for any new use without some compensation for the upheaval. This will tend to ensure that the price paid for the land for redevelopment must be significantly higher than current-use value. Moreover, attempts to tax away this difference, by means of a development gains tax or a betterment levy of some kind, will tend to slow down the rate of development and increase the price of land as owner occupiers attempt to see that they are properly compensated. Fifthly, the ownership of land will affect the rate of development. Landlords may be more willing to sell, displacing their tenants, than owner occupiers who would have to displace themselves. The rate of development depends not only on ownership but also on the legal rights of tenants, i.e. whether they have security of tenure and whether there is rent control of some kind.

Finally, we note one other way in which the pattern of ownership of land will affect the rate of development. The redevelopment of land may require the acquisition of several contiguous sites. This may only be possible within a reasonable period of time if the land is compulsorily purchased from the owners and so local and central government will usually be involved in extensive schemes of comprehensive redevelopment and urban renewal.

PLANNING CONTROLS

Throughout the analysis of the pattern of location and land use in the preceding chapters of this book, we have almost invariably assumed that land would be used by the activity which could pay the highest current rent, so that location and land values are mutually determined. In a monocentric city the land value gradient (or the rent gradient) would, therefore, have the shape shown in Figure 9.1. Since proximity to the centre is highly valued, land values would be lower further from the centre; moreover, they would decrease at a

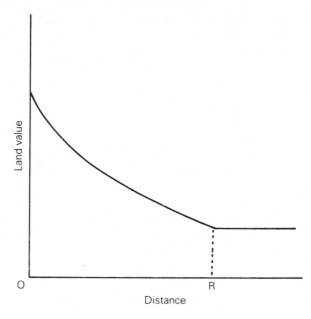

FIGURE 9.1

decreasing rate as distance from the centre increases. All land less than a certain distance from the centre, OR in the figure, will be developed and all land further from the centre will not and will be used for agriculture. Any change in the economic conditions will result in a smooth transition of the land-value gradient to a new equilibrium. As we showed in chapter 7, if the cost of travel is reduced the land-value gradient will become less steep and the boundary of the city will move outward as land values fall in the inner areas and rise in the outer areas. Land which lies outside the old boundary but within the new boundary will quickly be developed and converted to an urban land use that now yields a higher rent. Rents and land values within this kind of model are wholly demand-determined; there is no real theory of land supply other than that land is supplied to whoever happens to be the highest bidder.

In practice this assumption is almost invariably incorrect, because few governments allow land transactions to take place in this unfettered way. They impose planning controls or zoning regula-tions which limit the way in which pieces of land can be used. The effect is to restrict the supply of land for some uses below what it would be in a free market, so that land zoned for these uses will have a value higher than it otherwise would be. Moreover, by preventing the conversion of some land into other uses it increases the supply of land in some uses above the free market level and ensures that its value is lower than it otherwise would be. The resultant pattern of land values is indicated in figure 9.2 which shows a cross-section through the land-value gradient of a city in which planning controls are enforced; instead of the smooth gradient implied by the assumption of a free market a serrated pattern is more likely.

One result of zoning is that planning permission for a change of land use – a rezoning of a site – can become valuable, indeed can be equal to the difference in value of the land in one use rather than another. This tends to cause political and economic problems as landowners and would-be developers attempt to persuade governments to award them planning permissions. These problems as well as the possible economic reasons for zoning are discussed in chapter 12. In this chapter we are primarily concerned with land values and land use.

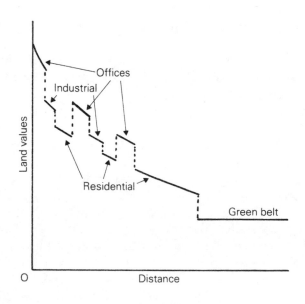

FIGURE 9.2

SPECULATION AND INERTIA

Apart from planning controls, the most obvious explanation for urban land use not conforming to the pattern predicted by the static, free-market theory mentioned earlier is that those owning land are 'speculating' by holding land off the market in anticipation of a higher price at a later date. One instance is the urban sprawl at the edge of American cities. This can be explained as being due to owners being unwilling to sell for development, anticipating that the price of land will rise so that at some future date a developer will be willing to pay them a higher price. Witte and Backman (1978) found that in the early stages of the urban development of previously rural areas, vacant land – land which had been 'leapfrogged' by urban development – was often owned by farmers, whilst in the later stages it had been acquired by professionals in the land business, i.e. 'speculators'.

It should be remarked here that, despite the generally bad press that it receives, speculation need not necessarily be harmful. The term originated as a reference to the owner speculating (i.e. thinking) about the future and such speculation may be correct or incorrect. If farmers sell their land at the first opportunity and congratulate themselves on the price they receive because they believe that they could not sell it more profitably later, then they too are speculating in just the same way as the person more usually described as a speculator who waits for a higher price. Furthermore if a farmer's enthusiasm, and that of the original developer, leads to land being developed at, say, too low a density so that it has soon to be redeveloped, then the precipitate sale has resulted in just as much waste of scarce resources as the speculator would cause who kept land vacant when it could profitably be used.

The differing views of the future held by the various sellers and of the possible buyers result in the process of urban land use change being neither as smooth nor as sharply defined as is implied in the theories outlined earlier in this book. Changes in land use will be extended over a period of time with the pattern of development being rather less uniform than one would have expected from the earlier analysis.

Speculation may in part be explained in terms of differing expectations. Theories explaining the Phillips curve – the apparent long-run relationship between the level of unemployment and the rate of increase in wages – can also be used to explain and predict the relationship between the amount of real property in the market at any one time and the rate of increase in the price of real property. Indeed Gordon and Hynes (1971) use the property market to explain by analogy the way in which the labour market is presumed to work, since both labour and real property are heterogeneous rather than homogeneous.

> Consider the problem of selling a house as contrasted to that of selling a relatively homogeneous asset [such as shares in a company]. We may suppose that for any buyer there is some price at which he would buy the house, but because of dissimilarities of taste the distribution of [the prices of the possible buyers] may have a wide range. If the seller can sample only a small number of buyers in a time period, no matter how many total buyers would buy at any particular price, he would have to lower the price drastically to raise the probability of selling in the period close to unity. On the other hand, because of the homogeneity of different shares ... a relatively small drop in price will raise the probability close to one. (Gordon and Hynes, 1971, p. 379)

Given the distribution of buyers' prices, and the uncertainty about the price which can be obtained, the seller will set a price and wait for it to be accepted. If, in general, prices are rising the seller is likely to set the asking price relatively low so that an acceptable offer will be received relatively quickly. If, on the other hand, prices are falling a relatively high asking price is more likely to be set and to have to wait some time before an acceptable offer is received. Indeed, since the asking price becomes higher over time relative to market prices, it is probable that it will have to be reduced eventually in order to effect a sale. Sellers may be particularly reluctant to lower prices if they have only recently bought the property and, therefore, stand to make a capital loss, and even more reluctant to do so if they have a large loan outstanding on the property which has to be repaid on a sale, and which may even be greater than the prices offered.

The economic effect of the relationships between prices, price changes, and the time taken to sell a property, is that the amount of property 'on the market' at any one time is likely to be inversely related to the rate of change of prices, as illustrated in figure 9.3.

Because there are few statistics collected on the amount of property for sale at any one time, we have no way of testing this hypothesis, despite the general availability of data on property

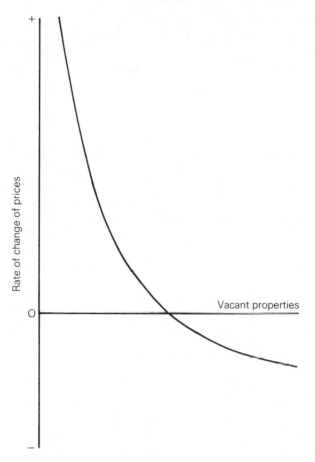

FIGURE 9.3

prices. To anyone who has house hunted, however, casual empiricism suggests that the predicted relationship does exist. When prices are rising strongly, for example at the height of the 1971/72 property boom in Britain (Mayes, 1979) real-estate agents have almost nothing to show possible purchasers, and anything that comes on the market is quickly sold. When prices are static or falling agents have large numbers of properties on their books.

This analysis suggests that even in the absence of overt speculation, the speed of change of prices will depend upon its direction. If economic or technical change causes property prices to rise on the periphery of the city and fall in the inner area, the speed of change in the outer area will be more rapid. In the inner areas properties are likely to remain vacant for long periods as owners seek to obtain prices closer to what they had been able to obtain in the recent past.

PROPERTY DEVELOPMENT

The rate of change of land use also depends on the profitability of redeveloping sites, demolishing existing buildings to erect others. The construction of a building on a site in a sense prevents or pre-empts other uses. The situation implied in much of the preceding analysis where any change in the level of rents and land values results in a change of land use of some kind never actually occurs in practice because it is rarely profitable to demolish new buildings. In recent years considerable effort and mathematical ingenuity has gone into the creation of economic models of urban development in which buildings are of varying ages or vintages (see e.g. Brueckner, 1981; Arnot, 1980) but here we will limit ourselves to a simple diagrammatic analysis (see Harvey, 1981).

When a building is new we would expect the gross annual return (the rents receivable) to be high and the operating costs (the cost of running and maintaining the building) to be low. Over time, however, as the building aged and became obsolete we would expect the rents receivable to fall – in real terms at least – and the cost of maintenance to rise. The changes are represented in figure 9.4(a) where time is indicated on the horizontal axis and rents and costs on the vertical axis.

The vertical difference between the two lines represents the expected net annual return at any time. The lines intersect when the net annual return falls to zero, as it is shown as doing after OZ years in the figure. This expected cash flow, the net annual return in each year over the life of the building (i.e. over OZ years), can be discounted to obtain the present value of the building in its existing use. This too falls to zero after OZ years on the implicit assumption that when the cost of maintaining the building exceeds the rent which would be received if it were let the building would, if practicable, be abandoned.

The present value of the existing building over a life of OZ years is shown in figure 9.4(b). In most cases buildings will be redeveloped

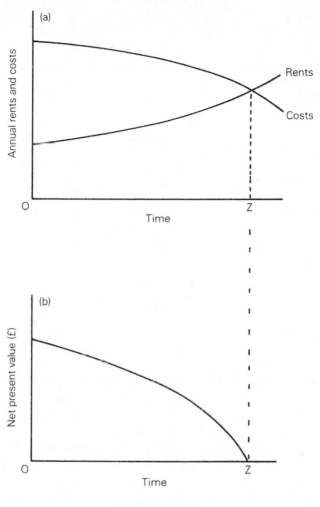

FIGURE 9.4

well before any possibility of abandonment. At all times some best alternative use for the site is possible, although this alternative use may be merely the construction of someting identical to the existing building, particularly when it is relatively new. The present value of the net annual returns from this best alternative use at the date of development is shown as a function of the date of development in figure 9.5. The date of development is shown on the horizontal axis,

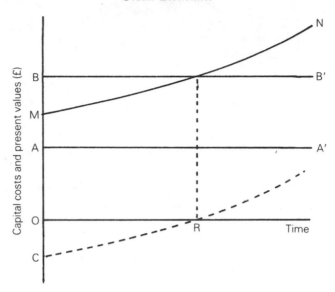

FIGURE 9.5

and the present value is represented on the vertical axis. The present value of the best alternative development will vary over time and is shown in the figure by the curve MN to be increasing over time. The cost of demolishing and clearing the existing buildings and the cost of constructing the new ones also have to be taken into account. These are shown in figure 9.5 by the vertical distances AB and OA respectively, and are assumed not to vary over time (though in practice they will vary as the best alternative use varies and as technology changes). The total cost of demolition, clearance and construction as a function of time is, therefore, shown by the horizontal line BB'. The value of the cleared site is found by deducting the cost of demolition, clearance and construction from the present value of the new building in the best alternative use. In figure 9.5 this is represented by the vertical distance between the curves MN and BB' which is initially negative but becomes positive after the curves intersect after a time OR. The value of the cleared site is, therefore, indicated by the curve CR.

In practice the value of the cleared site may never be negative. It depends upon the cost of demolition and clearance. If this is low then

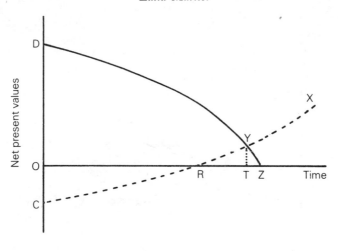

FIGURE 9.6

the value of the cleared site is likely to be positive throughout the life of the existing building. Moreover, in practice its value is irrelevant since, whether positive or negative, provided it is less than the value of the existing building it is not profitable to consider redevelopment. The position is illustrated in figure 9.6. The downward-sloping curve DZ shows the value of the existing building as a function of time, as in figure 9.4(b), and the upward-sloping curve CR shows the value of the cleared site as a function of time, as in figure 9.5. These intersect at Y after a period of time OT. After this date the owner of the building would obtain a higher price for the site if it was sold for redevelopment than the value of the existing building in its current use. So at time T the site would be redeveloped.

This analysis can be used to show that redevelopment will occur more quickly in areas where rents are rising than in areas where rents are falling. In figure 9.7 the lines DZ and CR are as in figure 9.6. Suppose that rents increase in the area. The value of the cleared site increases, at all dates, so that the curve CR is shifted upward to a new positon C'R'. The value of the existing building also rises but not as much as the value of the cleared site. It rises because the rent obtainable increases, but by less because of inflexibility; floor space of a given quantity and characteristic already exists and would be difficult and expensive to modify. So DZ shifts upwards to D'Z'. The

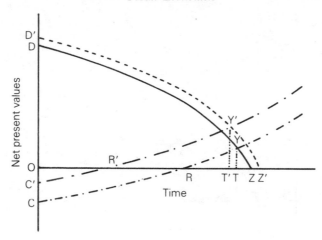

FIGURE 9.7

change in circumstances mean that it is now profitable to redevelop at an earlier date T'.

Falling rents may delay development, on the other hand. Because the existing building is already there – no demolition or building costs are involved – the fall in the value of the existing building will be less than the fall in the value of the cleared site. In particular large old buildings may remain in use long after they are apparently obsolete because of the amount of space they contain. The most profitable new development would be uneconomic because much less space would be built (see also Evans, 1973a, chapter 10).

At the limit redevelopment may never be worth while if the costs of demolition and clearance are high relative to the rent obtainable in the best alternative use. This may seem surprising but the result is very relevant in view of the concern over vacant and drelict sites in inner urban areas, particularly in areas such as United Kingdom and the north-east United States where industrialization occurred early.

The position can be seen from figure 9.5. If the cost of demolition and clearance, AB in the figure, is high relative to the present value of the rents available, then the present value of the cleared site may never be positive. If the date indicated by the point Z is passed, the existing building may, therefore, be abandoned and left derelict, and no new use may be found for the site.

In the past this sort of situation is more likely to have occurred in rural areas. An obvious and familiar example is the derelict filling situation on a main road which now carries less traffic because of a new road elsewhere. Because of the fall in traffic the filling station became uneconomic and was abandoned. The ruins of the building remain, however. The only alternative use is agricultural but the cost of clearing the site and recovering it with topsoil would be greater than the price at which the land could be sold for agricultural use. Therefore, it remains a derelict site. Dereliction has been rare in urban areas in the past because, particularly in inner areas, the cost of demolition and clearance has been low relative to the rent which could be obtained in the best available alternative use. But the technological changes which we discussed in chapter 7 have meant that the real value of these inner-city sites has fallen, particularly those most suitable for manufacturing development. The value of many sites, after demolishing the existing buildings and clearing the site, is less than the cost of this demolition and clearance so that redevelopment is just not·profitable. The value of the land for development is less than zero. If the cost of holding on to the site is low, however, its value as a vacant site is zero and the owner has little to lose in leaving it empty and waiting for something to turn up.

An example of this kind of dereliction on a massive scale is the area known as the London Docklands. Containerization and the introduction of bulk carriers resulted in the abandonment of the nineteenth-century docks on the Thames to the east of the city, as the dock trade moved downstream. The cost of clearance to achieve 'green-field' sites was too high relative to the value of the cleared site to make development profitable so that as the recession of the 1970s deepened the area became increasingly decayed and derelict. Development is only now taking place through government intervention either directly through the London Docklands Development Corporation or indirectly through various tax incentives. In the Docklands Enterprise Zone firms will not have to pay any property taxes (rates) for 10 years, and the cost of construction of new industrial and commercial buildings can be written off against tax immediately. These incentives make development more profitable – the freedom from rates means that a higher rent can be charged, the tax allowances reduce the cost of construction to companies paying tax.

There is every reason to suppose that vacant land and derelict buildings will continue to be a problem in the next few years, as technical change results in the continuing displacement of manufacturing from inner urban areas. The scale of the problem will depend to a great extent on the general level of economic activity. In a period of boom and prosperity rents and optimism are high and redevelopment is more likely to occur with no need for government intervention. When the economy is depressed rents remain low and sites remain derelict.

LAND OWNERSHIP

The static theory of land rent assumes that land is freely transferred into the use which gives the highest return. The sections above have indicated some of the reasons why this may not occur quickly. A further possible reason for delays in the transition of land in an area from a less-profitable use to a more-profitable use is the pattern of ownership. The owners and/or occupiers of land may be unwilling to transfer it without being compensated for doing so – the supply of land has to be taken into account as well as the demand.

For the occupier of a site their piece of land acquires, over time, attributes which differentiate it from all other sites. Its physical properties become familiar and social and economic relationships are built up with people and firms in the neighbourhood. Because of this the value of the site to the occupier becomes higher than its market value – the value to others. In the terminology of Marxian economics the use value of the site exceeds its exchange value. An illustration of this was provided by the research for the Roskill Commission on the Third London Airport. Householders were asked what they would require to compensate them, if they had to move, over and above the market value of their home – most would require large amounts to compensate them, some would require very large amounts.

The would-be purchaser of a site is not in the same situation as the seller. For the former one site is much the same as another and there would normally be no reason why he should be willing to pay anything more than the normal market price. The seller can, therefore, only rarely extract a monopoly rent from a buyer in the sense suggested by Harvey (1973), following Marx. Marx gives as an example land on which a particularly esteemed variety of wine can be grown; clearly a monopoly of this land is possible, but it is difficult to think of similar examples if the term monopoly is to have the same meaning as in mainstream economics (i.e. that a reduction in the quantity rented by a single seller, or group of sellers acting in combination, will allow a higher rent to be charged for the rest).

Because of the higher use value put upon land by occupiers most land will not be on the market. In an area which is not changing most land will be held by the owners for a long time. Some will be sold when the occupier dies, or retires, or moves for some reason, and the market price will be determined by the return from the use of land in the area. The situation is illustrated in figure 9.8. The amount of land in an agricultural area near to the built-up area of a city is measured along the horizontal axis – i.e. the number of hectares is indicated by OB. The price of land is indicated by the vertical axis. The market value of agricultural land in the region is OP, so that buyers will be willing to pay OP and no more for land. The demand curve for land for agricultural use is then the horizontal line PP'.

Most of the farmers in the area will be unwilling to sell their land at a price OP, because for them use value exceeds exchange value, but by varying amounts. For some the price they would accept

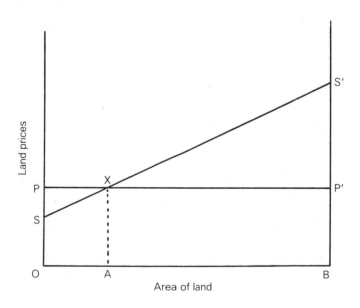

FIGURE 9.8

would be just above OP, others would hold out for a larger price. Their situation is represented by the section XS' of the supply curve SXS'. Some farmers will be 'in the market', and will be willing to accept a price of OP, possibly even less, for their land. Their situation is represented by the section SX of the supply curve SXS'. OA acres are then traded in the period, being sold at the market price OP and retained in agricultural use.

Suppose now that because of falling transport costs the demand for land for residential use increases in this area at the edge of the city; the line DZD' in figure 9.9 represents this demand. The line slopes downwards because if less land is developed at this site in this period then other land will have to be developed which is less favourably situated – it may be further from the city for example. The price of land at this more favourable location will therefore be higher. The demand curve DZD' intersects the supply curve SXS' at the point Z, and so the price of land for residential development will be OP₁

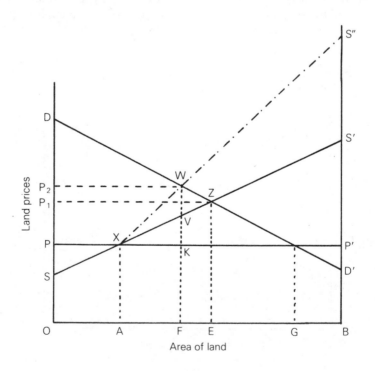

FIGURE 9.9

which is higher than OP, the market value of land for agricultural use. The higher price causes more land to come onto the market since some of the landowners who were unwilling to sell at the lower price are now willing to trade. The higher price compensates them for the loss of their social and economic connections at that location. So in addition to the OA hectares which would come onto the market anyway, a further AE hectares are developed, although EB hectares remain in agricultural use.

In principle the same argument applies to any conversion of land from one use to another, particularly from residential use to commercial or industrial, though less so perhaps from industrial to commercial and *vice versa*.

Therefore, even in the absence of overt speculation the unwillingness of the occupiers of land to be displaced, without compensation, will mean that the price of land for redevelopment into another use will tend to be higher than if it is to be maintained in the same use. Moreover, at the edge of the city, in the absence of planning controls such as green belts, urban sprawl will occur as some owners are willing to sell and some are not.

TAXATION

Prices and sprawl may be still greater if there is a tax on development gains, or a betterment levy, as it was sometimes called. This kind of tax reduces the gain to the owner from selling, usually through taxing the difference between the so-called current use value of land and its value for development. In figure 9.9 this is represented by the difference between OP and OP_1. But in terms of the analysis set out above this is not just pure profit but is for many sellers a compensation for the loss of a site at that location. Therefore, if this is reduced by taxation owners will be less willing to sell. The situation is represented in figure 9.9 by rotating the section XZS' of the supply curve anti-clockwise around X. A tax of 50 per cent would require the slope to be doubled, one of 25 per cent that it should be increased by a third. Owners will be unwilling to sell unless they receive the same compensation after tax as they previously did before a tax was introduced so a new supply curve must allow for the new economic relationship.

In figure 9.9 the line XWS" shows the effect of a 50 per cent tax. As indicated by the point W, the price of land is raised, because of the tax, to a new level OP_2 at which only OF acres come onto the market. The 'development gain' is KW of which half, KV, is taken in tax, and half, VK, remains to compensate the sellers.

If the tax is raised to take 100 per cent of the development gain, as with the development charge instituted by the post-war Labour Government in 1947, the effect will be to raise the price of development land still more and further reduce the amount sold. In figure 9.9 the supply of land would be represented by a vertical line above X. No more land would be sold for development than would normally be sold for agricultural use. The price, however, would be considerably higher.

Certainly the 1947 Town and Country Planning Act inhibited development 'since sellers had no incentive whatever to part with their land when it was wanted by a builder' (Parker, 1965, p. 65) although the anticipated return of a Conservative Government pledged to abolish the charge was also partly to blame, as indeed it was blamed at the time, since owners had only to wait for the repeal of the Act in the early 1950s for the whole development gain to accrue to themselves.

OWNERSHIP AND OCCUPATION

In the discussion above we have implicitly assumed that each site is owned and occupied by the same person or household. The farmer both owns and occupies the farm, the resident of a house is not a tenant but an owner-occupier. As occupier the owner acquires social and economic relationships which lead him not to wish to move, and as owner the occupier is in a position to demand compensation for moving by demanding a high price for the land.

When the land is owned by a landlord but occupied by a tenant the situation is different. The tenant acquires the social and economic relationships but the landlord is the person who sells the land. Therefore unless the landlord had to pay compensation to the tenant, he would probably accept a lower price than would his tenant were he the owner-occupier. The market price may not only be lower if the land is rented by tenants but also may be considerably less predictable than if it is occupied by the owners. The political and economic strengths of landlords and tenants in any conflict will determine the outcome as well as the economic costs and benefits summarized in the supply and demand curves of figure 9.9.

Keeping the same example of an agricultural area on the edge of a city, the rent of this agricultural land will generally be determined by its profitability in agricultural use. In principle therefore landlords would be willing to sell for development at any price above agricultural market value, OP in figures 9.8 and 9.9. Tenants, however, will be unwilling to move. Therefore landlords may attempt to obtain higher rents from the tenants since the price for which they could sell the land, its opportunity cost, is now higher, but tenants will be unwilling to pay these rents because rents elsewhere will be determined by the price of land for agricultural use. On the other hand, tenants will be willing to pay somewhat higher rents rather than move. As I indicated above, the end result will be determined by their political and economic strengths, largely as reflected in the legal system.

Three possible solutions may be outlined. First, security of tenure for tenants and 'fair rent' legislation which holds rents down to the level prevailing elsewhere would mean that no tenant would leave before he wished to. Only a small amount of land would come onto the market and, as a result, it would be sold for a high price. In figure 9.9 the situation would be represented by a supply curve which was a vertical line above X, since the amount of land coming onto the market, OA in the figure, would be no greater than if there was no demand for development land. Landlords would feel very hard done by since all would wish to sell but very few could do so. And those few would not perceive that the price they received for the land was higher than it would be in the absence of legal powers favouring the tenant.

Second, lack of security of tenure but a willingness to pay higher rents by tenants would result in the same amount of land being sold for development by landlords at the same price as if they were owner-occupiers, i.e. in figure 9.9, OE hectares at a price OP_1. The maximum rent tenants would pay would be that which would be just equal to the use value of the land to them including both its agricultural use and the value of continued occupation.

Third, lack of security of tenure coupled with an unwillingness to pay higher rents, either for personal, social or political reasons, would result in considerably more land being brought forward than in the other cases. Thus in figure 9.9 OG hectares would be sold at a price just above the market price in its existing use, namely OP.

These three cases do not indicate the only possible solutions but merely serve to indicate the range of possibilities. They also indicate the way in which landlord/tenant relationships can cause conflict. These conflicts are more usually highlighted by neo-Marxian or neo-Ricardian commentators (see e.g. Harvey, 1973; Scott, 1980) but are ignored in most 'neo-classical' studies. The above analysis shows that the form of property ownership and the interests of the different classes may also be important even within what is otherwise a non-Marxian neo-classical analysis.

COMPULSORY PURCHASE

The ownership of land may be important in another case, again because one piece of land is not the same as another, but this time from any user's point of view, not just the seller's. Each piece of land has a particular location. We have argued above that buyers can be considered to be indifferent between pieces of land at different locations and this will usually be true. But there are situations when it will not be true, and these occur when a buyer wants one piece of land because of its location relative to another, or indeed several pieces of land with a particular configuration relative to each other. The most obvious example of this is the strip of land required to build a railway or a road.

Buyers may attempt to purchase each piece of land as it comes onto the market, but this might take a very long time. Moreover, as soon as the buyer's intention became evident, some sellers could attempt to obtain extortionate prices for their properties if they thought that the buyer might be willing to pay this price rather than start again buying another set of pieces of land and writing off the costs previously incurred. Often, therefore, developments of this kind are carried out, in the United Kingdom, by public authorities who are given powers of compulsory purchase. In the United States private and public authorities may be given powers of 'eminent domain' under which they can compel a sale but the price must be agreed by a court (see Munch, 1976).

The social costs which can be imposed by compulsory purchase should not be ignored. Clearly the owners do not feel that the market price would fully compensate them for the loss of their land. Otherwise there would be no need to compel them to sell. Because of these social costs – the difference between the owner's use value and the exchange value – the law usually provides for some compensation over and above the market value of land to be paid to occupiers or owners by organizations allowed to purchase land compulsorily.

In some circumstances it is profitable for large areas to be redeveloped as one site, even by private developers without powers of compulsory purchase. This will happen where the existing land-use pattern has become obsolescent and/or there are economies of scale to be obtained by development on a large scale. Examples are large office blocks or shopping centres in town centres. In each case the various adjacent sites are worth more if they can be developed as one than if they are developed individually, simply because a higher rent per square foot can be charged by the developer for the larger area of space. Office space can be let to a single user; shopping precincts or malls can be created or space let to large chain stores or supermarkets. Once again, however, excessive prices may be demanded for the last key pieces of property as sellers become aware of the situation, these ultimate sellers attempting to obtain all the possible profit from the development for themselves. The buyer can attempt to force down the sellers, or, if they wish to avoid this, may set up a number of 'front' companies each of which appears to be acting separately. An alternative which has been used often in recent years in Britain for the development of town-centre shopping facilities involves the creation of a partnership between a property development company and a local authority. The local authority exercises its powers of compulsory purchase to put together the site. The development company uses its skills to ensure that the development will be profitable. Both share in the profits from the development. Such a partnership scheme ensures that the development is carried out expeditiously but the conflict between the interests of the owners of the land and the interests of society in obtaining a more efficient use of land is solved at the expense of the original owners and occupiers of land.

Powers of compulsory purchase have also been used in the past to expedite the development of large housing schemes. It was argued that the original housing was a slum or near-slum, the road lay out obsolescent, and the area deficient in open space. Moreover, large developments could be carried out by large companies using industrial building systems. The arguments may have been correct when they were applied to the worst housing of the 1940s and 1950s, but by the mid-seventies large schemes of this kind were no longer carried out. In part this was because massive maintenance problems on some earlier developments revealed that systems building might not be that economical, but also because some of the occupiers of housing which was scheduled to be redeveloped protested that they did not want to move; they regarded their existing house and location as adequate. In the terminology used earlier, use value exceeded exchange value, and political and economic pressure by these occupiers ensured that these social costs were taken into account.

SUMMARY

As we indicated in chapter 7, where we discussed urban change, the impact of change may be primarily felt in the labour market, the land market, and the finance of local government. In this chapter we have discussed the land market and shown that, contrary to the assumptions which are usually made in urban economics, the land market does not necessarily always work smoothly and efficiently to ensure that each piece of land is used by the activity which could pay the highest current rent.

In part this may be because of the deliberate intervention of central and local governments through the imposition of planning controls, but it may also be for other reasons, effective even in a market economy. The owners of land may be unwilling to sell at the price they are offered either because they think the market value is higher or because the price, though fair, would not compensate them for the costs and disruption of moving. The costs of demolishing the existing buildings, clearing the site, and building anew may also delay redevelopment; indeed where the costs of demolition and clearance are high, but, because of the decline of an area, the rents obtainable are low, it may be more profitable to an owner to leave the site derelict rather than redevelop. The ownership and tenancy of land may also delay redevelopment; in particular tenants with security of tenure and benefiting from rent controls would be extremely reluctant to move to make way for any more economic use of the land. And the dispersed ownership of large sites may delay their development on a large scale necessitating the use of powers of compulsory purchase.

FURTHER READING

Harvey (1981) is a good basic text on the economics of real property. A history of land value taxation up to the mid 1960s is given by Parker (1965). Prest (1981) gives a wide ranging economic analysis of the problem of the taxation of urban land. The discussion in this chapter, however, is heavily dependent on Evans (1983). On land rent and a Marxist approach to the topic see Harvey (1973) or, more recently, Ball *et al.*, (1985).

10

Local Governments and their Finance

> Cecily: From the top of one of the hills quite close one can see five
> counties.
> Gwendolen: Five counties! I don't think I should like that. I hate
> crowds.
> Cecily [sweetly]: I suppose that is why you live in town?
> *The Importance of Being Earnest* Act II

Local governments and their finance are usually regarded as being of
little general interest. The phrases 'parish pump policies' and 'only of
parochial interest' exemplify this view. The paradox is that at the
same time local government and its finances are endlessly debated. In
the United Kingdom within the last 25 years there have been Royal
Commissions on the government of London, Scotland, England and
Wales, a Committee of Inquiry into Local Government Finance, and
continuous and continuing arguments as to whether central government could or should impose its will on local authorities controlled
by opposition parties, by, for example, a Labour Government
compelling Conservative controlled local authorities to institute
systems of comprehensive education, or a Conservative Government
compelling Labour controlled authorities to raise rents or reduce
expenditure. Latterly the Conservative Government elected in 1983
was pledged to abolish the Councils controlling Greater London and
the other major English conurbations and to take powers to limit the
expenditure of recalcitrant local authorities.

In other countries, particularly in the United States, the roles of
central, state, and local government and the relationship between
them may be laid down constitutionally and might therefore be
thought to be less open to argument and discussion. However, even

apart from an extensive academic literature on the subject, the taxpayers' revolts exemplified by Proposition 13 in California indicate that, at the least, a degree of interest and concern exists elsewhere.

In this chapter we will first review the role and functions of local government, the evidence on the proper size of a local-government area and the relationship of local to central government. In the second section we discuss the problems of financing local-government expenditure – the reliance on a tax on property for locally produced revenue and the problems of creating an efficient and equitable system of central-government grants. This discussion is necessarily prior to the discussion of the fiscal effects of urban decline in the third section since government grants may exacerbate or compensate for these effects. Finally we consider the problems of the incidence of taxes. Are differences in taxes between areas borne by the residents or are they capitalized into the value of land and property so that the value of land in a high-tax area is lower than in a low-tax area? What are the implications of Tiebout's hypothesis that taxpaying households might reveal their preferences for different packages of local-authority expenditure by movement between areas?

THE ROLE AND FUNCTIONS OF LOCAL GOVERNMENT

There are two significant questions related to urban local government. What functions should local authorities carry out? What area, or rather how many people, should each authority serve? The two questions and their answers are necessarily interrelated since the area served is determined by the functions carried out, and vice versa.

In Great Britain the pattern is that there are two tiers of local government, although the division of responsibilities between the tiers is not uniform. Of the various functions carried out at a local level – education, housing, transport, fire, police, refuse disposal, social services, planning and environmental control – the most important, at least in terms of total expenditure, is education, but this is carried out at the district level in the Metropolitan Counties (i.e. the larger English conurbations) but at the county level outside these conurbations and at a regional level in Scotland. In the area of Greater London it is carried out by boroughs in outer London but by an *ad hoc* authority in inner London.

Ad hoc authorities or boards of this kind further complicate the structure of local government, though they are more numerous in the United States than in the United Kingdom. The most important in Britain are the various water authorities which raise money through imposing rates or property taxes to deal with the provision of water and the disposal of sewage. Serving areas larger than the counties, they are run by non-elected boards, as indeed are the Health Authorities which similarly occupy a shadowy position between central and local government.

These examples serve to illustrate the range of possibilities, a range which is enlarged when it is realized that the whole system was reorganized in the 1960s (in the case of London) and the early 1970s (in the case of the rest of the country) following the Reports of Royal Commissions, and that the 1983 Conservative Government was committed to the abolition of the Metropolitan County and Greater London Councils, intending to devolve their responsibilities to the lower tier of district and London borough councils which would then become the only level of local government in the major conurbations.

It seems, however, to be generally true that there are a number of functions which would seem to be best organized at a local level, and that the most important of these, in expenditure terms, is education. Which level of local government should carry out these functions is less clear. The economic reasons for this would seem to be that the empirical evidence as to the optimal size of a local authority is inconclusive. As a result decisions are more likely to be made on political rather than economic grounds.

Economic evidence which might be useful in determining the size of local authorities would relate to the economies and diseconomies of scale in the provision of local-government services. Up to what size are there economies of scale? At what size do there start to be diseconomies of scale? If the answers to both these questions were the same this would be the optimal population of a local authority, the population at which services could be provided at the minimum cost per head. In fact the evidence indicates that the cost curves for most functions have very long flat sections – costs vary very little with variations in the populaltion served by local authorities. The one point that seems to be agreed is that economies of scale reduce the costs of administration up to a population of at least 50 000 (see Bennett, 1980, pp. 122–6), and that the economies of scale in water and sewage and the other 'utilities' – gas, electricity, telephone, and transport – continue to increase with population size considerably beyond this point, one reason why these functions are usually organized at a national or regional rather than a local level.

The diseconomies of population size in local government must be distinguished from the diseconomies of city size. As we noted in chapter 5 and 6, the latter exist but are balanced by the known economies of city size. Moreover, the diseconomies of city size will exist whether the city is governed by one local authority or several. It is clear, however, that there exist some diseconomies of scale in local government, as an increase in the size of the population (or the administrative area) increases the number of units, for example, schools, which have to be controlled by the authority. As Bennett (1980) concludes 'most analysts now agree that diseconomies lead to greatly increased costs by the level of about 300 000 population, if not before' (p. 125).

The economic evidence is, therefore, that provided the population of a local authority lies between 50 000 and 300 000 its costs per head of population will be at or near the minimum. Between these two limits the optimal size of a local authority is more a question of politics than economics. On the one hand the smaller the authority the more responsive it would appear to be to local wishes, and therefore in a sense the more democratic. On the other, it would appear to be unnatural to divide up a city of moderate size into small governmental units. Moreover, some services have to be provided on a city-wide basis for the whole metropolitan area – strategic planning, the organization of the transport system, the provision of facilities used by the population of the whole urban area such as museums and large parks. At some city population size, therefore, it becomes natural to organize government on a two-tier system with some services being organized for the whole urban area either by a metropolitan county, a board appointed for the purpose, or an upper level of government whether state, regional or central.

A problem which arises out of the existence of different levels of government, and which is again political rather than economic, is that of conflicts between the different levels, in particular between local and central government and between different concepts of democracy. If the voters of district A have elected a majority of councillors belonging to party X, committed to one policy, but at a general election the population of the whole country elects party Z to form a government, which takes precedence? Both, in a sense, can claim that they are the rightful democratic government representing 'the voice of the people'. The British 'first past the post' system of elections may probably exacerbate the problem in that neither party X nor party Z need necessarily have been elected by a majority of the electorate, but neither may be constrained by any need to take into account the opinions of that wider electorate, since each has a majority of the elected members in Council or Parliament respectively.

The size of the local authority may be important in determining the result of any conflict. A small authority may be more easily ignored or overriden by the upper tier of government. A larger authority constitutes more of a challenge which must be dealt with. Witness the conflicts in the early eighties between the Labour controlled Metropolitan and Greater London Councils and the Conservative Government which resulted in the proposal to abolish them. Witness also the reluctance to create metropolitan counties to govern the large cities of America and Australia. In a state such as Victoria where the vast majority of the population live in the Melbourne metropolitan area, the creation of a metropolitan government would merely be a recipe for confrontation between state and metropolitan government.

FINANCING LOCAL GOVERNMENT

The main source of tax revenue for local authorities in the United Kingdom, as in most other countries is a property tax, called in Britain 'the rates'. As a tax this tends to be unpopular but, as we shall see, one difficult to replace. The reasons for its unpopularity are several. The first is that since it is a tax on real property it is not related to the ability to pay. The same rates may be paid whether a house is occupied by a married couple with grown-up children all of whom are working, or by a widow living alone. The evidence is, however, that the tax is not noticeably regressive. The rebates which can be claimed by those with low incomes in order to reduce the rates paid by them have eliminated the strongly regressive element in the tax for the poorer and poorest households and converted the tax into one which is more or less proportional to income (Department of the Environment, 1981).

A second reason for its unpopularity appears to be that unlike virtually all other taxes it is assessed on the householder and has to be paid directly by him or her. Each householder, therefore, knows precisely how much is paid. No other major sources of tax revenue are collected in this way. Income tax is usually deducted at source, value added and sales taxes are included in or added to the price paid, as are most customs and excise duties. In none of these cases does the tax payer actually pay over the cash or instruct his bank to pay, as he must with the rates. Moreover, whilst the rates paid are known, it would require effort, sometimes a lot of effort, to calculate the amount paid in a year in the case of other taxes.

Allied to this is the third reason for the unpopularity of the tax, the belief of many of the population that the rates are a payment for the services provided by local government. Those who receive little benefit from these services may, therefore, feel hard done by. The amount that they have to pay is clear as is their lack of use of local-government services. Thus the widow mentioned earlier whose rates bill may be high relative to her income because of her continued occupation of the former family home may feel doubly aggrieved because, for example, she derives no current benefit from local expenditure on education.

It is because of this unpopularity that political parties have sought to replace the rates by some other form of taxation. The problem is, however, that though unpopular, a large amount of money is raised through the tax on real property, and the costs of collection and administration are very low. Moreover, the arguments against the rates do not stand up well to close examination. The property tax should not and cannot be considered on its own. It is only part of the whole system of taxation. For this reason the regressivity of the tax is irrelevant if other taxes are more progressive so that the whole system is made progressive. For the same reason it is to a large extent irrelevant that it happens to be the tax collected by local authorities. It is collected by them because it is administratively easy for them to do so. It does not pay for all local-government expenditure; much of it is financed by other taxes collected at higher levels of government and paid to local authorities as grants. In Britain nearly half of all local-government expenditure is financed in this way by grants from central government.

Moreover, when the rates are seen as part of the whole system of taxation, the difficulty of abolishing them becomes evident since the revenue lost must be raised through some other form of taxation.

The Green Paper *Alternatives to Domestic Rates* noted that replacement by a local income tax would involve additional rates of tax of about 5 per cent, i.e. raising the basic rate of income tax at that time from 30 to 35 per cent, whilst a local sales tax would have to be at a rate of about 7½ per cent, additional to Valued Added Tax at the rate then of 15 per cent. Neither of these alternatives was politically acceptable so that the rates, for the present, remain.

It would, of course, be possible to allow local government to raise money through other taxes as well as the rates, for example, through a local income tax or sales tax, in such a way that the total level of taxation would remain approximately the same but central government grants would be replaced by local taxes. In countries other than the United Kingdom it is usual for a higher proportion of local-government expenditure to be covered by locally administered taxes. But local governments in all countries are usually in receipt of some central-government grants primarily because these grants are administered and awarded by central government in pursuit of policies other than local-government independence, and which might be negated by that independence.

In the context of public finance the functions of central government have been characterized as being those of allocation (of goods), distribution (of welfare) and stabilization (of economy), and it carries out all of these functions in deciding the grant that it will make to each local authority (Musgrave and Musgrave, 1976). The allocation function can be seen in the giving of specific grants, for example, subsidies for housing, which are designed to maintain or increase the consumption of specific goods and services. In Britain most central-government grants are not specific but general, and primarily related to distribution, secondarily to stabilization.

The method introduced in the early 1980s to determine the block grant to each local authority involves, in essence, two calculations. First, central government estimates from a number of formulae what should be the standard expenditure for any authority given the needs of the population of that authority. Secondly, it estimates the amount the authority could raise in revenue by levying a standard rate poundage on the rateable property in its area. Deducting the second sum from the first gives an initial estimate of the amount of the grant to that authority. Obviously authorities with greater needs – more children, more old people, and so on – should receive more than those with high property values per household, who should receive less. Thus the poorest areas with the greatest needs should receive larger grants and this of course should ensure the provision of services in those areas – the allocation function of central government. It also should ensure, indeed is designed to ensure, that these local authorities can provide all services at just as high a level as richer boroughs with less needs – the distribution function of central government.

The Conservative Government elected in 1979 has also actively tried to use the grant system to control and reduce local-government expenditure as part of its declared aim of limiting public expenditure to promote growth in the private sector. Thus it is part of the general macroeconomic policy of the government – the stabilization function.

Under the present system of control, in calculating the grant to each local authority, central government compares the current expenditure of the authority with the estimated standard expenditure, and authorities which are overspending have their grant cut. One justification for this process of 'tapering' grants, as it sometimes called, is that receipt of a large grant may encourage local authorities to increase their expenditure, financing it through higher rates. From the local government's point of view, since most of the services provided are being financed by central government, why should it not 'top up' these services by raising more funds on its own account? This is particularly likely to occur if most of the rateable value in an area is in the form of commercial and industrial property so that increases in the rate are largely paid by industry, which has no vote, but used to provide services for residents, who do have votes.

The advantages to local voters or local politicians of 'topping-up' grants by raising rates were increased by the system of grants existing in Britain before the present 'block grant' system was introduced. Under the previous system the total central-government grant to one authority was made up in the main from two separate elements. The first was related to the measured needs of the area (the needs element) and the second was inversely related to the rateable value per head of population in the area (the resources element). The latter was calculated as being the difference between the amount an authority actually raised with the rate poundage that it charged, and the amount that it would have raised with that rate poundage if the rateable value per head in the area had been some standard amount. If the first was lower than the second the difference was the grant paid, but no grant was paid if the first was equal to or higher than the second. Clearly local authorities in receipt of the resources element had an incentive to charge a higher rate than they might otherwise have done since this would result in them receiving a larger grant from central government.

In both sets of circumstances outlined about the 'price' to residents of voting for increased services for themselves is low. Either much of the cost is paid by industrial and commercial firms or it is met by central government. We would expect, therefore, that voters or politicians would respond by spending more, and this is what appears to have happened under the old system. Foster *et al.*, (1980) concluded after an extensive survey of the subject that 'there is evidence that the higher the proportion of grant, the greater the propensity for a local authority to spend' (p. 302).

Central government responded, as we have indicated, by changing the system of grant allocation, a change which would probably have occurred even without the change of government from Labour to Conservative in 1979, since the proposal, in essence, was contained in the 1977 Green Paper (see Foster *et al.* 1980, p. 436). This change only solves one part of the problem, however, since it is still true even under the new system that the 'price' of increased services is low if much of the cost is borne by industrial and commercial firms. Of course these firms may leave the area or go out of business, or the higher rates may be capitalized into lower land values or passed on in higher prices. In all these cases the incentive for commercial investment in the area is reduced, and so the area will become more residential so raising the cost to residents. Such changes are long term, very long term indeed, however. The attempts of the 1983 Conservative Government to limit local-government expenditure and rate levels are a way of solving this part of the problem. These policies, of imposing financial penalties on high-spending authorities by reducing or 'tapering' grants, or of limiting the rate poundage which could be charged by local authorities – so called 'rate capping' – may be part of that government's attempt to limit total public expenditure, but they are also a way of protecting the non-voting but rate paying industrial and commercial firms.

URBAN DECLINE

Discussion of the finance of local government and the system of government grants were necessary, as we shall see, before we could discuss the fiscal consequences of urban decline. It has been argued that the process of urban change described in chapter 6 – the decentralization of industry and population from the inner areas of the large conurbations – could set off a process of cumulative decline through its interaction with the finance of local government. This view was put forward in the United Kingdom by Eversley in 1972, and the apparently imminent bankruptcy of New York City at the time lent force to the argument.

In essence that argument runs as follows. The outward movement of industrial and commercial firms from the inner areas reduces the rateable value of those areas. One consequence of this decentralization, as we showed in chapter 9, may be that land and property is left empty and derelict for some time so that no property taxes can be collected. In one way or the other therefore the tax base is reduced in the central city. The outward movement of jobs is accompanied by an outward movement of the resident population.

One effect of this process of decentralization is, therefore, a reduction in the utilization of the existing social infrastructure. For political if not economic reasons, however, it may be difficult to dispose of any of it in order to reduce costs. The resistance to the closure of schools in the inner areas of the British conurbations, particularly London, despite falls of a third or more in the number of children of school age is an illustration of this difficulty.

Moreover, those moving are likely to be skilled rather than unskilled. A consequence of this population decentralization may therefore be a change in the characteristics of the resident population of the central city – the elderly, the unemployed and the unskilled remain but younger families move out. Therefore, another possible effect of decentralization and urban decline is that the services which need to be provided for the resident population do not fall in line with either the decline in the total population or the fall in the rateable value. In order to provide the same level of service to the differing population, i.e. to provide the greater services now required, the local authority must raise money through higher taxes. In turn these higher taxes may cause more firms to go out of business or to move out of the city, and make the area less attractive to new firms. The more employable residents may therefore move to jobs elsewhere. And so taxes will have to be raised further.

The paragraphs above present a persuasive model of urban decline, but the model is not necessarily applicable to every large city. The extent to which it is applicable depends upon the extent to which any system of central government grants of the kind described in the preceding section counter-balances the forces described in the model. It will be realized that the current British system, as well as the previous British system, were both designed so as to ensure that the model is inapplicable. If the needs of the population increase in the inner cities relative to other areas, so the level of grant to these local authorities should also increase. If the total rateable value or resources fall in the inner-city local authorities, then the grant should increase to make up for this.

In the absence of such a system of government grants, the model may partially represent the process of urban decline. There is little evidence, however, that the process of decline can go on continuously and cumulatively in the way the model suggests. The fiscal problems of local government probably exacerbate the problems of urban decline in the short run rather than being the prime cause of the long-run process. The impact of higher taxes is limited by the fact that in the medium term differences in tax levels, and in benefits, will be reflected in differences in property values. Higher taxes will, eventually, result in lower rents and lower land values with no real difference in the cost of space to the occupier. The effects of higher rates may be short term, therefore, and last only until rents are adjusted after a rent review. The longer-run impact of differences in taxes and benefits is, therefore, on property owners rather than on the firms occupying the properties, and it is this problem of 'capitalization' that we consider in the next section.

CAPITALIZATION AND THE TIEBOUT HYPOTHESIS

Who bears the property tax? We know who actually pays it – the occupiers of property, but who actually bears the cost? To use economic jargon, What is its incidence? Before trying to answer this question we have to make a slightly artificial distinction between 'onerous' and 'beneficial' taxes. In principle 'onerous' taxes are those which are paid to provide goods and services which benefit other people, or are spent on things which appear to benefit no one (e.g. local-government administration). 'Beneficial' taxes, on the other hand, pay for goods and services which benefit the tax payer. Of course one person's beneficial taxes may be another's onerous taxes which is why the distinction is somewhat artificial. Nevertheless, for analytical purposes it is a useful distinction to make, as we shall show.

An example of a generally onerous tax might be a higher rate poundage levied by a local government to pay for the provision of subsidized housing to a small number of residents in its area. The tax certainly benefits the occupiers of the housing, the availability of the housing might possibly be thought to confer some slight benefit on other residents of the borough, particularly the occupiers of rented property, but the policy seems not to benefit at all, save altruistically, the occupiers of industrial and commercial property. Suppose that the adjacent borough in the metropolitan area did not levy such a rate, providing no subsidized housing; then, *ceteris paribus*, the cost of occupying property is cheaper in the adjacent borough, borough B, compared to the first, borough A. Presumably industrial and commercial tenants and unsubsidized residents would therefore prefer to locate in B rather than A. It is unlikely that existing occupiers would attempt to move if the differences in tax levels were small, but people and firms choosing a new location would prefer to move to B rather than A. As a result rents and property values would fall in A relative to B. The fall in rents in A might take some time since it could only take effect at the end of a rent-review period, and until that time the tenant of property in A bears the cost of the higher level of rates in A. When the relative adjustment of rents and property values has been completed, however, the higher level of taxation in A rather than B is borne by the owners of land and property in that area. Note that it is borne by the owners of property at the time the tax differences are capitalized, not by future owners of property in A. Any purchasers of property in A pay a lower price for the property because of the higher taxes. The lower price just compensates them for the lower rent they receive or the higher tax they have to pay. Of course if, in the future, the level of taxes in A were to be reduced relative to B, say because the housing subsidy were reduced, then the new owners would benefit from this tax reduction through an increase in the value of their property.

Thus one answer to our original question as to who bears the cost of higher levels of taxation in some areas rather than others is that, in general, it is the land and property owners at the time the higher taxes are imposed who bear the cost, at least in the case of onerous taxes.

But what about beneficial taxes? The analysis of these in the context of local government goes back to a paper by Tiebout (1956) which was itself a response to the analysis of the economics of public goods by Samuelson (1954). Samuelson had argued that certain goods were public, in the sense that if they were available for one they were available for all the members of a specific economy, the most often cited example being national defence, and that in the case of these public goods no one had any incentive to reveal how much of each good they wanted and how much they were willing to pay. Indeed there was a strong incentive not to pay anything but to rely on everyone else providing the good so that one benefited from its provision but without cost. This 'free rider' problem has exercised the minds of economists a great deal since then. The general problem does not concern us here, however, only Tiebout's suggestion that if a public good were provided locally by each local authority only to its own taxpaying resident households, then the households would choose the amounts of the good they wished to consume by choosing a location in a particular local-government area. In this way people would in fact reveal their preferences as to the package of public goods which they wanted and were willing to pay for, by their location in particular local-authority areas, since each local government, so far as the consumer is concerned, would be providing a different package of local public goods and taxes. All this of course is subject to certain conditions – there are a very large number of local authorities within any metropolitan area, that people are otherwise indifferent as to where they live, that people are fully informed about the alternative packages in different authorities and can move freely between the areas, and that each local authority is optimal in size (so that there are no economies of scale available from being larger or smaller).

In Tiebout's model the taxes are beneficial taxes since the consumer only chooses to live in a higher tax area because they gain the benefit of a greater expenditure on local public goods. Under these conditions it can be shown that, in the long run, differences in the level of taxation between areas are not capitalized into differences in property values (Edel and Sclar, 1974; Hamilton, 1976). One authority may levy higher taxes than another but it also provides greater benefits. The two should cancel out and land values should be the same in each area. It is possible that differences in the level of taxation (or of benefits) between areas may be capitalized into differences in land values in the short run, if a particular tax/benefit package is only available in relatively few areas so that demand exceeds supply. The pressure to locate in these areas will push prices up in them in the short run, but in the longer run voting in other areas by those unable to buy property in the areas providing the desired services should force some of these other areas to provide the desired tax/benefit package and the price differences should be eliminated.

The Tiebout hypothesis and the associated question of the capitalization of tax and benefit differences have stimulated a large number of empirical studies, commencing with a paper by Oates (1969). These studies have been almost exclusively American, largely because the necessary conditions, as outlined earlier, are more nearly met in the larger metropolitan areas of the United States than elsewhere. Whether or not these studies confirm the correctness of the Tiebout hypothesis as a representation of voter choice, they do confirm, at the least, that differences in taxes and benefits between local government areas in the American conurbations are capitalized into differences in property values.

The evidence that these differences are capitalized in other countries is very much slighter. One reason is that the conditions mentioned earlier make the model less applicable – there may be fewer local authorities in a conurbation or the population may be less mobile. Another is that in more centralized economies, such as the United Kingdom, local authorities have much less freedom to vary the level of services which they provide. If central government lays down a minimum standard, and also attempts to limit total local-government expenditure this eliminates a lot of the possible variation in service levels. Moreover, the system of government grants outlined earlier tends to minimize, indeed was largely designed to minimize, differences in the level of taxation in different local authorities. Since the level of services varied little as did the level of taxation, and since there were relatively few local authorities in any metropolitan area, British voters had less reason, and were less able, to choose to locate in areas on the basis of differences between tax/benefit packages. Nevertheless, there is some evidence that people do tend to move away from high tax areas (Davies, 1982) and that what differences have existed in the past have to some extent been capitalized into property values (Foster *et al.*, 1980). Recently, however, and paradoxically as a result of attempts by central government to ensure still greater uniformity in local government expenditure, wider differences in tax/benefit packages between areas have started to become evident. The Conservative Goverment's attempts to make local governments reduce their expenditure have relied to some extent on persuasion and to some extent on reductions in the level of government grant. This grant covered 63 per cent of local-government expenditure in 1975/76, but this proportion had fallen to 48 per cent in 1983/84. In addition it has imposed penalties on high-spending authorities by reducing the grant which would otherwise be paid to them. Some Labour controlled authorities have chosen to maintain a high level of expenditure, incur the consequent penalties, and finance the expenditure by a higher level of rates. As a result, a number of authorities have had higher levels of expenditure and significantly higher rate poundages than the rest. These large and well-publicized differences in tax/benefit packages are more likely to be capitalized into property values than the smaller, less-well-known, differences existing in the past. Already there is some evidence that office rents in Camden, a high-spending authority controlling a part of central London, have fallen relative to office rents in Westminster, an adjacent lower-spending authority, so that the cost of the occupation of space – rent plus rates – is similar for office users on either side of the boundary between the boroughs. Moreover, the reduction in the level of central government grant, and the consequent increase in the general rate level has increased the relative importance of the rates as a cost of occupying property, at least for commercial and industrial property (Debenham, Tewson, and Chinnocks, 1983).

SUMMARY AND CONCLUSIONS

The discussion in this chapter of the finance of local government suggests that concern that urban decline may be reinforced and made cumulative by the fiscal problems of local government is generally misplaced. Despite the reliance of local government on the property tax as a source of revenue, much of its finance comes from higher levels of government in the form of grants. In Britain at least, these grants are designed to be greater when paid to areas which have low resources and areas which have greater needs. Thus any urban decline which results in either, say, derelict and vacant property, or an older, unemployed, population, should be compensated by higher grants: there should be no need for local governments to raise taxes in response.

The discussion of the capitalization of taxes in the last section suggests another reason why urban decline is unlikely to be made cumulative. Suppose the grants system does not compensate for changes to the economy of the inner-urban areas, so that property taxes become relatively higher in these areas. This may cause occupiers to reconsider their location, but if they are tenants they can argue at the time of the next rent review that the rent should be lower because of the higher rates bill, and if they own the property they occupy, the tax increase will cause a fall in the value of the property, so eliminating the incentive to move, since move or stay, they still have to bear the capital loss. Thus the capitalization of property-tax differences should also tend to prevent urban decline becoming cumulative, even if the grant system does not. The initial decentralization of firms need not cause further moves because of higher rates.

There is one possibility, however. Property taxes may become so high that the capital value of some properties is effectively reduced to zero. The economic benefit of occupation is less than the rate which any occupier would have to pay if they occupied it. The rent they would be willing to pay would, therefore, be less than zero. We showed in the preceding chapter that if the cost of demolition and site clearance is high this may cause property to remain derelict; the possibility of high property taxes if it is rebuilt or occupied may exacerbate this problem. In the Enterprise Zones created in several areas of urban dereliction in the United Kingdom, development has been encouraged not only by tax incentives to reduce the cost of construction to the developer but also by exemption from rates for a 10-year period so reducing the cost of occupation to tenants.

In principle, of course, if this problem occurs it implies a breakdown in the system of valuation used for calculating rateable values. If the possible rent is low the rateable value and the rates should also be low. When revaluations for rating purposes are carried out only infrequently, however, as they are in Britain, and when the system of valuation is largely hypothetical, as it is in Britain, this problem is likely to occur in some areas and locations.

FURTHER READING

A useful survey of local government economics has been published by Topham (1983). Bennett (1980) covers the geography of public finance in still greater depth, as he also covers the topic of central grants to local government in Bennett (1982). Most economic work in the field has been stimulated by the hypothesis put forward by Tiebout (1956), but the literature on capitalization is based on the work of Oates (1969). On this topic Edel and Sclar (1974) are worth reading on the differences between the short term and the long term and the problem of spillovers. The Green Paper on *Alternatives to Domestic Rates* (Dept. of the Environment, 1981) is commendably brief; Prest (1981) is also relevant to this topic.

11

Urban Transport

Lady Bracknell: Come dear, we have already missed five, if not six trains. To miss any more might expose us to comment on the platform.

The Importance of Being Earnest Act III

As we indicated in the introduction to this book, concern over the urban transport problem, in particular the effects of transport and transport improvements on the location of urban activities, was a major influence on the early development of urban economics. The impact of changes in transport systems has in turn been a recurring theme of this book. In various chapters we have discussed the way in which towns came originally to be located on transport routes, the way in which manufacturing was likely to develop at trans-shipment points, and the effects of transport improvements on the location of manufacturing and offices and on the pattern of residential location.

In these analyses we have, however, tended to take the urban transport system as being determined exogenously. Changes in the pattern of location have been assumed to occur as a result of changes in the speed and cost of transport which occur independently. But in fact the characteristics of the urban transport system, and in particular the price of transport, are to a large extent a matter of choice and public policy. Moreover, the factors which enter into this choice are to a large extent economic, so that we can use economic analysis to show how the urban transport system ought to develop, although, since its development is a political matter, this may not be what happens in practice.

In the first section of this chapter we discuss the relationship between city size, residential density, employment density, and the characteristics of optimal modes of transport. The transport problem endemic to cities is congestion, since the concentration of people and jobs in urban areas necessarily creates such congestion. The welfare economics of congestion are analysed in the second section as a necessary preamble to the possible solutions to the transport problem which are discussed in the succeeding sections, namely road pricing, road construction, parking controls and traffic restrictions, and the improvement and/or subsidization of public transport. The discussion, though general, relates primarily to the transport of passengers.

MODES OF TRANSPORT AND CITY SIZE

A feature of all modern transport systems is that there are great economies of scale. All systems require a very large capital investment to operate efficiently and public passenger transport systems tend to have high fixed costs. The system with the greatest economies of scale, and the highest fixed costs is a rail system. These costs include the cost of constructing the route, whether overground or underground, the cost of vehicles and their maintenance, and the cost of collecting fares and maintaining stations. To a very great extent these costs are quite independent of the number of passengers carried. The cost of actually running a train is also to a large extent independent of the number of passengers carried. Moreover, the passenger-carrying capacity of a rail system is very high once it has been constructed. In consequence it is used most economically if a large number of people have to be transported between points along routes – i.e. if the density of traffic along a transport corridor is very high. In the case of intra-urban passenger transport this traffic density is only likely to be great enough to make a rail system economical in a very large city, for only there will the numbers wishing to travel be high enough. The city must not only be large, however, the density of development must also be high, so that the numbers wishing to travel from any station will be great enough. The urban spatial structure is most favourable to rail transit where jobs are concentrated at a single city centre and residential densities are also high, for example, in cities such as London or New York. If residential densities are low and workplaces are scattered, the construction of a railway system becomes more difficult to justify economically because the number of trips desired between any two locations is not high enough.

The fixed costs and economies of scale of a bus system are somewhat lower than those of a rail system. The costs of construction of the road system may be high, but it is usually a cost borne long before, and is anyway shared with private-car transport. A combination scheme is possible under which the buses use a 'busway' for the main part of the route but come off the busway at each end to collect and distribute passengers without their having to change vehicles. Such a system is closer in terms of its cost structure to a rail system. Even in the case of a normal bus system, however, certain of the costs are fixed and independent of the number of passengers carried. A bus may be varied in size, of course, but the costs of operation, particularly the driver's labour costs, are more or less fixed. Once again, therefore, as in the case of the rail system, a higher density of development will allow the system to be more economical. Vehicles can be larger, more passengers can be carried per vehicle, and a more frequent service can be provided.

At low densities the private car comes into its own. In one way the same costs apply as to a bus system. The roads have to be built and maintained, the vehicles have to be built and maintained, and the driver has to be paid. All these costs tend to be lower for the private-car owner, however. Track costs are not charged directly. The vehicle costs are low since the driver uses the vehicle for other purposes, and tends to consider only the additional cost of the journey, ignoring the fixed costs which would be incurred anyway. Travelling time is also valued by drivers at a rate much lower than their wage rate.

The economics of the problem are illustrated in figure 11.1, which is derived from a study by Meyer *et al.* (1965). In a high-density city the cost per traveller per mile is represented on the vertical axis and the number of passengers travelling the route is represented on the horizontal axis. It can be seen that the private car is cost effective for traffic flows up to about 7000 passengers per hour, but bus or rail travel is then most economical for traffic flows between 7000 and 30 000 passengers per hour, and the train may only be cost effective for very high traffic flows.

The private car is not merely less economically efficient for high traffic flows, but if these traffic flows are to a single destination it becomes virtually physically impossible to provide the necessary space – not merely the road space when a number of routes converge, but also parking space for the automobiles. In economic

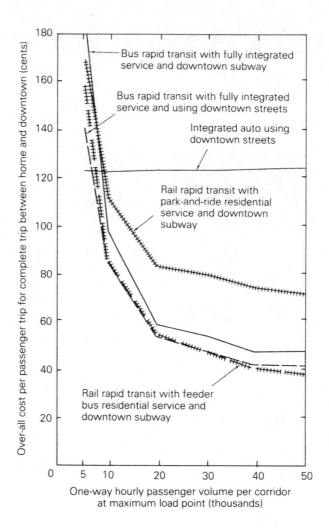

Source: Meyer et al. (1965)

FIGURE 11.1

Over-all home – downtown passenger-trip costs for high residential density
corridor, hourly downtown passenger-trip originations of ten per block at
the home end, 10-mile line-haul facility and 2-mile downtown distribution
system route length

terms the cost of the land required for the construction of roads and the provision of parking places becomes so high as to make car travel uneconomic.

Because of the interrelationship between the use of space, the cost of space and the flow of traffic the age of the city is relevant to its transport system. Many cities which developed in the nineteenth century grew at a time when rail transport was the main method of bringing a large number of workers to a central business district – indeed these cities developed rapidly because of rail transport. The radial transport routes created by the railways and the still relatively high cost of transport coupled with a need for stations to be within a short distance of homes led to high residential densities. Land at the centre became still more valuable because of the stress on centrality given by the radial transport created by the railways and perpetuated by the motor bus. When private-car ownership increased in the mid-twentieth century, and there was a demand for facilities for car travel, it only appeared to be economic to construct urban motor-ways when they could be built alongside existing rail routes or across parks or elsewhere where the financial cost of construction was low. It was too costly to purchase property to demolish it for road construction unless this could be justified on other grounds. For example, the Glasgow inner-ring motorway was planned to go through areas which were scheduled for comprehensive redevelop-ment because of the poor character of the housing.

As the high cost of land and space in nineteenth-century cities makes road construction relatively uneconomic, so it makes the construction of underground railways more economic. The cost of tunnelling may be high but it is still cheaper than buying buildings to demolish them and otherwise using up the scarcest resource – inner-urban land. So as cities throughout the world cut back on the construction of urban motorways in the early 1970s, this coincided with a boom in the construction and extension of urban under-ground systems.

With cities which developed mainly in the twentieth century in areas where car ownership was already widespread, the position was different, the main examples being the American cities of the mid-west and west. The growth of strong centres was not promoted by any pre-existing radial transport systems. Indeed the growth of such systems was discouraged by the fact that many or most journeys were undertaken by automobile; non-radial journeys were easy and workplaces need not be concentrated together at a high density. The lower density of development in these cities made it uneconomic, as they became larger, to construct rail transport systems for commuters, because the traffic density along any transport corridor was not high enough. It was, however, relatively cheap to build urban freeways. The cost of purchasing and demolishing property was relatively low since inner urban land values were low and pre-existing buildings were smaller and more widely spaced.

CONGESTION

The main urban transport problems, in the age of the automobile, are first, the cost and extent of the public-transport system, and, secondly, congestion on the road system. We shall comment on the first later but before that it is necessary to discuss, as the primary problem, the welfare economics of congestion.

Congestion is caused, to state the obvious, by the presence of a large number of vehicles all trying to travel the same route at the same time. Any one of the vehicles could get to its destination considerably faster if the other vehicles were not on the road. So each additional traveller is both slowed down by other vehicles and slows them down. But when deciding whether to make a journey travellers only take into account their own private costs, the way congestion affects them, and do not take into account their own impact on the costs of other travellers.

The economic analysis is represented in figure 11.2. Traffic flow (the number of vehicles travelling along a particular route per hour) is indicated on the horizontal axis, and costs are represented in money terms on the vertical axis. These costs include the opportunity cost of time spent travelling – several empirical studies have reported that commuters appear to value travel time at about 25–30 per cent of their wage rate in choosing, say, between travelling along a route which is cheaper but slower and one which is faster but more expensive (see Harrison and Quarmby, 1972).

The costs which the traveller does take into account are indicated by the solid line marked MPC (marginal private cost). This line is initially horizontal, i.e. the cost of an additional vehicle is constant if the traffic flow is light so that there is no congestion. If the traffic flow increases, however, congestion begins to slow down the traffic so that the cost of travelling along the route increases, and this is

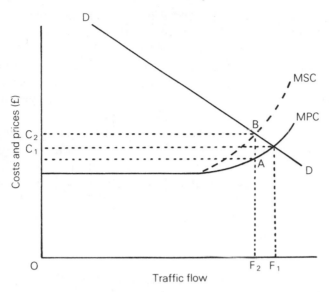

FIGURE 11.2

represented by the upward slope of the line MPC. At any point in time the demand for travel along the route can be represented by some such demand curve as the line DD. This slopes downwards to the right in the usual way because if the cost of travel along the route is low more people would wish to travel, either transferring from other routes or transport modes or making extra trips.

The actual, equilibrium traffic flow is indicated by the intersection of DD and MPC. The cost of travel is then indicated by the vertical distance OC_1. The number of people wishing to travel generates a traffic flow, indicated by the horizontal distance OF_1, which will create the congestion necessary for the cost to be OC_1. The private costs, as the name implies, ignore the congestion costs which each traveller may impose on others by slowing them down if the traffic flow is high. The social costs are indicated by the dotted line MSC. If traffic flows are light there is no congestion so that social costs are coincident with private costs. As traffic flows increase the costs of the congestion imposed on others have to be added to the private costs, and this is represented by the line MSC rising above and more steeply then MPC.

From a welfare maximizing view point the Pareto optimal traffic flow is that given by the intersection of the demand curve DD and the line MSC, represented in figure 11.2 by the distance OF_2. At this traffic flow the social costs of the marginal journey are just equal to the value of the journey to the marginal traveller. At greater traffic flows, including the equilibrium flow OF_1, when only private costs are considered, the social costs of the marginal journeys are greater than the value of those journeys to those making them. The economic and political problem is therefore one of limiting the traffic flow to the welfare maximizing level, or if it is decided that this is not politically or technically feasible, choosing acceptable alternatives.

ROAD PRICING

The analysis above points to a system of control by taxation or 'road pricing'. A tax would be imposed, the level of which is indicated by the vertical distance AB in figure 11.2. The tax would raise the cost of travel and reduce the number of people wishing to travel. The correct tax would reduce the traffic flow to OF_2 in the figure so that the cost of the marginal journey would equal its social costs and would be equal to the value of the journey to the marginal traveller.

Although economists have tended to favour such a system of taxes and the economic analysis points to it, it has never been put into practice. The reasons for this are several. First, to ensure the optimum traffic flow and congestion at all points in the city, the tax would have to vary throughout the city being highest at the centre and in sub-centres where congestion was greatest. Secondly, to ensure the optimum traffic flow and congestion at all times, the charge would also have to vary over time at all points since congestion is greatest at some peak times and may be low or non-existent, even in city centres, at other times of the day or night. Failure to charge the correct tax or road price at all times and places would mean either, if the tax were too high, that the traffic flow would be too low, and journeys which were valued at greater than the true social cost would not be made or, if it were too low, that congestion would be too great and journeys would be being made which were valued at less than their true social cost. A third problem is that of collection. Even if road use could be priced accurately, how would the tax or toll be collected without the collection process itself causing congestion, as may happen even on inter-urban toll roads at peak times, on the Italian autostrade and French autoroutes, for example.

In the 1960s a committee was set up by the British Ministry of Transport, under the chairmanship of Professor Smeed, to investigate the feasibility of road pricing. This committee reported that road pricing would be technically possible using a system of meters attached to cars, and a remote-control system built into urban roads so that the meter on a car would register the fact that it was travelling within a congested area. The meters could be read periodically and the tax collected without causing further congestion (Ministry of Transport, 1964).

Following the Smeed Report road pricing as a solution to the urban-traffic problem appeared very possible, even probable. Nearly 20 years later, despite whatever technical advances may have been made in the meantime, road pricing does not look remotely likely. Its unacceptability appears now to be for political reasons rather than because of any technological gap or economic scruples over its accuracy. Any new tax is always unpopular, and it would seem that road pricing would be particularly unpopular. Most would feel that they would suffer from the tax. The wealthier, who own and drive cars in congested areas, would be aware that they would be paying the tax, and not immediately aware that they would gain through a reduction in congestion. Moreover some would lose, presumably those at a middle-income level, since they would be forced back onto the public transport system by the tax. And lower-income households who do not drive would be aware that they might wish to and that such a tax would make it less likely that they could.

So any government considering introducing road pricing would be aware that there would be considerable political opposition with relatively little political advantage. Furthermore since the 1960s the whole economic climate has changed so that whilst the British government of that period was concerned with distributing jobs and people away from the major conurbations, since the 1970s British governments have been trying to encourage investment in the major cities and to create new jobs there. Any new tax which appears to discourage inner-city employment is not a possibility.

ROAD CONSTRUCTION

If road pricing is not likely for technical, economic, or political reasons, a possible way of solving the congestion problem is the construction of roads in order to eliminate congestion by providing enough road capacity. The difficulty is, as we shall show, that it is almost invariably not possible to eliminate road congestion in larger cities in this way at a cost which is politically acceptable.

In figure 11.3 the lines DD, MPC and MSC are as in figure 11.2. The assumption lying behind a policy of road construction is that by increasing capacity the lines indicating marginal private cost and marginal social cost can be shifted to the new positions shown as MPC' and MSC'. Traffic flow can be increased from OF_1 to OF_3 and traffic congestion eliminated.

The problem is that for any particular route within the congested part of the urban area the demand curve is not as inelastic as DD appears to be in figure 11.3. Indeed for any particular route the demand for road space will be highly elastic, and the demand curve could more accurately be represented by a nearly horizontal line such as D'D'. In effect, therefore, congestion could not be eliminated by a small addition to capacity but only by adding some large multiple of the existing capacity.

This is because any particular stretch of road is only a small part of the urban transport system. Its improvement leads drivers to divert

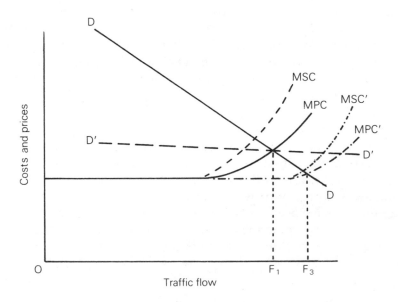

FIGURE 11.3

to it from other routes until speeds along that stretch are once again the same, or nearly the same, as they are along alternative routes. The previous bottleneck is replaced by 'a stretch of motorway with a bottleneck at each end' as London's Hyde Park Corner underpass is described. Furthermore the balance of costs will have been equalized not only between alternative road routes but also between road and rail or bus, as public transport users are encouraged to use private cars by the (eventually slight) improvement in road speeds.

The benefits of the road improvement to road users will be greatest when congestion is low, outside peak hours. At these times demand is low and more inelastic. The improvement in road capacity may therefore noticeably increase traffic speeds outside peak hours. This, however, further exacerbates the public-transport problem. Road improvements will draw some traffic away from public transport during peak hours but a lot more outside these peak hours. This will lead to increases in fares to cover the fixed costs, and reduced services because fewer passengers are being carried. This in turn will cause a further diversion of traffic from public to private transport, and so further reduce any reduction in congestion which might have occurred.

In effect cities hoping to build their way out of congestion would have to do so by creating a road-transport system which will not merely complement but will virtually replace any existing public-transport system. At the same time the city will have to cope with the reconstruction caused by the relocation of economic activities caused by the switch from a high traffic density radially oriented public-transport system to a low traffic density grid-like private-transport system. Not surprisingly with costs of this order of magnitude, although many cities have begun a policy of increasing road capacity, few, with the exception of some already low-density American cities, have wished to go far down the path which the policy signposts.

PARKING CONTROLS AND TRAFFIC RESTRICTIONS

If road construction is too expensive, and road pricing is not politically acceptable, a third possibility is the imposition of controls in order to limit traffic flow by other means. In practice traffic control in the developed economies is usually attempted through parking restrictions. Leaving aside a policy of limiting traffic congestion by limiting car ownership through rationing, taxes, or import restrictions, a policy pursued in most East European countries as well as in some developing countries (on Lagos and Bogotá see Thomson, 1978), the only country in which direct traffic control (and a form of road pricing) is practiced successfully is in the small city state of Singapore where a charge is imposed on cars entering the central area unless the car carries four persons.

Policy with respect to the provision of parking spaces has varied between cities and over time in the same city. The question at issue is whether parking is being provided to get the cars off the streets and speed the flow through the centre (or sub-centre) or whether parking spaces are being limited in order to discourage people from driving into the central area so speeding the flow of traffic into the centre (or sub-centre). In London, for example, there were no forms of traffic limitation until the late 1950s and parking meters were introduced only in the 1960s. The first post-war boom in office construction occurred after 1956 when controls were relaxed. At that time new offices had to provide parking spaces, possibly in basements, before planning permission would be given.

Later, in the 1970s, in order to discourage commuters from driving to work, the provision of parking spaces in new buildings in central London was no longer encouraged. In addition, many of the parking-meter spaces which had been designed earlier in order to provide for short-term parking needs were removed in order to discourage people from travelling by car to the central area.

Two difficulties with parking controls as a policy are relevant, the one administrative, the other more general. First, the controls may be ineffective if the restrictions merely encourage illegal parking. The elimination of parking spaces in central London was followed by a period during which there were relatively few traffic wardens. As a result many motorists chose to pay for parking by risking an occasional fine, and this seemed the more morally acceptable because they were often parking where it had previously been legal to park. Clearly, however, parking controls can be enforced if the penalties are great enough and/or the risk of incurring them is high enough.

But, parking controls, even if they are effective, may not in the end reduce congestion significantly. The second, more general, problem is that as the policy reduces travel to and from the centre or sub-centre and so reduces congestion on the routes to and in the (sub) centre, this actually encourages travel across the (sub) centre. Traffic which might otherwise avoid the congestion by travelling around now finds that it can as easily take a direct route through the centre.

PUBLIC TRANSPORT

If parking controls are a blunt weapon lacking discrimination, road construction is too expensive, and road pricing is not politically feasible, the alternative is to attempt to persuade people to travel by public transport instead of using their cars. One way of doing this is to improve the public transport system so that it gives a better service, and this is the policy pursued by a number of cities since the late 1960s, from Vienna to Washington, in constructing new underground railways in order to allow the continued prosperity of their city centres.

The difficulty is one of cost. Public transport may be expected to charge a fare which will cover all its costs – the cost of construction of the track, the purchase of rolling stock, the cost of manning the service – and to provide the level of service at which it can expect to break even. This puts it at a disadvantage compared with the private car and bus systems. Urban roads are provided virtually free to these users. There is an implicit contribution towards the cost of road use through various forms of vehicle taxation, particularly taxes on petrol, but though revenue from these taxes might more than cover the cost of using rural roads, it remains just a contribution to the cost of using congested urban roads on high cost inner-urban land. As we have shown the social cost of congestion is not taken into account by individuals making travel decisions. Moreover, car owners quite rationally regard the capital cost of their vehicle as a sunk cost. In deciding whether to travel by car or by train, they will only take account of the marginal private costs of travel in deciding the costs of the former, whereas the fare on the latter may be set to cover all the costs of the transport undertaking as it attempts to break even.

The construction of new 'rapid transit' facilities, as for example with the San Francisco Bay Areas Rapid Transit system (BART), no matter how advanced technically, will not solve the congestion problem if the fares are high or the service is poor, so that car drivers are unwilling to relinquish the use of their cars and travel by train. (On the history of BART as a 'Great Planning Disaster' see Hall, 1980.) As well as constructing new transport routes, and often instead of new construction, governments wishing to discourage the use of private vehicles tend, therefore, to be forced into a policy of subsidizing the public-transport system. Indeed subsidization, sometimes quite heavily, seems to be the rule rather than the exception in most cities in the developed economies (see Thomson, 1978, Table 9).

Although policies of subsidization may have been embarked upon by governments accidentally or unwillingly, or, sometimes, for political reasons, in order to subsidize the travel of the working classes, such policies can be justified in terms of welfare economic analysis, using what has come to be called 'the theory of the second best'. Although the non-economist may think that economic efficiency is maximized if the economy is characterized by competition between activities in which those that make losses go out of business, this is not necessarily so. Although Adam Smith may have written, in a well-known passage, that if each individual maximizes his own profits, he is 'led by an invisible hand to promote an end which was no part of his intention·. . . By pursuing his own interest he frequently promotes that of the society more effectually than when he really intends to promote it' (Smith, 1776, p. 400), welfare economists since the eighteenth century have spent considerable effort in defining the conditions under which this will be true, and hence when it will not be true. Their conclusion is that Smith's statement will be correct if, as a result of competition or otherwise, the prices of goods and services are each equal to their marginal social costs. The cost of providing an additional unit of a good or service will then be equal to the value put upon it by the customer. It is by applying this conclusion that road pricing is justified, as we showed above, for then the price of each road journey will be equal to its marginal social cost.

In the 1950s various authors, but particularly Lipsey and Lancaster (1956), showed that if prices were not equal to marginal social cost in some parts of the economy, and if for political or technical or other reasons these prices could not be made equal to marginal social cost, then economic efficiency would be increased if the prices of other goods and services which were closely competitive or complementary differed systematically from marginal social cost. If 'first best' is achieved when price equals marginal cost everywhere, then the 'second best' is the best that can be achieved when some prices cannot be equal to marginal cost.

The systematic nature of the differences implied by the theory between prices and marginal costs can be seen by looking further at the case of commuting into a central city with which we are mainly concerned. As we have shown, road traffic is likely to be paying less than its marginal social cost. The theory of the second best suggests that the price of competitive goods and services should, therefore, also be priced at less than marginal cost (and though we are not here concerned with them, that complementary goods should be priced at more than marginal costs). Since public transport and private transport are competitive it follows that public transport should, therefore, be priced at less than marginal cost. The justification for this can be set out as follows. Suppose that the price of public transport was initially set at a level which covered all its costs, but then subsidization allowed fares to be reduced. The reduction in fares would encourage commuters to shift from travelling by car to travelling by train (or bus). As a result road congestion would be reduced. The argument can be looked at in terms of figure 11.2. In that figure the demand curve for road transport shifts leftwards as car users now travel by public transport. The shift in the demand curve means that equilibrium is reached with a smaller traffic flow at which there is less congestion so that the difference between marginal private cost (the line MPC in figure 11.2) and marginal social cost (the line MSC in figure 11.2) is reduced. There are fewer car users and each of those users imposes less unpriced social cost on the others. The reduction in these unpriced social costs is greater than the cost of the subsidy and so more than makes up, in welfare terms, for the gap between price and marginal cost in the public transport system which is financed by the subsidy.

Second-best theory can also be used to justify further investment in the system. Thus, Foster and Beesley, in one of the pioneering studies in cost-benefit analysis, showed that the construction of a new underground railway in London (the Victoria Line) could be justified in that the benefits exceeded the costs. Much of the benefit arose because of reductions in congestion on the roads. If, however, fares were raised to try to recoup the costs of the railway, its construction would not be worthwhile because these benefits would be less even though the financial revenue raised might be greater (Foster and Beesley, 1963; Beesley and Foster, 1965).

More recent events in London, as political and judicial decisions caused fares to be cut and increased by substantial amounts, have shown the effects of fare cuts can be substantial. A 25 per cent cut in

London Transport fares reportedly resulted in a 14 per cent increase in the number of passengers carried. Moreover evidence for West Yorkshire, where fares have been held at low levels, suggest that low fares and improvements in service can, in the longer run, lead to a reduction in car ownership (Button *et al.*, 1980).

There is of course one problem which second-best theory does not resolve. The subsidization may be economically justifiable, but the above analysis ignores the important question as to who is going to pay the cost of the subsidy. Any taxes imposed to pay this cost have effects of their own, both in terms of efficiency, by raising the price of some goods, and in terms of distribution, by making some worse off. In the absence of any tax everyone appears to benefit from the subsidy – public transport passengers benefit from lower fares, those who transfer from private to public transport benefit as is shown by their transfer, and continuing road users benefit from reduced congestion. Whatever tax is imposed obviously reduces the benefits to one or more groups and will make some worse off than in the absence of the policy. In Britain subsidies to local transport are financed by local government through local taxes, particularly the rates. This means that the group gaining the most are those living just outside the local government area but commuting to the city centre. Those losing the most are those living within the local government area but in parts which are badly served by the transport system being subsidized. So when the Greater London Council introduced a policy of heavy subsidization in 1981 it was the London Borough of Bromley which fought the policy in the courts, for that Borough had no underground services in or near its boundaries. The ratepayers of Bromley clearly lost from the policy. Although welfare economics can justify the subsidization of public transport, the distributional effects of such a policy make its implementation a political rather than an economic problem.

SUMMARY AND CONCLUSION

In this chapter we have shown that the form of the transport system in a city cannot necessarily be taken as determined by the available technology. Rail systems are suited to higher-density, older cities. Low-density cities in the affluent west of America can cope with the dominance of the motor car. But the nature of the system may not only depend on the age and density of a city, but also on political decisions which may be made with respect to the control of congestion. Cities may pursue policies of road pricing, traffic and parking control, road construction, or the improvement and subsidization of public transport.

The policy which is chosen will also affect the location of economic activities. Road pricing would result in a smaller, more compact city, subsidies will lead to a more wide-spread metropolitan area, and road construction will create still further sprawl. The nature of this relocation in the absence of controls will have been seen in the earlier chapters of this book. The amount of relocation which is possible will also be affected by the strength and direction of planning controls and planning policy. The British planning system with a general policy of urban containment and the preservation of a clear distinction between urban places and rural areas has discouraged urban sprawl. In doing so it has discouraged car transport, and implicitly, if not explicitly, encouraged public transport by ensuring higher-density development than would otherwise have occurred. The economic rationale for such a system of planning we consider in the next chapter.

FURTHER READING

Thomson (1978) provides a good introduction to the transport problems of cities, providing as he does, not only a basic analysis of the transport problem but also much empirical and institutional information about cities in all parts of the world. Wider ranging texts on transport economics are by Glaister (1981) and Button (1982).

Economics and Town Planning

In most of this book we have tended to assume away government intervention by concentrating on the economic forces, particularly the market forces, which create and mould cities. But at various points we have had to note the importance of government intervention, and to recognize that although the economist may suggest what kind of intervention might be most effective or efficient on economic grounds, in the end government policy is decided on political grounds. The discussion of the problems of urban transport in the preceding chapter is only the most obvious example of this.

In this chapter we look at the most explicit form of government intervention, namely land-use planning or town-planning. In my view the relationship between economics and planning is not simple, since the introduction of planning means that planning decisions have to be considered as well as economic and political factors. Despite the fact that planning decisions have to be implemented by governments, planning controls may be decided only partially on political grounds; the basic characteristics of the controls are primarily determined by what are considered to be sound planning principles by the planning profession. Since this profession, as we noted in the first chapter of this book, developed independently, and during most of its life largely rejected economics, regarding it as being of no use to planners, town planning and economics are not as closely related as one might possibly have expected.

There seem to be three ways in which economics relates to land–use planning. First, the economic analysis of how cities work, i.e. positive urban economics, should allow planners to predict more accurately what will happen in the future and what the effects of their actions will be. Most importantly it should also predict what the unintended effects of planning controls will be, showing that if X is done not only will the intended effect Y occur but market forces will also lead to Z happening which might not be wanted. It is this field of positive urban economics with which we have primarily been concerned in most of this book. It is this which has been recognized by the planning profession as being the useful contribution to land-use planning of the economist.

Secondly, the methods and analyses of welfare economics can assist the planner in indicating the policies which can or should be adopted. Instead of saying that if X is done the results will be Y and Z, the welfare economist is saying that A should be done, because the consequences will be B and C. The prediction that the construction of a new rapid transit system will affect location patterns and relative land values in particular ways would be an application of positive urban economics. The use of the theory of the second best in the preceding chapter to show that the improvement and subsidization of the public-transport system should increase welfare is an application of welfare economics, indeed could be called normative urban economics.

Welfare economics can be applied to land-use planning in two ways, either the urban economy can be analysed in terms of the findings of welfare economics with respect to the failure of a market economy to maximize welfare (in effect the exposition of welfare economics using land-use examples), or the various instruments of land-use control used by the planner, particularly various types of zoning, can be analyzed in economic terms to discover their effect on economic welfare. Although various studies of this kind have been carried out by economists, this work has had relatively little impact on land-use planning (see, for example, Harrison, 1977; Willis, 1980; Evans, 1974a). Why this should be raises questions which are difficult to answer but related to the independent development of economics and planning which we have already mentioned. Do planners feel that the work adds nothing to their knowledge, or is the advice unwanted, or is it that the advice cannot be acted upon or otherwise used?

Attempts to answer these questions bring us to a third way in which economics relates to land-use planning, namely the economic analysis of planning. This is the economics of planning strictly defined, but it is only beginning to be developed. In time progress should also include, if it becomes necessary, the assimilation into welfare economics of the principles and methods on which planning is based.

In this chapter we shall not deal with the first topic – positive urban economics – for this is, after all, dealt with at length in the rest of the book. We shall discuss the second topic – the application of welfare economics to town planning in the second section, and some examples of the economic analysis of planning instruments in the third section. Then, as an example of the economic analysis of planning we discuss the implications of the preference of British planners for restrictive zoning as a planning instrument. Finally, we analyse the objectives of planning and their relationship to the objectives of the economist.

PLANNING AND WELFARE ECONOMICS

Welfare economics has developed as the branch of economics concerned with three problems, first, the definition of economic welfare; secondly, the determination of the conditions under which welfare would be maximized; thirdly, if these conditions do not exist, so that welfare is not maximized, what policies could be pursued to improve welfare.

The first of these questions is important since only with an agreed definition can we discuss whether or not welfare is increased by any action. In discussions by economists the generally accepted criterion is that named after the Italian sociologist Vilfredo Pareto. Welfare is increased if one person can be made better off with nobody else being made worse off. Pareto optimality exists if no one can be made better off without somebody else being made worse off. This criterion does not define a unique welfare maximum, only a set of possible optima, each of which represents a different distribution of welfare (and income and wealth) amongst the population. The choice between different Pareto optima, therefore, becomes a problem of equity, in effect of choosing between different distributions of welfare. Though economists will occasionally represent this as an economic problem of maximizing social welfare, in fact the choice and the problem is not purely economic but primarily political.

Moreover, the Pareto criterion itself is not as useful as it might initially appear to be. Virtually any policy which might be suggested to move the economy to or towards a Pareto optimum, in brief one which will improve efficiency, will make some people worse off even though it may make more better off. In policy decisions there is an almost invariable conflict between equity and efficiency. There are no policies which would make some people better off and nobody worse off for a very obvious reason – any such policy can only win votes and not lose them so that it will have already been proposed and implemented by any reasonably competent politician.

The second problem discussed in welfare economics is the definition of the conditions necessary for welfare to be maximized. As is well known, it has been found that in a market economy of capitalist firms, welfare would be maximized in conditions which have been described as perfectly competitive – there are a large number of firms in each industry, the products of the firms in each industry are homogeneous, each firm maximizes profits, consumers act rationally, both firms and consumers have full information about the consequences of alternative courses of action, both present and future, and there are no externalities of any kind. It has also been shown that welfare would also be maximized in a socialist economy which was similar to a perfectly competitive capitalist economy except that the firms were publicly owned and run by managers told to minimize costs rather than maximize profits. Moreover, it could also be maximized in a centrally planned socialist economy if the commissariat had full knowledge of everyone's preferences.

The conditions described above are, of course, not achievable in any economy, whether socialist or capitalist – externalities exist in all economies, monopolies of various kinds exist in capitalist economies (and decentralized socialist economies), and commissariats are not omniscient. In the end, therefore, the statement of welfare conditions has few simple implications for the organization of the economy. (Indeed the conclusions imply that the organization of the economy is not relevant for people's welfare since they have no preferences regarding it, which seems somewhat strange in that the organization of the economy is one of the things elections and revolutions are fought over, and would seem to be something which is perceived, whether rightly or wrongly, as greatly affecting people's welfare).

The statement of the conditions necessary for the achievement of Pareto optimality is useful, not in giving a simple answer as to the way an economy should be organized in some once and for all way –

indeed it shows that this cannot be done – but in giving guidance as to what kind of government action of intervention in an economy might increase welfare. In practice, of course, more right-wing governments may choose to ignore this guidance. Non-intervention may be preferred to intervention on the grounds that government intervention *per se* is bad – 'he governs best, who governs least'. And the case for intervention may also be rejected because intervention itself is costly, or because the benefits of intervention are uncertain and variable because the costs imposed by the market imperfection being corrected are themselves variable and uncertain.

For example, referring again to the discussion of road congestion in the previous chapter, the installation of the machinery necessary for road pricing is expensive, so that the cost of intervention is high. Furthermore, the exact cost of congestion is uncertain, since it is dependent on the value of travel time and this is difficult to ascertain and varies from individual to individual. Finally, the cost of congestion is variable since the degree of congestion varies during the day from hour to hour and even from minute to minute, so that it would be impossible to accurately charge for congestion at all times. In practice the tax would be approximate and would on average tend to undercharge some of the time and overcharge most of the rest.

If, however, intervention is favoured, under what conditions, or for what reasons, would welfare economics suggest that governments should intervene? The reasons for intervention divide into two broad groups along the lines suggested earlier, equity reasons to alter the distribution of welfare from what it otherwise might have been, and efficiency reasons, to make the economy more nearly Pareto optimal.

Intervention for reasons of equity can also be considered to be of two kinds, some intervention being overtly concerned with the distribution of income as with many taxes and transfers, and some more concerned with consumer protection. In the context of land-use planning the provision of parks, swimming pools, and other recreational facilities is designed to ensure that they are available to all and not only for those who could afford them. The adoption of planning standards which recommend the provision of so many acres of recreation space per thousand population makes this explicit, since the provision is supposed to be the same for all.

Intervention in order to protect the consumer is necessary when the consumers of a good or service cannot be fully aware of what they are buying or the consequences of their actions. So the building regulations administered by local authorities in Britain, with periodic inspections of construction sites, ensure that, for example, the foundations and damp proofing are adequate and that the roof will provide adequate protection. Consumers, the eventual purchasers of the buildings, will not be able to carry out such inspections when they buy, and so are protected by the state. In this case even though consumers might be intellectually able to make their own inspections, or financially be able to pay an expert, neither consumer nor expert would be physically able to make a proper inspection. In other cases consumers of goods or services may be thought intellectually unable to understand the consequences of their actions. Compulsory schooling until a certain age is an example with implications for land-use planning, since the urban planner must plan for the schools to be provided for the predicted school age population.

The second broad group of reasons for intervention are those to promote efficiency because the market will otherwise fail to ensure Pareto optimality, if any of the conditions stated earlier do not exist. Of these the least important for planning is the existence of monopolies or some other kind of imperfect competition. Lack of competition does occur with respect to land, but it is rarely considered an important problem. From a land-use planning viewpoint the most important cause of market failure is the existence of externalities of one kind or another, either external economies or external diseconomies. With respect to land use in an urban area external effects are endemic. Transactions between one party and another can rarely be 'private' in the sense that they affect no one not a party to the transaction. Any development affects others, in its construction, in its appearance, and in its use. In its construction neighbours will be affected by the noise, dirt, and inconvenience. The building, when finished, will affect neighbours and passers-by aesthetically since it may be pleasing or displeasing in appearance. The use of the building will affect people in numerous ways. A new shop, for example, will affect other shopkeepers negatively by increasing competition, and/or positively by increasing the attraction of a centre to shoppers. A factory may affect people through the noise, dirt, and pollution caused by the production process. A new office building will attract users and visitors and may increase congestion.

These are only examples of the externalities created by land use and development, but each of them is controlled in some way, within the British planning system at least. Planning permission has to be obtained for any new development, and the decision to grant permission should take account of the appearance of the building and the effects of construction and the future use; permission may be refused or modifications to the design may be asked for before permission is granted. The zoning system will affect the location and intensity of use. Shops will usually be kept in existing shopping areas. Factories will be kept together in industrial zones separated from residential areas, and new offices will not only be kept in commercial areas, but the amount of floor space constructed on any site will be limited.

The extreme example of an externality is the public good – a good which if consumed by one is consumed by all in an area or group. Because they are extreme cases public goods are rare, but one local public good which is important to land use planning is the town plan itself. There has to be only one. Residents cannot each have separate town plans; plans have to be implemented one at a time and cannot even change rapidly. As a public good the town plan therefore has to be provided publicly or it will not be provided at all.

Apart from externalities, the 'market failure' which planning has most to do with is lack of information. As we noted earlier, one of the conditions for perfect competition is that consumers and firms should have complete information about alternatives both present and future. Obviously, in practice, even if information about the present were reasonably complete and accurate, information about the future could not be. If developers' 'speculations' about the future are inaccurate this will result in a waste of resources; for example, the construction of a shopping centre ahead of residential development is wasted if few of the houses materialize, and equally a waste if residential development in the area is so successful that the capacity of the centre has to be expanded. The planner in providing a plan of future development which can be expected to be adhered to in effect provides information about the future which ensures that current development is not wasteful.

The information content of the planning process has been stressed by some economists as being the more important economic function (see Keogh, 1981) but the role of planning in the control of externalities is rather more obvious. In the next section we shall discuss the welfare economics of three different examples of planning controls in practice – density controls on residential development, plot ratio control of office development, and green belts to limit the spatial expansion of cities.

PLANNING CONTROLS: THREE EXAMPLES

One example of the analysis of a type of planning control was given in chapter 2. There we showed that welfare economics could be used to justify the control of the density of residential development if households preferred living at lower densities to living at higher densities. The analysis need not be repeated in full here, as it has already been given. Briefly, the empirical evidence does suggest that households prefer lower densities to higher, since statistical studies of property prices show that people seem generally to be willing to pay more for houses in lower-density areas. The analysis showed that in these circumstances, if land were owned and developed piecemeal, the density of development would be too high (in the absence of any controls) because each developer would not take into account the impact of their (high-density) development on neighbouring sites. If, on the other hand, land were owned and developed as a unit the developer would take this impact into account because a higher density of development on one site would result in having to charge a lower price for dwellings on neighbouring sites.

From a welfare economic viewpoint, planning authorities are justified in laying down maximum densities for residential development. It is true that if an area is controlled by a single developer then, as we have shown, the controls should be superfluous, but a general control is easier to administer than one which would be *ad hoc*. Although the control can be justified in this way, the problem for the economic analyst is that there is no evidence that planners actually think of residential density control in this way. Rather it is considered to be good planning practice that there should be controls on density. The argument through which this conclusion is reached appears to start with the old Victorian high density slums, the existence of which was one of the factors encouraging the pioneers of British planning in the construction of low-density garden cities and suburbs. The slum densities were clearly too high but resulted from the unfettered operation of market forces. Therefore, though the market may suggest that densities should be at some level, it would be better if they were lower. In the end this mode of thought reaches almost the same conclusion as the economist but by a slightly different route.

The important difference is, however, that the economist is thinking in relative terms – densities should be proportionately lower than would be determined by market forces, and if the demand for housing increases so that prices rise, the permitted (optimal) density should also increase. The planner on the other hand is thinking in absolute terms – the permitted residential density in each part of the city should be set at a certain level whatever market forces are and should be changed only if the plan changes. In other words, the market is overriden by the plan, in the planner's view, rather than modified, as in the economist's view. Of course when standards were originally laid down the existing densities were taken into account by the planners as an indication of what they could realistically expect, but changes in market forces since that time have not been reflected in changes in density controls.

Another kind of control is the limitation of the amount of office space which can be built on a given site or plot, through setting a maximum ratio of the floor area to the area of the plot, called the floor area ratio in the United States and the plot ratio in the United Kingdom. Study of the planning literature suggests that although aesthetic considerations regarding building size might also be relevant, plot-ratio control is primarily intended to be a method of controlling congestion (Evans, 1974b). If a smaller amount of office space is allowed on a given site, fewer people will be working there or visiting these offices – in other words the fewer will be the number of journeys originating or terminating at that site and so, presumably, the lower the level of congestion in the area.

This view of the problem can be illustrated diagrammatically and analysed in welfare economic terms. In figure 12.1 the amount of floor space in an office development on a given site is indicated along the horizontal axis and costs and prices are represented on the vertical axis. The curve marked MPC represents the relationship between the marginal private cost of each additional unit of space and the density of development. As the building gets higher each additional floor is more expensive to build so the curve slopes upwards. In the absence of any intervention by planners, the developer will maximize profits by developing the site up to the point that the price received for a unit of space is equal to its marginal (private) construction cost. In

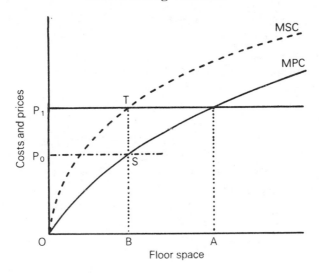

FIGURE 12.1

the figure the price per unit is P_1 and so the developer builds OA units of floor space.

The view in the planning literature mentioned earlier implies that each additional unit of space will cause social costs since additional trips starting or ending at the site will be generated through the occupation of the additional floor space and these trips will cause congestion. This view is represented by the curve marked MSC, lying above MPC, which depicts the relationship between marginal social costs (including private costs) and the amount of development on the site. If this is correct, the optimal scale of development is indicated by B on the horizontal axis since at this density the price of space is just equal to its marginal social cost. This analysis therefore provides an economic explanation of the planning process – plot ratio control is an attempt to limit development to this optimal level.

There are two problems with this view of things, however. The first is that, again, in practice, planners do not appear to act as though this is their mode of thought. Plot ratios once set for an area are rarely changed. But according to the economic analysis plot ratios should change if market forces change. The planner's mode of thought appears to be absolutist – this plot ratio would be best – whereas the economist's is relative – compared to what would result from market forces this plot ratio would be better. Once again, as with residential densities, in practice plot ratios differ both within cities and between cities and the level set has depended on what market forces resulted in before any plot-ratio controls were imposed. Plot ratios in the City of London are considerably lower than they are in the centre of New York City. The planner's absolutism is, therefore, in practice rather relative.

A second problem with this analysis of plot-ratio control is that a more sophisticated, general, analysis suggests that the conclusions reached through the partial analysis set out above are actually incorrect. In the partial analysis the problem is conceived of solely in terms of a single site but a more general analysis would be concerned with the whole city centre. Suppose a number of office users have to be housed within a city centre. They can be housed within a few tall office blocks with high plot ratios, or a large number of smaller office blocks with low plot ratios. Since the reason for choosing and paying for a location in the city centre is to facilitate meetings and transactions with other office users, particularly those also located in the centre, many of the trips terminating at one office will have originated at another located in the same area. If the office users are housed within a few tall blocks, more of these trips will take place within these blocks, and fewer between them than if there were a large number of smaller office blocks. Furthermore, with fewer sites used for offices the city centre will be spread over a smaller area so that more journeys can take place on foot or over a short distance by taxi or public transport. If the city centre is spread over a large area trips are less likely to be made on foot and more likely to be made by taxi, or even private car. So more, smaller, office blocks may result in fewer trips ending at a given site but in more trips being made, using more space-intensive modes of transport, over the central area. It is for this reason, I believe, that the congestion observed in high-density office centres such as Hong Kong or Manhattan is not noticeably greater than in lower-density centres such as the City and West End of London.

A third example of planning in practice is the system of green belts surrounding the larger British cities, first initiated in the 1940s, which prevents any major physical expansion of the contiguous built-up area of these cities. As we indicated in chapter 8 in the discussion of the definition of urban areas, the economic growth of these cities resulted in new development occurring beyond the green belts, with the city, as a functional economic unit, coming to include expanded towns on the other side of the green belt.

The economic process is represented diagrammatically in figure 12.2. Distance is represented on the horizontal axis and the value of land on the vertical axis. The land-value gradient before the green belt is defined is represented by the curve AB. The horizontal line through B represents the value of land in agricultural use. Suppose that transport improvements are made; these would lead, as we showed in chapter 7, to the land-value gradient becoming less steep. If at the same time the number of jobs in the city centre increases and rising incomes lead to an increased demand for space then these factors would lead to land values rising throughout the city. In the absence of a green belt the various factors would have resulted in the new land-value gradient indicated in figure 12.2 by the dotted line DE. But if there is a green belt around the city, BC in the figure, the predicted development between B and E in the figure cannot take

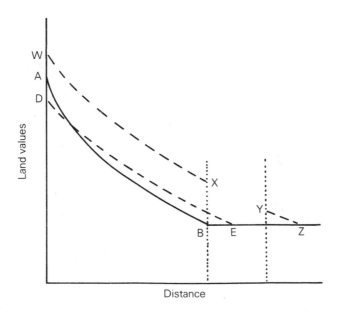

FIGURE 12.2

place. The restriction on the supply of land for development leaves the demand for land unsatisfied and causes land values to increase within the existing urban area until the demand for living space can be met through higher densities in the existing built-up area, particularly the suburbs, or, if the demand is great enough and land and property values rise sufficiently, through people living beyond the green belt and travelling across it to work. The new land-value gradient is WX within the old built-up area and YZ beyond the green belt; however X and Y land values are kept down to agricultural-use value.

Unlike the analyses of the two other examples of planning controls, the above analysis indicates the costs of the policy, but does not indicate what the social benefits of the control are, or, alternatively, what social costs are reduced by it. One benefit presumably results from the prevention of urban sprawl (i.e. disorganized scattered development on the fringes of cities and towns). The urban population also benefits from the fact that travelling out of the city will bring people more rapidly to a rural area with its recreational possibilities and visual appeal. Again, the urban population living on the edge of the existing built-up area, and those living in homes located in the green belt will gain from the certainty that the rural area near them will remain rural, and the owners of these houses will benefit financially from this. Finally there is presumably some aesthetic appeal in having a clear boundary between town and country.

The benefits of the policy would not appear to be of very great importance economically – that is to say, in a cost-benefit analysis it would be difficult to put a very substantial value on them. The costs, on the other hand, are obvious and economically important, at least if the constraint imposed by the policy is as effective as it is assumed to be in the analysis above. In the case of many British cities the green-belt policy has been effective. The demand for land and space in the urban area has been high, and the policy has resulted in higher property values and longer journeys to work. The higher land values and the unsatisfied demand for land have resulted in higher residential densities and the development of land within the existing built-up area which would otherwise have been unused and valueless (for example, because of its proximity to a busy railway line or because the land was on a hillside or otherwise difficult to build on).

These costs, the negative effects of the policy, were certainly not intended when the green-belt policy was initiated, nor would it appear that they were foreseen. What would appear to have happened is that what was thought of at the time as a prediction became, as circumstances changed, a control. When the green belts were first defined in the late 1940s it was being predicted that the birth-rate, after a post-war boom, would continue to be as low as it had been in the 1930s so that the total population would not increase very much. It was also expected that manufacturing would continue to be the most important employment sector and that new regional policies would ensure that manufacturing jobs would be decentralized out of the cities to the less-prosperous regions. The cities might even be reduced in population as slums were cleared and families moved to New Towns built beyond the green belts. In consequence there would be no need or demand to expand the built-up areas of the cities, and so the land surrounding these cities need not be developed. The green belts would make sure of this and prevent any unnecessary development by builders whose predictions of the future were less accurate than those of the planners.

In the event the birth-rate was higher than expected so that the population of the country increased, and although regional policies for the dispersal and decentralization of manufacturing were reasonably successful, services, and particularly office industries, became relatively more important. As a result the number of jobs in the cities did not fall to the extent that the resident population did. Moreover, as incomes and car ownership increased and roads and railways were improved, the demand for space within and beyond the existing built-up area also increased, with the effects on land values which we outlined in the discussion of figure 12.2 above.

Once again, therefore, there is a conflict between the relativism of the economist and the absolutism of the planner. An economist weighing up the costs and benefits of the policy would have suggested that the green-belt policy should be flexible, so that some land was released for development within the green belts. Recreational rural land would be preserved but land values and journeys to work would be lower. In this way the costs of the policy could have been kept in line with the benefits. Planners, on the other hand, having laid down the policy appear to have regarded it as fixed, to regard the green belts as first defined to be the best attainable, and to think that, since it is the best, there is little point in thinking of modifying it. Rather, that further controls might be necessary, as were taken in the 1960s with respect to office development, in order to reduce the demand for space in the cities and so bring the facts into line with the predictions rather than the other way round.

THE ECONOMIC ANALYSIS OF PLANNING

In the preceding section we have analysed the economic justification for three examples for planning controls. It is possible to go further in analysing the economics of planning in terms of its objectives, the tools used, and the consequences of using these instruments. As we said in the introduction to this chapter, very little of this kind of economic analysis of planning has yet been carried out, but here we will take the operation of plot-ratio control as an example to give some indication of the topics which need to be studied. Suppose then that the partial analysis illustrated in figure 12.1 is in fact correct, in that increasing the amount of space on a site does in fact increase congestion – marginal social cost does exceed marginal private cost.

The first question which must be raised is why the planner uses physical controls and rarely uses any other kind of instrument, particularly taxes or subsidies. The diagrammatic analysis in figure 12.1 suggests that the optimal density would also be attained if a tax per unit of space were levied at a level indicated by ST in the figure. The tax would reduce the revenue per unit received by the developer. At the price received after tax, P_o, the profit-maximizing density would also be the optimal social density. Moreover, a tax system would have the significant advantage over a system of controls in that the government administering it would receive a revenue.

There are several possible reasons for the use of controls by planners instead of taxes, despite the major obvious advantage of the latter. The first is that the use of controls rather than taxes is a legacy of planning history, a result of the way the planning system originally developed as an architectural cum legal institution, as we indicated in chapter 1. The second is that as we showed in the discussion of green belts in the preceding section planning may slip unintentionally from prediction to control. If it is expected originally that the system will not limit development but merely make it more orderly, then the yield from a tax system would be expected to be low and so there would be little point in creating such a system. Moreover a tax system might be less effective in making development orderly than a control system. As prediction changes into control as the original expectations are proved wrong it becomes difficult to add a tax system to the original system of controls.

The third reason is that where the social costs of an externality are uncertain and variable, a control may be more effective than a tax. The formal economic analysis of this is due to Weitzman (1974). The point is this: the diagrammatic analysis based on figure 12.1 assumes that the social costs per unit of floor space are known and certain; suppose, however, that although the expected average value of these social costs is known, the actual social costs may turn out to be considerably higher or considerably lower. In these circumstances a control may be more economically efficient than a tax, since a control will certainly prevent these cases when the social costs may be very high, which a tax might not. Whilst a developer might find it profitable, even after paying a tax, to build a very large building at a location where it would cause very great congestion, this can be prevented by controls.

For a final reason for the planners preference for controls we come back again to the difference between the economist's relativism and the planner's absolutism that we stressed in the preceding section. A system of controls ensures that what the planner wants is more likely to be achieved. A tax would only ensure that the actual density of development would be a certain amount less than it would otherwise be. A control sets the actual level of development.

It is probable that all these reasons have played a part in ensuring that controls are used instead of taxes, and they may be valid reasons outweighing the loss of any tax revenue. There are, however, other costs associated with the planner's preferences for controls over taxes. The controls restrict the supply of land or floor space for particular activities. As demand increases for these uses but the supply remains restricted, the price of land which can be used for these uses increases. In the end if the controls are imposed stringently enough and for long enough the differences in prices between pieces of land zoned for different uses may become substantial. Cheshire and Leven (1982) report that the estimated value of land for agricultural use on the outskirts of the town of Reading, some 30 miles west of London, was £1750 per acre in 1982. If it could be used for housing its price was £50 000 per acre. In more favoured areas in Reading the value of land for residential use was £100 000 per acre but £600 000 per acre if it could be used for industry. Clearly planning permission for residential or industrial use can be worth a substantial sum of money to the owner of the land.

When planning permission is worth a substantial sum it becomes worthwhile for the land owner to spend equally large sums on obtaining this permission. This expenditure, called rent-seeking expenditure in the economics literature (Krueger, 1974; Evans, 1982), does not in any way increase economic welfare; it does not directly result in generally increased production nor does it make consumers better off; in economic jargon it is a dead-weight loss. In the attempt to obtain planning permission such expenditure includes the payment of lawyers and real-estate experts, architects and public-relations firms, in order to persuade the local planning authority. Sometimes these attempts at persuasion may go beyond expensive media publicity and 'splash' presentations of the proposed development to political pressure, expensive gifts, holidays disguised as fact-finding tours, and outright bribery.

When this kind of activity comes to the public notice, as with the Poulson case in the 1970s, it brings no credit to the planning system and discredits those who operate it, but the primary cause of this expenditure, the method by which the planning system operates is not usually brought into question.

The existence of the huge profits which can be gained from an award of planning permission has, however, had repercussions. One response, at central government level, has been the creation of a Development Gains Tax under which profits on the development of land are taxed at a rate of 60 per cent, this tax rate contrasting with the rate of 30 per cent charged as Capital Gains Tax on other capital transactions of this kind.

Another response, at the local-government level, has been a semi-formalized system of trading planning permissions for large developments in exchange for some addition to the scheme of benefit to the local community. This 'planning gain' may be land for road widening, a community centre, some public housing, etc. Such a system has the advantage that it is more flexible than a tax system (see Keogh, 1982). On the other hand the location of the 'planning gains' is determined by the preferences of developers as to sites which it is worth developing for other reasons. The system is still developing, however, and may be expected to become more sophisticated as local authorities become more adept in their bargaining.

THE OBJECTIVES OF PLANNING

The discussion in the preceding section suggests that at a political economic level the system can adapt to some extent to accommodate the planners preferences for controls over taxes or subsidies. But this adaptation merely serves to accommodate the stresses on the system caused by this preference and the rigidity with which the controls are applied. Instead of the controls being adapted to changing circumstances, as the economic analysis in the second section suggests that they should, the economic system has to adapt to the economic forces created by planning. The planning system, in other words, is the fixed point in the system, everything else has had to adjust or be adjusted to take account of it. We return, therefore, to the problem that we have already stressed, the difference between the absolutist approach of the planner and the relativist approach of the economist.

It is as though welfare economics and planning are unrelated – out of joint. Seen from a distance the planner and the economist look to be on the same track heading for the same destination. A closer approach reveals that though they are both heading in the same direction, they are in fact on different tracks and these tracks are some distance apart so that communication between them is difficult and only occasionally possible by shouting very loudly. Moreover, there is no guarantee that these tracks actually reach the same destination in the end, though both the planner and the economist claim that they do; a look at the signposts suggests that their eventual destinations in fact lie many miles apart.

Welfare economists claim that their objective, the eventual destination on their track, is the maximization of welfare, but in practice, as we noted earlier in the chapter, this means primarily the maximization of economic efficiency, with the distribution of income and wealth being given only secondary consideration, whilst things such as the economic organization of society seem to be entirely excluded from consideration.

Planners would also argue that their objective is the maximization of welfare, but in practice they largely limit themselves to consideration of the physical environment, and, since that environment already exists – is already given, to minimizing the impact of change on that environment. For example, as Foster and Whitehead (1973) note in their review of the Layfield Committee's Report on the

Greater London Development Plan, that Committee appeared to explicitly exclude many factors from consideration for planning purposes in view of their comment that 'we do not accept the statement that the improvement of London depends on the Londoner's well-being'.

The absolutist approach of the planner also helps to explain the fuzziness or uncertainty over whether planners attempt to predict what will happen or whether they intend to determine what will happen. In the discussion of planning and welfare economics earlier in this chapter we suggested that from a welfare economist's viewpoint planning might help to avoid wasted resources by providing information about the future, and, indeed, planning the future. But in practice it would appear that the planner wishes to both predict and determine. Both objectives co-exist so that it is easy to slip from one to the other without noticing – i.e. from a 'will' to an 'ought'. Much planning starts with predictions of things largely outside the control of planners – demographic change, employment in manufacturing and services, etc. – and moves on to lay down what would be the optimal pattern of land use if these predictions are correct. But once having planned the future pattern of land use it is easier to ensure that it is achieved, even if the predictions prove wrong, than to replan because circumstances have changed.

The earlier discussion of green belts is an extreme example of this. The original controls were prepared on the basis of certain predictions. These predictions were incorrect but little or no attempt was made to modify the controls laid down on the basis of these predictions. Indeed, so far from needing modification green belts are usually regarded as one of the great successes of post-war British planning.

This brings us to the core of the problem. What is the criterion of success? In what sense is a plan a success? So far as I can see there are three possible alternatives.

The first is the sense in which the Apollo programme to land a man on the moon was a success, or the ascent of Everest, or the Normandy landings. The cost is largely irrelevant, success is achieved if the objective is attained.

The second is the sense in which a business is successful. Its product is in demand at a price which allows the business to continue to be profitable.

The third is the sense in which the Anglo-French Concorde is/is not a success. This is not really a separate sense, but a mixture of the first two. Supporters of the Concorde enterprise point to the fact that a supersonic transport was designed and built – a success in the first sense. Critics point to the fact that its construction and sale has had to be heavily subsidized and that very, very few have been sold. As a business venture it was not a success – in the second sense.

The achievements of British planning seem usually to be considered in the first sense. The objectives are attained, therefore the planner has been successful. The economist wishes to apply criteria to determine its success in the second sense – to question whether the benefits exceed the costs, whilst the supporters of the system, as with the supporters of Concorde, regard this questioning as mere niggling and carping in the face of a great achievement.

In my view this situation is unfortunately not likely to change, for cost benefit criteria are even less likely to be accepted as applicable to planning than to Concorde. The great planning disasters, as illustrated by the examples in Hall's (1980) book, tend only to be recognized as such if the costs are obvious – if cash actually flows out of the public exchequer. However, the costs of planning are social costs – less housing space, longer journeys to work, etc. – and are not immediately identifiable as being due to the 'planning achievements'. The economist thus appears to be like some war reporter following the campaign of a victorious general, and pointing out that each victory is a Pyrrhic victory and makes eventual success in the war less likely not more. Beside such glorious victories who should listen to such a mean carping fellow!

FURTHER READING

Both Harrison (1977) and Willis (1980) have written texts on the economics of land use planning, mainly dealing with planning as an aspect of applied welfare economics. The discussion of the economics of plot ratio controls in this chapter is based on Evans (1974b), and of residential density controls and green belts on Evans (1973a).

13

Afterword: Cities in Less Developed Countries

Miss Prism: The chapter on the Fall of the Rupee you may omit.
   It is somewhat too sensational.
                              The Importance of Being Earnest Act III

In the preface I stated that, for the purpose of this book at least, topics were regarded as part of urban economics if they were related to location and land use in cities. There is another limitation in the scope of the book which will have become obvious to the reader; it is almost wholly concerned with the economics of cities in the developed, capitalist, countries. There has been no discussion of the economy of the cities of Eastern Europe and almost no reference to the economic problems of cities in the less-developed countries.

The first omission is fairly easy to justify. First, the book is unlikely to be used by readers in Eastern Europe to study their own economic problems, and, secondly, including a discussion of the economics of these cities is not likely to help those who do read the book who are concerned with cities elsewhere. As chapter 12 has shown, a discussion of planning in the context of a mixed economy like that of Britain is quite complicated enough. A discussion of the situation where the state has almost complete control is going to be that much more complex, unless it is to be merely a piece of description.

The second omission is less easy to justify, and that is the reason for this afterword. It less easy to justify mainly because some of those responsible for understanding the urban economies of the less-developed countries are likely to read this book, and it would be misleading to imply that the urban economic analysis of cities in the developed capitalist countries is wholly applicable to cities elsewhere. The problem is, however, that it is not clear, to me at least, to what extent it is applicable. But it would seem right to outline here the main economic problems which cities may face in the less-developed countries which might affect the relevance of the analysis.

The first problem is a very rapid rate of expansion in the size of the larger cities in part because of a rapid rate of natural increase in the population, whether urban or rural, but mainly because of migration to the cities from the rural areas during development (see Ledent, 1982a). The result is a high positive correlation between development, represented by GNP per capita, and degree of urbanization, represented by the percentage of the total population living in urban areas (see Berry, 1973; Ledent, 1982b; Wheaton and Shishido, 1981). The relationship is shown in figure 13.1.

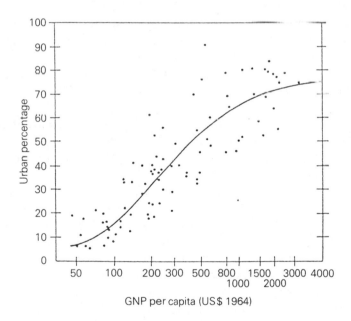

Source: Ledent (1982b)

FIGURE 13.1
Relationship between degree of urbanization and GNP per capita for 88
non–centrally planned countries, 1965

This rapid rate of expansion means that in the case of these cities it is less reasonable to assume that the urban economy is in some kind of static equilibrium, as we have implicitly assumed in most of this book. We showed in chapter 9 that rapid change will certainly affect the land market. There is no reason to assume that it will not affect other parts of the economy, so reducing the applicability of theories which may depend on the assumption that there is no change.

The nature of this urban–rural migration has been recently surveyed by Yap (1977). In her paper she stressed the attractions of cities to the rural migrants, and concluded that migrants do benefit from the move they make. Thus it is not safe to assume, as some have done, that the migrants are merely rural dwellers who have become surplus to the labour requirements of the rural areas and so have moved to the cities. The migration occurs because of the attraction of cities, but not because of the repulsion of the countryside. However, the migration is not necessarily permanent, as one would assume it to be in a developed country. There is a high rate of return migration, so that many migrate to the cities, live and work there for a short time and then return to their original home areas with their savings.

This circular migration flow has been stressed by others, as has the fact that the migrant will maintain contact with those of the extended family who remain at the original home. Crampton (1982) points out that in Jakarta much migration is virtually on a week-by-week basis with the male migrants living in makeshift accommodation in the cities and maintaining their families in their home villages to which they return at frequent intervals, often weekly. On a large scale this kind of migration will affect urban structure. The analysis of the economics of city size in chapter 5 assumes that the diseconomies of size increase as the population increases, in part at least because the demand for space by the population increases land rents and land values. If in fact the families of many workers do not have to be accommodated within the city, the space required to house the workers will be much less than it would otherwise have to be. Since the diseconomies are less, the city may become larger in terms of jobs, if not total population.

Another factor which distinguishes most cities in the less-developed countries from others is the existence of squatter settlements or shanty towns of one kind or another. The squatters do not have a full legal right to the land they occupy. So no rent is paid for the land, and because of the poverty of the squatters and because their rights of tenure are fragile if not non-existent, the shanties remain only temporary constructions. There is no incentive for anybody to put more capital into them than is necessary since they may soon be torn down. If nothing happens, however, the settlements may become semi-permanent, being monitored by the authorities (Gilbert, 1981) and tolerated by the land owners (Crampton, 1982). The latter notes that in Jakarta railway land alongside the tracks is a favoured location. The land is not going to be built on, but 'the railway company could not receive payment for the occupation of the land without acknowledging in some measure the rights of the individuals living within a few feet of the track' (Crampton, 1982, p. 12). Informal systems of self-government and control of the use of land may grow up. Naipaul (1977) relates how in a Bombay squatter settlement efforts are made by the squatters to prevent the last remaining pieces of open land being occupied so that some open space is left for the community. But 'a squatter's hut could go up overnight, and it was hard then – since all the huts were illegal – to have just that one pulled down' (Naipal, 1977, p. 68).

From an economic point of view the problem with the squatter settlements is that since the site is occupied outside the market system, normal market forces do not determine who lives where and what is paid for the land. Once again, as with periodic migration, expansion of the city will not necessarily drive up land values. This is particularly so if the squatters move into the city and live on land which would not otherwise be occupied, e.g. land alongside railway tracks, land liable to flooding, etc. The increasing population will not necessarily lead to increased land values. On the other hand the greater population and the increase in economic activity will lead to greater external economies, and so will make the large city an attractive location for additional economic activities leading to a further increase in its size. Thus squatter settlements, periodic migration, and of course the low demand for space because of low incomes even from those living in housing in the market sector, all three together provide a possible economic explanation for the large size and economic dominance of the largest cities in the less-developed countries.

A reason why migration into these large cities might be imbalanced, if not excessive, is suggested by the two-sector model of the urban labour market proposed by Harris and Todaro (1970). They argued, largely on the basis of experience in African cities, that one should distinguish between the formal labour market of the major cities and the informal system operating in most of the rest of the economy. For various reasons – the influence of the central government and the policies of multinational companies for example – wages are likely to be higher in the formal sector than incomes elsewhere in the economy. As a result, they argue, people will migrate to the cities in search of higher incomes. There will be more seeking these jobs than there are jobs available and the result will be high levels of unemploment in the cities. In the end a balance will be reached when migration is no longer attractive. This will occur when the higher probability of being unemployed in the cities cancels out the attractiveness of higher rates of pay. Incomes will be higher in the cities but so will unemployment.

A problem with the Harris–Todaro model is that it is assumed that migration is more or less permanent. But the high rates of return migration, as well as the extent of circular migration and periodic migration pointed out above, make it not altogether clear why those who migrate should remain if they are unemployed rather than returning to their home villages.

The Harris–Todaro model implies that the formal and informal sectors are largely coincident with the urban and rural sectors and to a limited extent this is so. But the final factor which distinguishes the city in the less-developed country from its counterpart in a developed country is the large size of the informal sector *within* the city, this sector including both individual and family enterprises, with the formal sector dominated by corporate enterprises. Of course the informal sector is smaller in the cities than in the country; the corporate sector dominates but the informal economy exists, with enterprises, whether individual or family, operating largely without formal records on a cash or exchange basis, paralleling and often largely coincident with the squatters and their settlements.

Development, as it occurs, will tend to make the cities in the less-developed countries more like those in the developed economies. One would expect rising real incomes to lead to a desire for better, more permanent accommodation than can be obtained in the squatter settlements and for there to be a decline in the importance of the informal sectors as incomes increase and 'development' spreads to more rural areas. This will occur only in the later stages, however. As we have indicated, the evidence confirms that development initially leads to increased urban concentration, only in the later stages of development does concentration not increase rapidly.

What happens to cities 'after development', in countries like Britain, Australia or the USA is what this book has been about. We do not need to recapitulate it here. The reader may agree or disagree with that analysis. Though I am human enough to hope for agreement, still, whether he or she agrees or not, I should have achieved what I should have wished if the reader is now better able to express his or her own independent views on the development and planning of cities and towns.

FURTHER READING

The problems of very large cities in the less developed countries are discussed by Gilbert (1976). The extent to which this urban growth is caused by immigration rather than natural increase is examined by Ledent (1982a), and Yap (1977) surveys the literature on the nature and causes of this rural–urban migration. Berry (1973) discusses the human consequences of urbanization.

References

Abercrombie, Patrick (1959) In D. Rigby Childs (ed.), *Town and Country Planning*, 3rd edn, London: Oxford University Press.

Alexander, I. (1979) *Office Location and Public Policy*, London: Longman.

Alonso, William (1964a) *Location and Land Use*, Cambridge, Mass: Harvard University Press.

Alonso, W. (1964b) Location theory. In J. Friedmann and W. Alonso (eds), *Regional Development and Planning: A Reader*, Cambridge, Mass: MIT Press.

Alonso, W. (1971) The economics of urban size, *Papers and Proceedings of the Regional Science Association*, **26**.

Armstrong, H. and Taylor, J. (1978) *Regional Economic Policy*, Oxford: Philip Allan.

Armstrong, Regina B. (1972) *The Office Industry: Patterns of Growth and Location*, Cambridge, Mass: MIT Press for the Regional Plan Association.

Arnot, R. (1980) A simple urban growth model with durable housing, *Regional Science and Urban Economics*, **10**, 1 (March).

Ball, M., Bentivegna, V., Edwards, M. and Folin, M. (1985) *Land Rent, Housing and Urban Planning*, Beckenham, Kent: Croom Helm.

Baran, P. A. and Sweezey, P. M. (1966) *Monopoly Capital*, New York: Monthly Review Press.

Bassett, K., and Short J. R. (1980) *Housing and Residential Structure*, London: Routledge and Kegan Paul.

Beckmann, M. J. (1958) City hierarchies and the distribution of city size, *Economic Development and Cultural Change*, **6**.

Beckmann, M. J. and McPherson, J. C. (1970) City size distribution in a central place hierarchy: An alternative approach, *Journal of Regional Science*, **10**.

Beesley, M. E. and Foster, C. D. (1965) Victoria Line: Social benefit and finances. *Journal of the Royal Statistical Society*, Series A, **128**, 1.

Beguin, H. (1982) City-size distribution and central place models: a suggestion, *Journal of Regional Science*, **22**, 2 (May).

Bennett, R. J. (1980) *The Geography of Public Finance*, London: Methuen.
Bennett, R. J. (1982) *Central Grants to Local Government*, Cambridge: Cambridge U.P.
Berry, B. J. L. (1964) Cities as systems within systems of cities, *Papers and Proceedings of the Regional Science Association*, **13**.
Berry, B. J. L. (1967) *Geography of Market Areas and Retail Distribution*, Englewood Cliffs N.J: Prentice Hall.
Berry, B. J. L. (1973) *The Human Consequences of Urbanisation*, London: Macmillan.
Berry, B. J. L. and Horton, F. E. (1970) *Geographic Perspectives on Urban Systems*, Englewood Cliffs, N.J.: Prentice Hall.
Bliss, Barbara (1945) *The New Planning*, London: Faber and Faber.
von Böventer, E. G. (1969) Determinants of migration into West German cities 1965–61, 1961–66, *Papers and Proceedings of the Regional Science Association*, **23**.
von Böventer, E. G. (1975) Regional growth theory, *Urban Studies*, **12**, 1 (February).
Brueckner, J. K. (1981) Testing a vintage model of urban growth, *Journal of Regional Science*, **21**, 1 (February).
Burgess, Ernest W. (1925) The growth of the city: An introduction to a research project. In R. E. Park, E. W. Burgess and R. A. McKenzie (eds), *The City*, Chicago: University of Chicago Press.
Button, K. J. (1982) *Transport Economics*, London: Heinemann.
Button, K. J., Fowkes, A. S. and Pearman, A. D. (1980) Car ownership in West Yorkshire: The influence of public transport accessibility, *Urban Studies*, **17**, 2 (June).
CALUS (1983) *Property and Information Technology – the Future for the Offices Market*, Reading: Centre for Advanced Land Use Studies, College of Estate Management.
Cameron, G. C. (1973) Intra-urban location and the new plant, *Papers of the Regional Science Association*, **29**.
Cameron, G. C. (1980) The inner city: New plant incubator? In A. W. Evans and D. E. C. Eversley (eds), *The Inner City: Employment and Industry*, London: Heinemann.
Cameron, G. C. and Evans, A. W. (1973) The British conurbation centres, *Regional Studies*, **7**, 1, (November).
Cameron, G. C., and Wingo, L. (eds) (1973) *Cities, Regions and Public Policy*, Edinburgh: Oliver and Boyd.
Carlino, Gerald A. (1979) Increasing returns to scale in metropolitan manufacturing, *Journal of Regional Science*, **19**, 3 (August).
Carlino, Gerald A. (1980) Contrasts in agglomeration: New York and Pittsburgh reconsidered, *Urban Studies*, **17**, 3 (October).
Carlino, Gerald A. (1982) Manufacturing agglomeration economies as returns to scale: A production function approach, *Papers of the Regional Science Association*, **50**.

Cheshire, P. C. and Leven, C. (1982) On the costs and economic consequences of the British land use planning system. University of Reading Discussion Papers in Urban and Regional Economics, No. 11.

Chicago Area Transportation Study (1959) *Final Report*, Chicago: Chicago Area Transportation Study.

Chinitz, B. (1961) Contrasts in agglomeration: New York and Pittsburgh, *American Economic Review*, **51**, 2 (May).

Christaller, W. (1933) *Die Zentralen Orte in Süddeutschland*. Jena: Fischer. Translated by C. Baskin as *The Central Places of Southern Germany*, Englewood Cliffs: Prentice Hall, 1966.

Clark, C. (1951) Urban population densities, *Journal of the Royal Statistical Society*, Series A, **114**, 4.

Clark, C. (1966) *Population Growth and Land Use*, London: Macmillan.

Clemente, F. and Sturgis, R. B. (1971) Population size and industrial diversification, *Urban Studies*, **8**, 1 (February).

Corkindale, J. T. (1980) Employment trends in the conurbations, In A. W. Evans and D. E. C. Eversley (eds), *The Inner City Employment and Industry*, London: Heinemann.

Crampton, G. R. (1982) The applicability of urban economic theory to the cities of developing countries: the case of Jakarta. University of Reading Discussion papers in Urban and Regional Economics, No. 13.

Cropper, M. L. (1981) The value of urban amenities, *Journal of Regional Science*, **21**, 3 (August).

Crowley, R. W. (1973) Reflections and further evidence on population size and industrial diversification, *Urban Studies*, **10**, 1 (February).

Curry, L. (1964) The random spatial economy: an exploration in settlement theory, *Annals of the Association of American Geography*, **54**, 1 (March).

Davies, H. (1982) Fiscal migration and the London boroughs, *Urban Studies*, **19**, 2 (May).

Davies, R. L. (1976) *Marketing Geography*, London: Methuen.

Debenham, Tewson and Chinnocks (1983) Rent and rates analysis: 1973–1983, *Journal of Valuation*, **2**, 1 (Autumn).

Dennis, R. (1980) The decline of manufacturing employment in Greater London. In A. W. Evans and D. E. C. Eversley (eds), *The Inner City: Employment and Industry*, London: Heinemann.

Department of the Environment (1981) *Alternatives to Domestic Rates*, Cmnd. 8449, London: HMSO.

Dyos, H. J. (1961) *Victorian Suburb*, Leicester: Leicester University Press.

Edel, M. and Sclar, E. (1974) Taxes, spending and property values: Supply adjustment in a Tiebout–Oates model, *Journal of Political Economy*, **82**, 5 (September/October).

Evans, A. W. (1972) The pure theory of city size in an industrial economy, *Urban Studies*, **9**, 1 (February).

Evans, A. W. (1973a) *The Economics of Residential Location*, London: Macmillan.

Evans, A. W. (1973b) The location of the headquarters of industrial companies, *Urban Studies*, **10**, 3 (October).

Evans, A. W. (1974a) Economics and planning. In Jean Forbes (ed.), *Studies in Social Science and Planning*, Edinburgh: Scottish Academic Press.

Evans, A. W. (1974b) Planning for offices, the economics of plot ratio control. In Jean Forbes (ed.), *Studies in Social Science and Planning*, Edinburgh: Scottish Academic Press.

Evans, A. W. (1975) A note in the intra-urban location of wholesalers and local market manufacturers, *Land Economics*, **51**, 3 (August).

Evans, A. W. (1976) Economic influences on social mix, *Urban Studies*, **13**, 3 (October).

Evans, A. W. (1977) Neighbourhood externalities, economic clubs, and the environment. In L. Wingo and A. W. Evans (eds), *Public Economies and the Quality of Life*, Baltimore: The Johns Hopkins University Press.

Evans, A. W. (1980) Poverty in the conurbations. In G. C. Cameron (ed.), *The Future of the British Conurbations*, London: Longman.

Evans, A. W. (1982) Externalities, rent-seeking and town planning. University of Reading Discussion Papers in Urban and Regional Economics, No. 10.

Evans, A. W. (1983) The determination of the price of land, *Urban Studies*, **10**, 2 (May).

Evans, A. W. (1984) Inside out down under? Outer city unemployment in Australia, *Urban Policy and Research*, **2**, 1 (March).

Evans, A. W. and Eversley, D. E. C. (eds) (1980) *The Inner City: Employment and Industry*, London: Heinemann.

Evans, A. W. and Richardson, R. (1981) Urban unemployment: Interpretation and additional evidence, *Scottish Journal of Political Economy*, **23**, 2 (June).

Eversley, D. E. C. (1972) Rising costs and static incomes: Some economic consequences of regional planning in London, *Urban Studies*, **9**, 3 (October).

Fagg, J. J. (1980) A re-examination of the incubator hypothesis: A case study of Greater Leicester, *Urban Studies* **17**, 1, (February).

Farbman, M. (1975) The size distribution of family income in U.S. SMSAs, 1959, *The Review of Income and Wealth*, **21**, 2, (June).

Foster, C. D. and Beesley, M. E. (1963) Estimating the social benefits of constructing an underground railway in London, *Journal of the Royal Statistical Society*, Series A, 126.

Foster, C. D., Jackman, R. and Perlman, M. (1980) *Local Government Finance in a Unitary State*, London: George Allen and Unwin.

Foster, C. D. and Richardson, R. (1973) Employment trends in London in the 1960s and their relevance to the future. In D. V. Donnison and D. E. C. Eversley (eds), *London: Urban Problems, Patterns and Policies*, London: Heinemann.

Foster, C. D. and Whitehead, C. M. E. (1973) The Layfield Report on the Greater London Development Plan, *Economica*, **40**, 160 (November).

Friedly, P. (1965) A note on the retail trade multiplier and residential mobility, *Journal of Regional Science*, **6**, 1 (Summer).

Gilbert, A. (1976) The arguments for very large cities reconsidered, *Urban Studies*, **13**, 1, (February).

Gilbert, A. (1981) Pirates and invaders: Land acquisition in urban Columbia and Venezuela, *World Development*, **9**, 7 (July).

Glaister, S. (1981) *Fundamentals of Transport Economics*, Oxford: Basil Blackwell.

Goddard, J. B. (1968) Multivariate analysis of office location patterns in the city centre: A London example, *Regional Studies*, **2**, 1, (September).

Goddard, J. B. (1973) *Office Linkages and Location*, Oxford: Pergamon Press.

Goldfarb, R. S. and Yezer, A. M. J. (1976) Evaluating alternative theories of intercity and interregional wage differentials, *Journal of Regional Science*, **16**, 3 (December).

Gordon, D. F. and Hynes, A. (1971) On the theory of price dynamics. In E. S. Phelps (ed.) *Microeconomic Foundations of Employment and Inflation Theory*, London: Macmillan.

Gould, P. R. and White, R. R. (1968) The mental maps of British school leavers, *Regional Studies*, **2**, 2 (November).

Gupta, S. P. and Hutton, J. P. (1968) *Economies of Scale in Local Government Services*, Royal Commission on Local Government in England, Research Studies No. 3.

Haig, R. M. (1926) Toward an understanding of the metropolis, I and II, *Quarterly Journal of Economics*, **40**, (February and May).

Hall, Peter (1971) Spatial structure of metropolitan England and Wales. In M. Chisholm and G. Manners (eds), *Spatial Policy Problems of the British Economy*, Cambridge: Cambridge University Press.

Hall, Peter (1980) *Great Planning Disasters*, London: Weidenfeld and Nicholson.

Hall, P. and Hay, D. (1980) *Growth Centres in the European Urban System*, London: Heinemann.

Hamilton, B. W. (1976) The effects of property taxes and local public spending on property values: a theoretical comment, *Journal of Political Economy*, **84**, 3 (June).

Hamilton, F. E. I. (ed) (1974) *Spatial Perspectives on Industrial Organisation and Decision-Making*, London: John Wiley.

Harris, J. R. and Todaro, M. (1970) Migration, unemployment and development: A two sector analysis, *American Economic Review*, **60**, 1 (March).

Harrison, A. J. (1977) *Economics and Land Use Planning*, London: Croom Helm.

Harrison, A. J. and Quarmby, D. A. (1969) The value of time. In Richard Layard (ed.), *Cost-Benefit Analysis*, Harmondsworth: Penguin.

Harvey, D. (1973) Use value, exchange value and the theory of urban land use, *Social Justice and the City*, London: Edward Arnold.

Harvey, J. (1981) *The Economics of Real Property*, London: Macmillan.

Haworth, C. T., Long, J. E. and Rasmussen, D. W. (1978) Income distribution, city size, and urban growth, *Urban Studies*, **15**, 1 (February).

Higgs, R. (1969) The growth of cities in a mid-western region. *Journal of Regional Science*, **9**, 1 (December).

Hoch, I. (1977) Climate, wages and the quality of life. In Lowdon Wingo and Alan Evans (eds), *Public Economics and the Quality of Life*, Baltimore: Johns Hopkins University Press.

Holtermann, S. E. (1975) Areas of urban deprivation in Great Britain: An analysis of 1971 census data, *Social Trends*, **6**.

Hoover, E. M. (1948) *The Location of Economic Activity*, New York: McGraw Hill.

Hoover, Edgar M. and Vernon, Raymond (1959) *Anatomy of a Metropolis*, Cambridge, Mass: Harvard University Press.

Hoyt, Homer (1939) *The Structure and Growth of Residential Neighbourhoods in American Cities*, Washington: U.S. Government Printing Office; repr. Homer Hoyt Associates, 1968.

Hughes, G. and McCormick, B. (1981) Do council housing policies reduce migration between regions? *Economic Journal*, **91**, 364 (December).

Isard, W. (1965) *Location and Space-Economy*, Cambridge, Mass: MIT Press.

Isard, W. and Langford, T. W. (1971) *Regional Input–Output Study: Recollections, Reflections, and Diverse Notes on the Philadelphia Experience*, Cambridge, Mass: MIT Press.

Kain, J. F. (1975) Housing market discrimination and negro employment. In *Essays on Spatial Structure*, Cambridge, Mass: Ballinger.

Kain, J. F. and Quigley, J. M. (1975) *Housing Markets and Racial Discrimination*, New York: National Bureau of Economic Research.

Keeble, D. E. (1968) Industrial decentralisation and the metropolis: The North West London Case, *Transactions of the Institute of British Geography*, **44**.

Keogh, G. (1981) Land-use planning and the production of market information. University of Reading Discussion Papers in Urban and Regional Economics, No. 8.

Keogh, G. (1982) Planning gain: An economic analysis. University of Reading Discussion Papers in Urban and Regional Economics, No. 12.

Krueger, Anne O. (1974) The political economy of the rent-seeking society. *American Economic Review*, **64**, 3 (June).

Ledent, J. (1982a) The factors of urban population growth: net immigration versus national increase, *International Regional Science Review*, **3**, 2.

Ledent, J. (1982b) Rural–urban migration, urbanization, and economic development, *Economic Development and Cultural Change*, **30**, 3 (April).

Lee, Douglass B. (1973) Requiem for large-scale models, *Journal of the American Institute of Planners*, **39**, 3 (May).

Leone, R. A. and Struyk, R. (1976) The incubator hypothesis: Evidence from five SMSAs, *Urban Studies*, **13**, 3 (October).

Lichtenberg, Robert M. (1960) *One-Tenth of a Nation*, Cambridge, Mass: Harvard University Press.

Lipsey, R. G. and Lancaster, R. K. (1956) The general theory of the second best, *Review of Economic Studies*, **24**, 1 (January).

Lösch, A. (1945) *Die Raumliche Ordnung der Wirtschaft*, Jena: Fischer. Translated by W. H. Woglom and W. F. Stolper, as *The Economics of Location*, New Haven: Yale University Press.

McGuire, Martin (1974) Group segregation and optimal jurisdictions, *Journal of Political Economy*, **82**, 1 (January/February).

McKean, R. N. (1973) An outsider looks at urban economics, *Urban Studies*, **10**, 1, (February).

Marshall, Alfred (1920) *Principles of Economics*, 8th edn, London: Macmillan.

Martin, J. E. (1969) Size of plant and location of industry in Greater London, *Tijdschrift voor Economische en Sociale Geografie*, **60**, 6 (November/December).

Mathur, V. K. (1970) Occupational composition and its determinants: An intercity size class analysis, *Journal of Regional Science*, **10**, 1 (April).

Mayes, D. (1979) *The Property Boom*, Oxford: Martin Robertson.

Metcalf, D. (1975) Urban unemployment in England, *Economic Journal*, **85**, 339 (September).

Metcalf, D. and Richardson, R. (1980) Unemployment in London. In A. W. Evans and D. E. C. Eversley (eds), *The Inner City: Employment and Industry*, London: Heinemann.

Meyer, J. R., Kain, J. F. and Wohl, M. (1965) *The Urban Transportation Problem*, Cambridge, Mass: Harvard University Press.

Mills, E. S. (1970) Urban density functions, *Urban Studies*, **7**, 1, (March).

Ministry of Transport (1964) *Road Pricing, The Economic and Technical Possibilities*, known as *The Smeed Report*, London: HMSO.

Mirrlees, James A. (1972) The optimum town, *Swedish Journal of Economics*, **74**, 1 (March).

Mitchell, Robert and Rapkin, Chester (1954) *Urban Traffic: A Function of Land Use*, New York: Columbia University Press.

Morrissett, I. (1958) The economic structure of American cities, *Papers of the Regional Science Association*, **4**.

Moses, L. N. (1958) Location and the theory of production, *Quarterly Journal of Economics*, **73**, 2 (May).

Mumford, Lewis (1961) *The City in History*, London: Secker and Warburg.

Munch, P. (1976) An economic analysis of eminent domain, *Journal of Political Economy*, **8**, 3 (June).

Musgrave, R. A. and Musgrave, P. B. (1976) *Public Finance in Theory and Practice*, New York: McGraw-Hill.

Muth, Richard F. (1969) *Cities and Housing*, Chicago: University of Chicago Press.

Naipaul, V. S. (1977) *India: A Wounded Civilization*, London: André Deutsch.

Newman, P., Annandale, D. and Duxbury, L. (1984) The rise and decline of the Australian inner city? *Urban Policy and Research*, **2**, 1 (March).

Nicholson, B. M., Brinkley, I. and Evans, A. W. (1981) The role of the inner city in the development of manufacturing industry, *Urban Studies*, **18**, 1 (February)

Oates, W. E. (1969) The effects of property taxes and local public spending on property values: An empirical study of tax capitalization and the Tiebout hypothesis, *Journal of Political Economy*, **77**, 6 (November/ December).

Parker, H. R. (1965) The history of compensation and betterment since 1900. In Peter Hall (ed.), *Land Values*, London: Sweet and Maxwell.

Perloff, H. S. (1973) The development of urban economics in the United States, *Urban Studies*, **10**, 3, (October).

Pfouts, R. W. (1960) *The Techniques of Urban Economic Analysis*, West Trenton, N. J: Chandler Davis.

Prest, A. R. (1981) *The Taxation of Urban Land*, Manchester: Manchester U.P.

Price, C. (1978) Individual preference and optimal city size, *Urban Studies*, **15**, 1 (February).

Rhodes, J. and Kan, A. (1971) *Office Dispersal and Regional Policy*, Cambridge: Cambridge University Press.

Richardson, H. W. (1973a) *Regional Growth Theory*, London: Macmillan.

Richardson, H. W. (1973b) *The Economics of Urban Size*, Farnborough, Hants: Saxon House.

Richardson, H. W. (1976) Growth pole spillovers: The dynamics of spread and backwash, *Regional Studies*, **10**, 1.

Richardson, H. W. (1977) *The New Urban Economics*, London: Pion.

Richardson, H. W. (1981) National urban development strategies in developing countries, *Urban Studies*, **18**, 3 (October).

Robbins, S. M. and Terleckyj, N. E. (1960) *Money Metropolis*, Cambridge, Mass: Harvard University Press.

Robson, B. T. (1973) *Urban Growth: An Approach*, London: Methuen.

Royal Commission on Local Government in England (1969) *Report*, Cmnd. 4040 London: HMSO.

Rudé, George (1971) *Hanoverian London 1714–1808*, London: Secker and Warburg.

Samuelson, P. A. (1954) The pure theory of public expenditures, *Review of Economics and Statistics*, **36**, 4 (November).

Sarkissian, Wendy (1976) The idea of social mix in town planning: An historical review, *Urban Studies*, **13**, 3 (October).

Scott, A. J. (1980) *The Urban Land Nexus and the State*, London: Pion.

Scott, A. J. (1982) Locational patterns and dynamics of industrial activity in the modern metropolis, *Urban Studies*, **19**, 2, (May).

Sheppard, E. S. (1982) City size distributions and spatial economic change, *International Regional Science Review*, **7**, 2 (October).

Smith, Adam (1776) *The Wealth of Nations*, London: Dent and Sons, Everyman Edition.

Smith, D. M. (1981) *Industrial Location,* London: John Wiley, (2nd ed).

Smith, J. P. and Welch, F. (1979) Race differences in earnings. In P. Mieszkowski and M. Straszhelm (eds), *Current Issues in Urban Economics,* Baltimore: Johns Hopkins Press.

Stanback, T. M. and Knight, R. V. (1970) *The Metropolitan Economy,* New York: Columbia University Press.

Steinnes, D. N. (1982) Do 'people follow jobs' or do 'jobs follow people'? A causality issue in urban economics, *Urban Studies,* **19**, 2 (May).

Stephens, J. D. and Holly, B. P. (1981) City system behaviour and corporate influence: The headquarters location of U.S. industrial firms, *Urban Studies,* **18**, 3 (October).

Struyk, R. and James, F. (1975) *Intra Metropolitan Industrial Location,* Lexington, Mass: D. C. Heath.

Sveikauskas, L. A. (1975) The productivity of cities, *Quarterly Journal of Economics,* **89**, 3 (August).

Taaffe, E. J. (1956) Air transportation and United States urban distribution, *Geographical Review,* **46**, 2 (April).

Thompson, W. (1965) *A Preface to Urban Economics,* Baltimore, Md: The Johns Hopkins Press for Resources for the Future.

Thompson, W. (1968) Internal and external factors in the development of urban economics. H. S. Perloff and Lowdon Wingo (eds), *Issues in Urban Economics,* Baltimore: Johns Hopkins Press.

Thomson, J. M. (1978) *Great Cities and Their Traffic,* Harmondsworth, Middlesex: Penguin Books.

Thorngren, B. (1970) How do contact systems affect regional development? *Environment and Planning,* **2**, 4.

Tiebout, C. M. (1956) A pure theory of local expenditures, *Journal of Political Economy,* **64**, 5 (October).

Tiebout, C. M. (1960) The commodity income multiplier: A case study. In R. W. Pfouts (ed.), *The Techniques of Urban Economic Analysis,* West Trenton, N.J.: Chandler Davis.

Tinbergen, J. (1968) The hierarchy model of the size distribution of centres, *Papers and Proceedings of the Regional Science Association,* **20**.

Troy, E. F. (1965) Linear estimates of the export employment multiplier, *Journal of Regional Science,* **6**, 1 (Summer).

Van Slooten, R. and Coverdale, A. H. (1977) The characteristics of low income households, *Social Trends,* **8**.

Vernon, Raymond (1960) *Metropolis 1985,* Cambridge, Mass: Harvard University Press.

Wabe, J. S. (1966) Office decentralisation: An empirical study, *Urban Studies,* **3**, 1 (February).

Walker, B. (1979) Income distribution, city size, and urban growth: A comment. *Urban Studies,* **16**, 3 (October).

Walker, B. (1981) Income distribution, city size and urban growth: A rejoinder, *Urban Studies,* **18**, 1 (February).

Wärneryd, O. (1968) *Interdependence in Urban Systems,* Gothenberg: Regionkonsult Aktiebolag.

Warnes, A. M. (1980) A long term view of employment decentralisation from the larger English cities. In A. W. Evans and D. E. C. Eversley (eds), *The Inner City: Employment and Industry,* London: Heinemann.

Weber, F. (1928) *Theory of the Location of Industries,* edited and translated by C. J. Friedrich, Chicago: Chicago University Press.

Weitzman, M. L. (1974) Prices *vs.* quantities, *Review of Economic Studies,* **41,** 4 (October).

Wheaton, W. C. and Shishido, H. (1981) Urban concentration, agglomeration economics, and the level of economic development, *Economic Development and Cultural Change,* **30,** 1 (October).

Williamson, J. G. and Swanson, J. A. (1966) The growth of cities in the American Northeast, 1820–1870, *Explorations in Entrepreneurial History,* **4,** 1 (Supplement).

Willis, K. G. (1980) *The Economics of Town and Country Planning,* London: Granada.

Wingo, Lowdon (1961) *Transportation and Urban Land,* Washington, D. C: Resources for the Future.

Witte, Ann D. and Bachman, J. E. (1978) Vacant urban land holdings: Portfolio considerations and owner characteristics, *Southern Economic Journal,* **45,** 2 (October).

Yap, L. Y. L. (1977) The attraction of cities: A review of the migration literature, *Journal of Development Economies* **4,** 3 (September).

Yinger, J. (1979) Prejudice and discrimination in the urban housing market. In P. Mieszkowski and M. Straszheim (eds), *Current Issues in Urban Economics,* Baltimore: Johns Hopkins Press.

Zipf, G. K. (1941) *National Unity and Disunity,* Bloomington: Principia Press.

Index